Culture and Adult Education

Culture and Adult Education

A Study of Alberta and Quebec

Hayden Roberts

The University of Alberta Press

Published by
The University of Alberta Press
450 Athabasca Hall
Edmonton, Alberta
Canada T6G 2E8

ISBN 0–88864–027–7 (hardcover)
    0–88864–028–5 (paperback)

Canadian Cataloguing in Publication Data

Roberts, Hayden, 1922–
    Culture and adult education

    Bibliography: p.
    ISBN 0–88864–027–7 (bound). – ISBN
0–88864–028–5 (pbk.)

    1. Adult education – Alberta. 2. Adult
education – Quebec (Province) I. Title.
LC5254.2.A4R6   374'.97123   C81–091394–1

Typesetting by The Typeworks
Mayne Island, British Columbia

Printed by D.W. Friesen & Sons Ltd.
Altona, Manitoba

Contents

List of Tables   vii
List of Figures   ix
List of Abbreviations   xi
Acknowledgements   xv

Part I   **The Framework**
          Introduction   3
    1   The Context   5
    2   Adult Education and Culture: The Terminology   15
    3   Basis of Comparison   27

Part II   **Social Philosophies and Government Structures**
          Introduction   49
    4   Social Philosophies and Broad Policies   52
    5   Government and Government-Linked Structures
          in Alberta   78
    6   Government and Government-Linked Structures
          in Quebec   107

Part III   Non-Government Institutions
              Introduction   145
       7   Organizations of Native People   147
       8   Agricultural Organizations   179
       9   Trade Union Organizations   195
      10   Provincial Adult Education Associations   211

Part IV   The Outcomes
              Introduction   225
      11   The Ascription of Needs and Allocation
                of Resources   227
      12   Conclusion   250
      13   Postscript   261

Index   271

Tables

1 Alberta and Quebec: Main Population Origins 63

2 Courses and Participants in Non-Credit Adult Education:
   Alberta 101

3 Post-Secondary Education, Department of Indian and
   Northern Affairs, Alberta Region 153

4 Trade Union Membership and Affiliations in
   Alberta, 1976 199

5 Trade Union Membership and Affiliations in
   Quebec, 1976 204

6 Allocations of Government Expenditure to Various
   Programs of Adult Education, 1979–80 236

7 Registration in Non-Credit Part-Time Courses 245

Figures

1 Dimensions of the Learning Process   29
2 Purposes of Adult Education   31
3 Social Institutions   38
4 Forces Influencing Adult Education   43
5 Alberta Government Structures   87
6 Interlinking Government Structures: Quebec   119
7 Two Main Program Areas of the D.G.E.A. (Quebec)   121
8 Relationship Between Forces Influencing Adult
     Education   254
9 Purposes of Adult Education (Revised)   258
10 The Relationships of Cultures   259

Abbreviations

A.A.C.E.	Alberta Association for Continuing Education
A.B.E.	Adult Basic Education
ACCESS	Alberta Education Communications Corporation (Alberta Communications Centre for Educational Systems and Services), Edmonton
A.E.A.	Adult Education Association, Washington, D.C.
A.E.C.A.	Alberta Education Communications Authority, Edmonton
A.F.L.	Alberta Federation of Labor, Edmonton
A.F.U.	Alberta Farmers' Union
A.N.C.S.	Alberta Native Communications Society, Edmonton
A.P.I.T.C.	Alberta Petroleum Industry Training Centre
A.T.A.	Alberta Teachers' Association, Edmonton
C.A.A.E.	Canadian Association for Adult Education, Toronto

C.A.D.R.E.	Centre d'Animation, de Développement et de Recherche en Education, Montreal
C.A.S.N.P.	Canadian Association in Support of Native Peoples, Toronto
CBC	Canadian Broadcasting Corporation
C.C.F.	Co-operative Commonwealth Federation
C.E.G.E.P.	Collège d'Enseignement Général et Professionel
C.E.Q.	Centrale de l'Enseignement du Québec, Quebec City
C.E.R.I.	Centre for Educational Research and Innovation, Paris
C.L.C.	Canadian Labour Congress, Ottawa
C.L.S.C.	Centre Locale de Services Communautaires
C.O.F.I.	Centres d'Orientation et de Formation des Immigrants
C.O.R.E.P.S.	Comités Régionnaux de Planification Scolaire
C.R.T.C.	Canadian Radio and Television Commission, Ottawa
C.S.D.	Centrale des Syndicaux Démocratiques, Montreal
C.S.N.	Confédération des Syndicaux Nationaux, Montreal
D.G.E.A.	Direction Générale d'Education des Adultes
D.G.E.E.S.	Direction Générale d'Education Elémentaire et Secondaire
D.G.E.S.	Direction Générale d'Education Supérieure
ERIC	Educational Resources Information Centre
F.C.C.	Front Commun des Communications, Montreal
F.T.Q.	Fédération des Travailleurs du Québec, Montreal
F.U.A.	Farmers' Union of Alberta

F.U.C.D.A.	Farmers' Union and Co-operative Development Association
H.R.D.A.	Human Resources Development Authority
I.C.E.A.	Institut Canadien d'Education des Adultes, Montreal
I.L.O.	International Labor Organization, Geneva
I.T.N.	Inagtigut Tunngavinga Nunaminni, Sugluk, Quebec
L.I.P.	Local Initiatives Program
NAIT	Northern Alberta Institute of Technology, Edmonton
N.D.P.	New Democratic Party
N.F.U.	National Farmers' Union
N.Q.I.A.	Northern Quebec Inuit Association
O.E.C.D.	Organization for Economic Co-operation and Development, Paris
O.R.T.Q.	Office of Radio Telediffusion of Quebec
O.V.E.P.	Organismes Volontaires d'Education Populaire
P.C.	Progressive Conservative
P.Q.	Parti Québécois
P.S.A.C.	Public Service Alliance of Canada, Ottawa
R.E.D.A.	Rural Education and Development Association, Edmonton
S.A.G.M.A.I.	Secrétariat des Activités Gouvernementales en Milieu Amérindien et Inuit, Quebec City
SAIT	Southern Alberta Institute of Technology, Calgary
S.E.A.P.A.C.	Services Educatifs d'Aide Personelle et d'Animation Communautaire, Quebec City
STEP	Student Temporary Employment Program

SUCO   Services Universitaires du Canada Outre-mer,
Ottawa

T.A.N.U.   Tanzanian African National Union

T.N.I.   Tagramiut Nipingat Inc., Sugluk, Quebec

U.C.C.   Union des Cultivateurs Catholiques

U.F.A.   United Farmers of Alberta

U.F.W.A.   United Farm Women of Alberta

UNESCO   United Nations Educational, Scientific & Cultural
Organization, Paris

U.P.A.   Union des Produceurs Agricoles, Montreal

U.Q.A.M.   Université du Québec à Montréal

W.E.A.   Workers' Education Association

Y.M.C.A.   Young Men's Christian Association

Y.W.C.A.   Young Women's Christian Association

Acknowledgements

There are so many individuals in Alberta, Quebec, and Ottawa, who either provided me with information related to this study, or led me to sources of information, that I cannot thank them all personally. I wish, however, to acknowledge their help collectively. Some who were particularly helpful in making this study possible are, in Quebec, Mario Ferland of Laval University, Marie-Madeleine Devaux of the Ministry of Education, and my delightful hosts, Thérèse and Louise Archer, and, in Ottawa, Don MacNeill.

I am indebted to the University of Alberta Humanities and Social Science Research Fund for assistance in travelling to Quebec.

Finally, I am pleased to acknowledge that this book has been published with the help of a grant from the Social Science Foundation of Canada, using funds provided by the Social Science and Humanities Research Council of Canada, and with a grant from the Faculty of Extension of the University of Alberta.

Hayden Roberts
Edmonton

Part I
The Framework

Introduction

This book is a comparative study of adult education in the two Canadian provinces of Alberta and Quebec. The choice of these two provinces arises from the author's close acquaintance with the adult education scene in Alberta, and an interest in the Quebec scene, heightened by an earlier cross-Canada study of development projects in which the author participated. The latter was reinforced by written reports of studies conducted in Quebec found at UNESCO in Paris, an irony that underlined a feeling of a lack of knowledge in anglophone Canada of events and developments of an important province in our own country.

Also, it appeared that these two provinces provided an interesting contrast of history, demography, and economic development. On the other hand, they may be seen to share a long-standing antipathy against the seat of federal power in Ontario, but for quite different reasons: cultural and political in Quebec, and economic in Alberta.

This book, however, has a broader purpose, which is to explore some models that might provide a valid basis for comparative studies in adult education in any two or more regions. In other words, this study, while generating knowledge specifically of the Canadian adult education scene, might provide a model for other comparative studies. The perception of the author was that though there were many area studies focusing on aspects of adult education in separate countries and regions, there was little, if any, evidence of studies that compared two or more different regions or countries within a conceptual framework in terms of what Bereday calls a guiding hypothesis.

The three chapters in Part I set the scene for the comparative study itself, which is pursued in Parts II, III, and IV. Chapter 1 advocates a closer attention to the relationship between adult education practice, purposes, and underlying philosophies, and it draws attention to the main types of purpose as discussed in the literature in Britain and North America. It gives notice that this study will build its guiding hypothesis around the concept of purpose seen in the two broad categories of individual development and social development. Chapter 2 places the study within a scope defined by certain interpretations of the two terms used in the title, adult education and culture. It uses as its base the definition of adult education approved by the General Assembly of UNESCO in 1976, and a definition of culture in its broadest sense of a pattern of society as a whole. It deals with some of the terms relating to adult education in use in the two provinces, and explores their compatability with one another and with the UNESCO definition. Chapter 3 discusses in detail the two main elements of the model in terms of which the comparative study is conducted, that is, a continuum of purposes, and the relationship between factors that determine these purposes.

A list of references is included after each chapter.

1

The Context

The choice (of philosophies) shapes our thinking about the issues of the strategy, the tactics and the logistics of adult education. To which of the philosophical systems otherwise expounded in our country shall we commit ourselves? (Kallen, 1962:34)

Where adult education is discussed at the level of broad purposes, a common proposition is that such purposes divide into two broad categories: those related to personal development and those related to social development. The 1919 Report in England, which was one of the earliest attempts to place the practice of adult education in a broader social context, used the terms "personal development" and "social service," addressing the needs of the individual and the need for a better social order (Ministry of Reconstruction, 1956). Whether in Britain, North America, or elsewhere, writers in the field of adult education have continued to accept this broad categorization, but it is not entirely clear whether the distinction is simply descriptive, that is, that adult education activities appear to fall within one of these two broad purposes, or normative, that is, that adult education activities *should* be thus distinguished and categorized.

In some instances it is not entirely clear whether these two main purposes are seen to be compatible, or mutually exclusive and incompatible. In England, the 1919 Report proposed that adult education as a movement should be aimed at satisfying the needs of the individual and at the attainment of a better social order, (Ministry of Reconstruction, 1956:149) and in the U.S., Liveright proposed that there should be more and better programs of adult education for vocational and personal competence and self-realization, and for civic and social competence (1966).

While the implication here is that under the broad umbrella of adult education, there may and should be programs aimed variously at individual and social development, it is not clear whether the two aims could be met within any one program or series of programs. On the other hand, some writers clearly see the two purposes to be in competition. Sheats talks of the polarity of aims in America: community action and problem-solving on the one hand, *versus* (my italics) self-actualization on the other (1970:xxvi). And another American, Schroeder, points out in the same Handbook that "The major issue which has plagued efforts to derive goals deductively has been 'individual needs vs societal needs'" (1970:33). Writing from an English perspective, Paterson is quite adamant that social change must be repudiated as an aim of adult education (1973:353), and he is, in general, supported in this view by another English writer, Lawson, who has strong reservations about the social and political functions of adult education (1975).

Over the last few years in Britain a debate has taken place in the literature over this question of the broad purposes of adult education. On the one hand is the stand taken by Paterson, that "in Britain, and in any open society, it is to be expected that those engaged in adult education, both teachers and students, will be far from unanimous in their opinions on any given social issue" (1973:354-55), that "an adult educator who uses adult education to promote the social policies of his preference is betraying the educational engagement"—an engagement simply to "discover and unfold the meanings inherent in our common human experience." This seems to be supported by the Russell Report, which suggests that the adult educator will always maintain an essentially educational rather than a social or political role (Department of Education and Science, 1973:para. 282). On the other hand, British writers such as Jackson (1970, 1971), Lovett (1971, 1975), and Harrison (1974) suggest that a very legitimate, if not necessary, role of the adult educator, is to help people not only understand social problems but answer them. Thomas and Harries-Jenkins (1975) suggest that in the realities of adult education there is a continuum of attitudes towards the legitimacy of postulated aims, and therefore of strategies of learning activities, from conservation through maintenance and reform to revolution. And Fordham (1976), pointing out that some sort of political value-judgment seems inherent in practically all adult education activities, doubts that this kind of education can ever be politically neutral, in the broadest sense of the term, "political." He sees British adult education as having been predominantly reformist, in Thomas's and Harries-Jenkins's terms, but with a significant maintenance role – both of which stances are political.

Such debate at the level of broad purposes, and such investigation and discussion of underlying values inherent in adult education, is harder to find in North America. In the 1960s, the works of Bergevin (1967) and Kallen (1962) appeared, the latter of which is quoted at the beginning of this chapter. Philosophical considerations are present in Miller's brief discussion of the purposes of education from the special perspectives of the adult, where he refers to adjustment to social change on the one hand, and individual growth on the other (Miller, 1964:18–26). Again in the early 1960s, Knowles, in his study of the adult education movement in the U.S. proposed the creation of "educative communities," in which adult education would help people acquire attitudes and skills of civic participation. He suggested that the adult education of the future would serve a clientele not only of individuals, but of organizations and total communities (Knowles, 1962:278–79). A decade later, discussing theories of learning, Knowles relates them to certain world views or metaphysical systems, and suggests that two such systems have been pervasive in the social sciences and, by extension, in educational practices: the mechanistic world view, and the organismic world view (1973:chap. 2). But here Knowles's application of such theories to adult education practice relates rather to the field of methodology than of teleology, as part of his discussion of the difference between pedagogy and andragogy.

There are acknowledgements, of the sort referred to earlier, by

Sheats and Schroeder, of the broad division of purposes into those concerned with personal and social development, and there is from time to time an expression of uneasy feeling that adult education as a whole does not question dominant social values and practices. Sheats refers to the Achilles' heel of American adult education, "We are essentially 'establishment-oriented'," and he goes on to suggest that "unless adult education (in the 70s) gets closer to the 'action' it will suffer disfunction and the inevitable put-down by more socially relevant institutions" (1970:xxvii). Ten years earlier, Powell and Benne suggested that American adult educationists had done more educating than philosophizing about it, and "the kind of philosophizing that examines the competing assumptions, the value-consequences of alternative decisions.... becomes a vital concern of adult education" (1960:41–42).

A search of the literature in North America reveals a dominant interest, not in the philosophy and underlying purposes of adult education, so much as in methods and techniques, and "objective" research studies of such techniques and of the characteristics of client populations. In *Resources in Education*, published monthly by the Educational Resources Informational Centre (ERIC) during 1977 and between January and October 1978, the total number of references under the indicators, "adult education," "adults," "continuing education," and "continuous learning," was 299, of which only twelve were related to purposes in adult education. Of these twelve, three were not prepared by agencies seen primarily as adult education agencies, but by such bodies as the Institute of German Studies, Indiana University; the Aspen Institute of Humanistic Studies, Palo Alto; and the Union of Experimenting Colleges and Universities. In the journal of Adult Education Research and *Theory* [my italics], *Adult Education*, the score is somewhat better; of the twenty-two main articles published in volumes xxvi and xxvii between the end of 1975 and 1977, six were related to goals and purposes, including one by this author. This count excludes the Bicentennial Issue of 1976 in which five out of five articles were, as one might have hoped, devoted to more reflective and contemplative reviews of American adult education.

More recently, there are signs of increasing discussion of philosophies and purposes in American adult education. J. L. Elias, who sees the field in the light of "the quest of men and women for meaning and transcendance"—words he uses in his review of Lawson's book referred to above (1978)—conducted a critical but sympathetic review of the principles, motivation, and vision of Freire and Illich, in 1976. In 1980, together with Merriam, he identified certain philosophical themes in American adult education: liberalism, progressivism, behaviorism, humanism, analytic philosophy, and radicalism (Elias and Merriam, 1980). That this work may raise the tempo of discussion about this aspect of adult education is given some promise, in that a very recent examination of controversies in adult education in the U.S. begins with a chapter on Philosophies At Issue (Kreitlow et al., 1981).

The current literature in and about anglophone Canada is so sparse as to make it difficult to detect emphases in this way. The Canadian Association for Adult Education (C.A.A.E.) has periodically taken the initiative in publishing anthologies relating to the state of adult education in the country—in 1950, "Adult Education in Canada;" in 1962, "Learning and Society," and in 1978, "Coming of Age." One impression left by the latter publication is that the majority of efforts directed at social goals during the 1960s were initiated not by the recognized adult education institutions so much as by governmental and other agencies, and that the notable innovators and askers of basic questions, such as Corbett and Coady, were men of earlier generations (Kidd and Selman, 1976). In 1964 the C.A.A.E. also published a "White Paper on the Education of Adults in Canada," which saw national growth and development, and the welfare and happiness of our citizens, as being contingent on the establishment of an encompassing system of continuing education in the country. The basic philosophy here appears to be individualistic, with emphasis on the initiative of the individual—"Whatever an individual chooses to learn is important simply because he chooses to learn it" (C.A.A.E., 1964).

More recently, Boshier (1978) discusses the issue in the context of the growing uneasiness about biospheric crises, and suggests the necessity for adult educationists to take this new dimension of problems into account in their practice and research. He suggests that in future, adult educationists will be fulfilling functions which are more society- and planet-centred than at present.

The pursuit of these ideas is prompted by the author's experience as an adult education practitioner in western Canada, and an observer of and participant in provincial, regional, and national networks of adult education. Subjective perceptions of adult education in Canada, particularly after adult education work in a different milieu in Africa, were that it was generally characterized by a blandness, obscured by such notable exceptions of public commitment as the Antigonish Movement and Farm Forum, and the recent program, "People Talking Back," an attempt initiated by the C.A.A.E. to obtain dialogue across the country in relation to the issue of national unity. Adult education in Alberta appeared to conform to Sheats's American diagnosis of being establishment-oriented, and to Fordham's suggestion, related to Britain, that adult education has political and even ideological dimensions at four levels of decision-making in programming and administration: in the employment of staff (with certain interests, values, and competencies); in the criteria that are used in programming policy, selection, and planning; in the criteria for and selection of students; and in the nature of the involvement and identification of staff with students. It involved little of the examination of competing assumptions and value consequences of which Powell and Benne speak. Moreover, the pervasion in adult education practice of dominant values and behaviors in the encompassing economic and social environment showed itself in the strong tendency toward competitive, non-co-operative programming by different agencies, a reluctance to get involved in complementary and co-operative planning, and an overall operating principle that adult education was primarily a process of marketing—what has been called a goods and services approach (Marriott, 1972).

But things change, in terms of both time and place. In terms of time, Schroeder (1970:27) points out that in the U.S. there have been three periods of growth or rationale over the last sixty years or so: 1919 to 1929 was a period of idealism, of adult education as an instrument of social reform, social reconstruction, and social progress; 1930 to 1946 was a period of adjustment of such ideals to what professionals judged to be more realistic; and 1947 to 1964 was a period of greater professionalism and institutionalization—and, one might add, a further retreat from social idealism into educational technology. In Britain an era of socially responsive and socially directed adult education coincided with the early period of trade unionism, co-operativism, and working-class struggle generally, and continued into the first couple of decades of this century. In times of national struggles for independence in countries like Zimbabwe in the 1960s and 1970s, much of the emphasis in adult education among Africans was at the reform and revolution end of the Thomas/Harries-Jenkins continuum, while for the whites it was at the maintenance end of the continuum.

In Canada, at the same time that adult education in Alberta appeared to lie mostly at the maintenance end of this continuum, not stirring the dominant social values, there were signs that in Quebec other more socially directed practices were coming to the fore. The difficulty here is that knowledge of practices and developments in Quebec is minimal in anglophone Canada. Indeed, verbal communication—whether oral or written—is minimal as a whole, because of a widespread inability to overcome the language barrier, and a consequent weakness of commitment on the part of anglophones and anglophone institutions to provide themselves with information about Quebec developments. This does not work so powerfully the other way around, because most adult educationists in Quebec are bilingual, and many have trained in anglophone Canadian, American, or British universities.

From 1974 to 1975 a study of over thirty development projects in various parts of Canada was conducted by a group of Canadian researchers (Development Associates, 1975). The purpose of this study was to discover similarities and differences in approaches to and strategies for the development of human and natural resources, and to see if there might be any relationship between such strategies and the success of the projects. Success was broadly related to degrees of public participation and decision-making, consciousness-raising, as well as the attainment of economic development objectives. One of the impressions left by the study was that the projects based in the province of Quebec indicated a more radical approach than the others, radical in the sense of getting at root causes of underdevelopment in society, and involved more activity rooted in the communities involved. Of the seven Quebec projects included in the final report of the survey, six had a high degree of social animation and action, a community development approach to change, and the use of information and information media to increase peoples' awareness of their condition and their potential strengths.

These differences of practice based on different rationales and these movements in different times raise the general question of influences on adult education practices. The question has two parts: by what system, or according to what categories, can we make useful distinctions between such practices; and what factors appear to lead toward these distinctions? The differences, perceived at the level of first impressions, between the situations in Alberta and Quebec, appear to provide a good arena in which to pursue both these questions. The creation of models of investigation for this purpose can then, perhaps, have an application in comparative studies in adult education on a wider basis and between other regions, countries, or periods of time. As a leader in the field of comparative studies in education, Bereday suggests that a comparative study should have a guiding hypothesis, a framework of inquiry (1964:22). The guiding hypothesis for the study that follows is provided by the Development Associates survey referred to above, that adult education is more socially oriented, and in this sense more radical, in Quebec than in Alberta. In terms of that hypothesis, the purpose of this study is to examine policies, structures, and processes of adult education in the two provinces to see if they confirm the hypothesis or not, and to relate those policies, structures, and processes to forces in the respective environments.

References

Bereday, G.Z.F. 1964. *Comparative Methods in Education.* New York: Holt, Rinehart and Winston.

Bergevin, P. 1967. *A Philosophy for Adult Education.* New York: Seabury Press.

Boshier, R. 1978. "Future Functions of Adult Education." *Canadian Journal of University Continuing Education,* vol. v, no. 1.

Canadian Association for Adult Education. 1964. *A Canadian Policy for Continuing Education.* Toronto: Canadian Association of Adult Education.

Department of Education and Science, (U.K.). 1973. *Adult Education: A Plan for Development.* London: Her Majesty's Stationery Office.

Development Associates. 1975. *Documentation and Analysis of Development Programs in Canada.* Edmonton: Division of Community Development, University of Alberta.

Educational Resources Information Centre (ERIC). 1977–1978. *Resources in Education.* Washington: Department of Health, Education, and Welfare.

Elias, J.L. 1976. *Conscientization and Deschooling.* Philadelphia: Westminster.

———. 1978. Review of K.H. Lawson's "Philosophical Concepts and Values in Adult Education." *Adult Education* (U.S.), vol. xxviii, no. 3.

Elias, J.L. and Merriam, S. 1980. *Philosophical Foundations of Adult Education.* New York: Kreiger.

Fordham, P. 1976. "The Political Context of Adult Education." *Studies in Adult Education,* vol. 8, no. 1.

Harrison, J. 1974. "Community Work and Adult Education." *Studies in Adult Education,* vol. 6, no. 1.

Jackson, K. 1970. "Adult Education and Community Development." *Studies in Adult Education,* vol. 2, no. 2.

Jackson, K. and Lovett, T. 1971. "Universities and the W.E.A.—An Alternative Approach." *Adult Education* (U.K.), vol. 44 no. 2.

Kallen, H.M. 1962. *Philosophical Issues in Adult Education.* Springfield, Ill.: Charles C. Thomas.

Kidd, J.R. and Selman, G.R., eds. 1978. *Coming of Age.* Toronto: Canadian Association of Adult Education.

Knowles, M. 1962. *The Adult Education Movement in the United States.* New York: Holt, Rinehart and Winston.

———. 1973. *The Adult Learner: A Neglected Species.* Houston: Gulf Publishing.

Lawson, K.H. 1975. *Philosophical Concepts and Values in Adult Education.* Nottingham: Barnes and Humby.

Liveright, A.A. 1966. "Some Observations on the Status of Adult Education in the U.S. Today." *Adult Education* (U.S.), vol. xvi, no. 4.

Lovett, T. 1975. *Adult Education, Community Development and the Working Class.* London: Ward Lock Educational.

Lovett, T. and Jackson, K. 1971. "Universities and the W.E.A.—An Alternative Approach." *Adult Education* (U.K.), vol. 44, no. 2.

Marriott, S. 1972. "Society, Universities and Adult Education." *Journal of the International Congress of University Adult Education,* vol. xi, nos. 1 and 2.

Miller, H.L. 1964. *Teaching and Learning in Adult Education.* New York: Macmillan.

Ministry of Reconstruction (U.K.). 1956. *Design for Democracy.* London: Parrish.

Paterson, R.W.K. 1973. "Social Change as an Educational Aim." *Adult Education* (U.K.), vol. 45, no. 6.

Powell, J.W. and Benne, K.D. 1960. "Philosophies of Adult Education." In *Handbook of Adult Education in the United States,* ed. M.S. Knowles. Chicago: Adult Education Association of the U.S.

Schroeder, W.L. 1970. "Adult Education Defined and Described." In *Handbook of Adult Education,* ed. R.M. Smith, G.F. Aker, and J.R. Kidd. New York: Macmillan.

Sheats, P. 1970. Introduction. In *Handbook of Adult Education,* ed. R.M. Smith, G.F. Aker, and J.R. Kidd. New York: Macmillan.

Thomas, J.E. and Harries-Jenkins, G. 1975. "Adult Education and Social Change." *Studies in Adult Education,* vol. 7, no. 1.

2

Adult Education and Culture: The Terminology

Adult Education

In a Recommendation on the Development of Adult Education adopted by UNESCO general conference in Nairobi, October-November 1976, adult education

> denotes the entire body of organized educational processes, whatever the content, level and method, whether formal or otherwise, whether they prolong or replace initial education in schools, colleges and universities as well as in apprenticeship, whereby persons regarded as adult by the society to which they belong develop their abilities, enrich their knowledge, improve their technical or professional qualifications or turn them in a new direction and bring about changes in their attitudes or behavior in the two-fold perspective of full personal development and participation in balanced and independent social, economic and cultural development.

It is "an integral part of a global scheme for lifelong education and learning." And "lifelong education and learning.... denotes an overall scheme aimed both at restructuring the existing educational system and at developing the entire educational potential outside the education system" (UNESCO, 1976).

Thus, accepting this comprehensive definition, we are concerned with a range of experiences, organized as distinct from casual, incidental and/or spontaneous, that have as their objectives, either discretely or in some combination, vocational proficiency, inner satisfaction, personal growth, and social change. In other words, programs having a personal, individual purpose are equally included in the scope of the definition with those having a social collective purpose. It clearly envisages both personal and social development.

A number of points arise from this definition. First, what is not resolved by the definition is the extent to which the term "education" includes what are sometimes seen as merely recreational or leisure pursuits, for example, ballroom dancing, gardening, or embroidery. This can affect government attitudes toward funding of adult education activities. Secondly, the phrase, "persons regarded as adult by the society to which they belong" raises an interesting question about the distinction that is commonly made between adult education and post-secondary or higher education. According to other measures of adulthood, such as eligibility to vote in government elections, to purchase liquor, or to serve in the armed forces, it is accepted that persons from the age of eighteen are adults; this is so in both Alberta and Quebec. By these standards, the large majority of students attending institutions of post-secondary education full-time are regarded as adult. Yet the term "adult education," in English or French, is reserved in practice for processes that lie outside the regular full-time regime of college or university admission and study in which these adults are engaged, and such adults are not seen as being in the field of adult education. Moreover, they are often not treated as adults, so far as regimes of study and methods of teaching are concerned.

A third point of interest in the UNESCO definition is the proposition that adult education is an integral part of lifelong learning and education, and that the latter is aimed at the restructuring of the existing education system. It cannot be said, from the evidence of this study, that in either Alberta or Quebec the question of restructuring the existing education system in the light of the concept of lifelong learning has been addressed in earnest.

The fact that the Resolution, containing the definition set out above, was signed by the Canadian delegate to the General Conference of UNESCO in Nairobi, does not give it any force in Canada. In this country education is a matter falling exclusively within the jurisdiction of the provincial governments (Government of Canada, 1970: sec. 93). So, to discover whether the view of adult education expressed in the UNESCO definition corresponds in any way with that held in Alberta and Quebec, it is necessary to seek definitions, recommendations, or similar statements of policy produced in those provinces.

In Alberta an explicit policy on adult education was first articulated in April 1975 with the publication of the document, *Further Education Policy, Guidelines and Procedures,* by the Department of Advanced Education. The use of the term, "further education" by the government might, on the face of it, seem to indicate a limitation of the scope of the concept along the lines that have been followed for some years in Britain, where the term relates to learning activities pursued by adults in furthering their formal education or training, and where "adult education" has traditionally meant liberal, non-vocationally-oriented education. The use of the term, "further education," in Alberta appears to stem from the Report of the Commission on Educational Planning (1972). The term carried through from the commission's report into government usage probably because Dr. Walter Worth, the Commissioner and author of the report, became the first Deputy Minister of the Department of Advanced Education, which was established shortly after the report was published.

The meaning given to the term, "further education," by Worth is clearly broader than that in the traditional British usage. In the report the term is equated with what is "usually referred to as adult or continuing education" (1972:59). And the functions of further education are listed as: motivation, enhancing and maintaining each individual's urge and ability to keep learning; emancipation, providing the opportunities to be set free and to be able to function normally in society; career enhancement; and integration, developing a person's own identity and integrity with respect to the human community, and the social consciousness necessary to be an active and understanding participant in a democratic society.

The definition of the term in the government's *Further Education*

Policy Guidelines and Procedures is not as full as that in Worth's report, but it allows for the same kind of scope—"planned educational experiences designed to be integrated on a part-time basis into the on-going life styles of adults as part of a system of recurrent education." The statement goes on: "continued learning by adults is also needed to help Albertans better understand and cope with the development of a resource base to sustain and improve the quality of life in the Province in the decades ahead." And "lifelong learning is seen as an important necessary condition to any solutions to serious social problems that face our society" (Ministry of Advanced Education, 1975:1).

So, despite the different terminology, adult education is seen by the Alberta government in the same light as it is by the signatories of the UNESCO recommendation, bound into the context of a system of recurrent, or lifelong education and learning. It seems, likewise, to relate to individual and social development, and to vocationally-oriented as well as inner-oriented learning. One way in which it differs from the UNESCO definition is that it specifically relates to part-time educational experiences for adults. It is at this point that the UNESCO definition, which does not distinguish between full-time and part-time studies, takes on what may, for the present, be considered a quality of idealism—ideal in the sense that it does not yet find a response in the organizational and administrative realities of the Alberta education system.

As the Worth report indicates, the term favored by the Alberta government, "further education," means the same as the other two terms commonly used in the province—adult and continuing education. And apart from the general tendency to apply all these terms to part-time studies only, they all have the same general scope as the UNESCO definition of adult education. So the three terms can be, and are, used interchangeably in the province.

In Quebec there is also a plurality of terms in use, but in this case these various terms are not used interchangeably, but are used to make distinctions within the broad definition. The terminology begins to point to a difference between the two provinces, and to trace the genesis and development of this difference we can, as in Alberta, go back to the report of a commission of inquiry—in this case, the Royal Commission on Education in the Province of Quebec, which, insofar as it deals with adult education, was published in 1963. This Commission (named after Dr. A.W. Parent, its chairman) appears to have been influenced by the ideas of Bertrand Schwartz of France, who has been a central figure in the development of the concept of *éducation permanente* or lifelong education, and the commission expressed a preference for the term éducation permanente over *éducation des adultes*

> because we believe that what we are, in fact, proposing is really something new. We understand by the term, éducation permanente, a broader need and desire for personal and cultural improvement; we see it as a general education that not only offers to the adult population the necessary variety of courses and opportunities for personal and cultural development, but which also encourages that population to take advantage of them and which seeks to open up among adults a concern for and a habit of study. (Commission Royale, 1963:321)

This seems uncommonly like the Worth Commission's definition of the scope and function of further education, with its reference to motivation, emancipation, and so forth.

Following the establishment of the Ministry of Education in 1964, there were established in 1966 four divisions (*directions générales*) with responsibility for elementary and secondary education, college education, higher (university) education, and éducation permanente; in other words, the Parent Commission terminology was used to designate what corresponded to the field of further/adult/continuing education in Alberta. However, since then there has been a reaction in Quebec against the term, on the grounds that it confuses the issue of the education of adults as such. The view is held that while éducation permanente is a valid concept and should stand as an inspiration and a context for particular educational practices, it diverts attention from the particular and immediate needs for improving learning opportunities for adults. Hence, in 1971 the Direction Générale de l'Education Permanente became the Direction Générale de l'Education des Adultes. So "adult education" became the general term in use.

The discussion about terminology, and what it represents, appears to indicate a difference between Quebec and Alberta. On the one hand, there appears to be some attraction in Quebec toward the European—and particularly the French—penchant for conceptualization, for proposing ideas, discussing them, and hazarding the means of realizing them. Besides Schwartz, referred to above, perhaps Edgar Faure, as Head of UNESCO's International Commission on the Development of Education (1972), which produced a report titled *Learning to Be*, best exemplifies this characteristic. Certainly, the most active discussion of such concepts as éducation permanente, lifelong learning, and recurrent education, and of their implications for systemic change, appears to come from Europeans (Dave, 1976; C.E.R.I., 1973). On the other hand, there is also some attraction in Quebec toward the more typically North American pragmatism, which sees adult education more in functional, practical terms, emphasizing methods and techniques of management, programming, and teaching, and displaying almost a distrust of theoretical approaches. A number of leading adult educationalists in Quebec pursued their studies in adult education in American and Canadian universities, which tend to follow the U.S. models. They appear to reflect the two-way pull of Europe and of North America, and a resulting ambivalence. At any rate, in Quebec there is an awareness of and debate about the meaning and implications of terms and concepts such as éducation permanente, lifelong learning, and recurrent education.

In Alberta there is no evidence of such debate. Though the Worth Report and the government's *Further Education Policy, Guidelines and Procedures* refer to lifelong learning, the term could be replaced with "continuing education" without changing the sense. Alberta appears to reflect without any significant qualification the dominant North American view of adult education as a compendium of organizational and instructional techniques that make it possible for adults to take up various forms of learning where their "normal" education left off. With the possibly exclusive exception of E.A. Corbett, adult educationalists in Alberta have not been concerned so much with conceptualizing and influencing the direction of adult education as they have with the very practical process of providing forms of learning according to their perceptions of the demands.

To return to the practical situation in Quebec, the scope of adult education is to offer to all those who have left the (formal education) system, to all those who wish to follow a learning project suitable to their needs and capacities – personal development, collective research, academic upgrading, re-training, specialization, etc. – a wide range of instructional programs. (Quebec Government, 1975–76:511)

This, again, as in the case of Alberta, corresponds nearly enough to the scope and intention of the UNESCO definition of adult education, but again with a qualification, that adult education appertains to those who have left the formal, full-time education system. It excludes that increasing number of adults who are defined as full-time students in institutions of post-secondary education.

The annual report of the Ministry of Education, 1976, does not express this qualification, in stating the objectives of adult education as being "to assure to all adults in Quebec, conditions which permit them to expand in respect of their economic, social and cultural future, and to participate actively in guiding and developing Quebec society" (Ministère de l'Education, 1976:69). This takes into account the opportunities – both full-time and part-time – provided to adults for upgrading their formal education and/or vocational skills, that is, manpower development. But beyond this particular category of adult education, only part-time studies are classified and treated as adult education.

Where Quebec differs from Alberta in this matter of terminology and at the level of general intention, is that within the system of adult education, other more specific terms are used to denote particular aspects of the field. And such terms, with the activities they represent, show some of the features of Quebec practice. There are three broad categories of adult education: general education (formation générale), professional education (formation professionelle), and sociocultural or popular education (formation socio-culturelle or éducation populaire). The first two are, generally speaking, related to manpower development (and in this respect they have their equivalents in Alberta), while the third denotes activities of a non-credit nature guided by personal interests or directed at social and community matters. This distinction between personal and social purposes of education, and an emphasis on the latter, may have had its earliest expression and impetus in the Report of the Ryan Committee, which was set up in conjunction with the Parent Commission. One of the recommendations of this Committee was

> that a distinction be made between adult education considered as personal development (academic, professional and cultural) and adult education considered as a contribution to national and community planning; in other words, that a distinction be made between two different levels of adult education oriented toward change: one concerned with qualifications needed by adults to adjust to planned changes, and one concerned with qualifications needed by groups of people to participate actively and positively in both the preparation and execution of the (national) plan. (Comité d'Etude, 1963:133-34)

This distinction draws our attention to an emphasis in Quebec adult education that is not present in Alberta; this will be examined in more detail later.

This introductory discussion of the scope of adult education indicates that we can validly attempt to compare reasonably common concepts and fields of educational practice in the two provinces. The common comprehension is that we are dealing with educational opportunities provided by and/or for adults, which have as their purpose, either separately or in combination, vocational security or advancement, personal fulfilment, and social and community development. Within this, the distinctions made in Quebec, and different emphases in the two provinces, indicate a fruitful field for an analysis of comparisons and contrasts and their causes.

What this study will not attempt to examine is what is sometimes called informal education, the lifelong process whereby people acquire attitudes, values, skills, and knowledge from such agencies and environments as the mass media, libraries, theatres, and so forth (Coombs, et al., 1973), except insofar as such agencies and environments are purposefully used for the "organized eductional processes" of the UNESCO definition. Furthermore, there is a wide variety of purely private adult education programs, such as in-service training schemes in industry, and programs conducted by churches for their members, which as Verner and Booth (1964:2) suggest, far outnumber public programs, but for which adequate data are difficult to collect.

This study will relate almost entirely to public programs offered by institutions whose primary purpose is education, by government agencies, and by certain other important associations.

Culture

The use of the word "culture" as part of the title of this book requires definition for the purpose of the study, which is to relate patterns of adult education to the broader social context in which they are shaped. Accordingly, we use the term in a wide sense, wider than that used, for example, by the Federal Cultural Policy Review Committee in its *Discussion Guide* (1981). The committee focused on three types of culture: professional culture, including the "traditional and classical forms in art, literature and music"; community culture, encompassing those "amateur activities and community arts by which people come to understand themselves through creative expression"; and commercial culture, associated with "such activities as mass-market publishing, most film and commercial television." These types of culture are only a part of our field.

T.S. Eliot's definition of culture is one of the widest: "the pattern of the society as a whole" (1948:25). Writing as anthropologists, after citing 164 definitions, Kroeber and Kluckholm suggest the following one, more detailed but hardly less comprehensive:

> Culture consists of patterns, explicit and implicit, of and for behaviour acquired and transmitted by symbols, constituting the distinct achievement of human groups, including their embodiments in artifacts; the essential core of culture consists of traditional (i.e. historically derived and selected) ideas and especially their attached values; culture systems may, on the one hand, be considered as products of action, on the other hand as conditioning elements of further action. (1952:357)

Important features of this definition are that it refers to symbolic patterns of and for behavior, historically derived and selected ideas and their values, and conditioning elements of action; in other words, the broad set of forces that arise from the past and influence future actions, of whatever sort and by whomever in the orbit of that culture. This broad scope is reflected in the definition produced in the Canadian context by a group of scholars for the Canadian Commission for UNESCO. Their conclusion was:

> Culture is a dynamic value system of learned elements, with assumptions, conventions, beliefs and rules permitting members of a group to relate to each other and to the world, to communicate and to develop their creative potential. (1972:83)

This definition goes beyond the idea of a set of forces influencing future action in a somewhat restricting sense, to suggest a positive, creative, nurturing environment. It is in this broad sense that Quebec culture is seen by the francophone leaders in the province. The aspect of nurturing is taken up directly by the Minister of State for Cultural Development, in his definition of culture as, "the building and nurturing of a people by itself" (1978:153). His Blue Book on a Quebec policy for cultural development is an exploration of the spirit of Quebecois culture, and the place of that culture in the policy and decision-making process of the provincial government. Culture involves "styles of living, of creating, of educating" (1978:111); it is "a universe of knowledge and a certain philosophy of life" (1978:153).

The discussions under the aegis of the Canadian Commission for UNESCO Group produced two other concepts that are relevant to questions of culture in both Quebec and Alberta, though in different ways. "Cultural pluralism", that is, the cultural concerns of groups within a wider entity, is a concept taken up in Quebec in justification of a distinct and relatively homogeneous Quebecois culture in, and to some extent apart from, the rest of Canada. The thrust of much of the political, social, economic, and more narrowly conceived cultural energies is in support of that concept. The "right to culture," which includes the right to live creatively in one's culture of origin, stirs up the same energies.

The broad sense of the term "culture" and its nationalist spirit, as used in Quebec, is not so clearly or explicitly articulated in Alberta. The concepts of "cultural pluralism" and "right to culture" do, however, find their place and a voice in the concern of some of the ethnic groups in the province to preserve and encourage their culture of origin. This is principally at the level of language and creative arts – what the Federal Cultural Policy Review Committee calls community culture. However, overlying these multi-cultural strata, it is possible to discern in Alberta a dominant value system, a constellation of historically derived and selected ideas, values, assumptions, and conventions, which can be taken to indicate a culture in the sense of the broad definitions referred to above. Much of the remainder of this study, insofar as it relates to Alberta, will be an exploration of the influence of that dominant value system on patterns of adult education in the province, while the study of the Quebec scene will explore the effects of the relatively more homogeneous, and explicitly political, nature of the Quebec culture on adult education patterns.

This is not to say that these patterns are attributable only to the different cultures in the two provinces. Both provinces share many features of a common Canadian experience, for instance, the influence of certain federal government policies, and both feel the effects of broader influences, such as the surge in the human relations movement in North America in the 1950s and 1960s, which had widespread effects on management and adult education practices on this continent and in other countries.

References

Canadian Commission for UNESCO. 1977. "Definition of Culture." *Cultures,* vol. 4, no. 4. Paris: UNESCO Press.

Centre Pour la Recherche et l'Innovation dans l'Enseignement (C.E.R.I.). 1973. *L'Education Récurrente.* Paris: Organization de Cooperation et de Développement Economique (O.E.C.D.).

Comité d'Etude Sur L'Education Des Adultes. 1963. *Rapport.* Quebec: Ministère de l'Education.

Commission on Educational Planning. 1972. *A Choice of Futures.* Edmonton: Queen's Printer.

Commission Royale d'Enguête sur L'Enseignement Dans La Province de Québec. 1963. *Rapport —Deuxieme Partie.* Quebec: Editeur Officiel.

Coombs, P.H., Prosser, Roy C. and Ahmed, M. 1973. *New Paths to Learning for Rural Children and Youth.* New York: International Council for Educational Development.

Dave, R.H., ed. 1976. *Foundations of Lifelong Education.* Toronto: Pergamon Press.

Eliot, T.S. 1948. *Notes Toward the Definition of Culture.* London: Faber and Faber.

Federal Cultural Review Committee. 1981. *Speaking of Our Culture.* Ottawa: Federal Cultural Review Committee.

Government of Canada. 1970. *British North America Act: Revised Statutes of Canada.* Ottawa: Queen's Printer.

International Commission on the Development of Education. 1972. *Learning to Be.* Paris: UNESCO Press.

Kroeber, A.L. and Kluckholm, C. 1952. *Culture.* New York: Vantage Books.

Ministère de l'Education. 1976. *L'Education Au Québec en 1976.* Quebec: Editeur Officiel.

Ministre d'Etat au Développement Culturel. 1978. *La Politique Québécoise du Développement Culturel.* Quebec: Editeur Officiel.

Ministry of Advanced Education and Manpower. 1975. *Further Education Policy, Guidelines and Procedures.* Edmonton: Ministry of Advanced Education and Manpower.

Quebec Government. 1975-76. *Annuaire (Yearbook).* Quebec: Editeur Officiel.

UNESCO. 1976. *Recommendation on the Development of Adult Education.* Ottawa: UNESCO Canadian Commission.

Verner, C. and Booth, A. 1964. *Adult Education.* New York: Centre for Applied Research in Education.

3

Basis of Comparison

In Chapter 1 the guiding hypothesis of this study was that adult education as it is promoted and practiced in Quebec is more socially oriented than in Alberta. In order to pursue the hypothesis, a scale for measuring and comparing is needed. Then, to make the comparison useful, we need to examine the forces that cause the differences, and to make that examination pertinent rather than discursive we need to see those forces within a framework. The purpose of this chapter is to set out a scale to base the comparisons and a framework to examine the forces that influence what happens.

A Range of Purposes

In developing a scale to measure and compare adult educational systems and enterprises, we can profitably start from a very simple one suggested by Powell and Benne (1960:44), which is that change as a process of learning can be seen broadly in terms of two approaches, the rationalistic and the developmental. The rationalistic approach embraces the more traditional, didactic approach of liberal education, based on the premise that people are guided by reason and will change their opinion if presented with "objective" information and reasonable arguments. The developmental mode implies a more experiential involvement of the people concerned in the learning process; examples of this mode are community development and group dynamics sessions. Such a simple typology implies, in terms of the *mode* of learning, the dimension of passivity-activity. In other words, there is a continuum from a condition where the learner, in a position of relative ignorance and powerlessness, receives knowledge from someone who is considered to possess it, to a condition where the learner is assumed to possess some qualities that can contribute to the learning process, and is brought in to that process in an active capacity. There is, as well, a second dimension, which ranges from a condition where the knowledge imparted and acquired, the *content* of the learning, is focused on the inner personal satisfaction of the individual, to a condition where it is focused on social, collective issues. These two dimensions can be depicted in terms of two axes, as in Figure 1. The horizontal axis shows the movement from a passive to an active mode, while the vertical axis shows the movement from individual-focused content to collective-focused content.

These two axes, and the configuration of the model, recall a similar approach to the question of purposes by Miller (1964:20-24). But Miller's content axis moves from "adjustment" to "individual growth," and adjustment means helping the adult "adjust to some facet of change in the society which affects his performance in a social role." This equates adjustment more to what is referred to later in this chapter as coping, rather than to social development in the sense of having to do with social change.

Some examples from each of the resulting four quadrants of the diagram will illustrate the use of the model. Example 1 in the top left quadrant, could represent a course of lectures in psychology, taught in a didactic manner; the content is focused on personal understanding and the role of the learner is passive. A course in a foreign language on the other hand, would be likely to have some social purpose and to involve more active participation by the learner, and could be placed in position 2. A typical program of lectures on politi-

Figure 1

Dimensions of the Learning Process

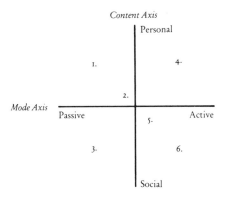

1. Lectures in psychology
2. A course in a foreign language
3. Lectures in political science or economics
4. Experiential learning – personal growth
5. Action research
6. Social action

cal science or economics would be represented by position 3 in the lower left-hand quadrant, the content being socially oriented but the mode being student-passive. If, on the other hand, the course in personal understanding were presented in a way that required the learner to participate in group experiences such as communication exercises and T-groups, the activity would fall in the upper right-hand quadrant, as shown by position 4, and if the program in political science or economics involved the learner in action research, it would be placed somewhere around position 5, while if it involved participatory social action, it would also fall within the same lower right-hand quadrant, near position 6.

It is, of course, one of the claims of adult education that adults respond better to active modes of learning, and that poor adult education is conducted at the passive end of the continuum. We would therefore expect most adult education to be at the active end, whether in Alberta or Quebec. It is difficult to know, from an outside and macroscopic viewpoint, what mode of teaching and learning is being followed in particular programs, and an investigation of similarities and differences in the two provinces will have to rely mainly on observation of the content and overt purposes of adult education activities, but will consider the other dimension in trying to discern differences in approach. For instance, programs based clearly on an action research or social action mode will give strong indications of social content and purpose.

There is another aspect of adult education that distinguishes some forms of it from education in the early years of life. The English comparative educationist, King (1957:14), points out that the most obvious reason for wishing to educate adults is seen where formal schooling has been limited—in other words, remedial adult education. Writing in 1957, King pointed out that the need for this was not confined to less developed countries with clearly inadequate schooling, but occurred in such countries as Germany, the U.S. and Britain. Over twenty years later it is still possible to say the same thing, certainly about Canada, where the 1976 census figures show that 5.5 percent of the population over fifteen years of age, or 856,000 people, had less than a Grade 5 education and that 28 percent of that population, or almost 4.5 million, had only a Grade 8 education or less.

King suggests that, in a sense, all adult education can be described as either remedial or evolutionary. It is not quite clear what "evolutionary" means, but the implication seems to be that remedial adult education is to be seen as relying on an outside teaching agency, as distinct from being able to evolve, or develop, from within the learner's own resources. This would place remedial education at the left end of the passive/active axis. If this were King's meaning, in the time since the late 1950s he may acknowledge that there are valid evolutionary or developmental techniques by which the lack of adult literacy, numeracy, and skills in problem-solving can be remedied—such as the Freirean process of action/praxis (1972), and participatory research projects (Participatory Research Group, 1978). What this suggests is that programs in remedial adult education could fit into any one of the four quadrants in Figure 1, depending on what kind of deficiency was being remedied and how the learning was organized.

If, on the other hand, King is thinking not in terms of modalities but of purposes, his suggestion is a useful one; there are, in other words, forms of adult education to remedy some deficiency in the learner's knowledge or skill, while other forms of adult education enable the learner to evolve or develop beyond a present adequate level of functioning, either as a person or in some role. We can therefore propose a continuum representing a variety of purposes, from remedying learning deficiencies to enabling a higher level of personal and social functioning, somewhat on the analogy of Maslow's model of deficiency needs and growth needs, culminating in self-actualization. In other words, such a continuum would enable us to refine and make more explicit the content axis in Figure 1, giving us more specific bench-marks along that axis.

Figure 2 represents a continuum from what may be considered a condition of inadequate personal functioning, in terms of the expectations of the dominant culture, toward a condition of adequacy, fulfilment, and social responsibility. An interpretation of each of the terms along the continuum will help toward an understanding of the model.

The term "remedial" refers to adult education programs designed, as King suggests, to make up for a deficiency in formal schooling. Such programs become necessary for people who for a variety of reasons have not acquired the basic skills to function in the society in which they now find themselves—either in economic or social terms, or both. For the most part, these are literacy and numeracy, but they also include an elementary familiarity with the norms and rules of the society that aid or restrain one in making decisions in that society—basic life skills. As far as literacy and numeracy are concerned, in the 1960s Statistics Canada defined functional literacy as having five years

Figure 2

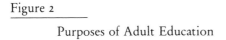

Purposes of Adult Education

Remedial   Coping   Personal   Social   Counter-cultural
                      Development   Development   Development

of schooling; by this measure, according to the 1976 Census, almost a million adults in Canada—over 5 percent of the population aged over fifteen years—were illiterate (Statistics Canada, cat. 92-827). The Canadian Association for Adult Education defines illiteracy as having had eight years or less of schooling; by this measure almost 4.5 million Canadians out of a total of 15.4 million aged over fifteen years, or 28 percent, were illiterate in 1976. In Alberta there were 240,000 out of a total of 1.2 million aged over fifteen years who had schooling up to Grade 8 or less—20 percent. In Quebec there were 1.5 million out of a total of 4.2 million—37 percent. This indicates a definite need for remedial adult education.

In addition, there are immigrants who require to learn English or French as their second language in order to function in Canadian society, and there are others whose upbringing in isolated areas or in a culture different from mainstream Canadian society makes it difficult to adapt. The programs at this end of the spectrum are adult literacy programs, English or French as a second language, and what are called Adult Basic Education programs.

There is not a clear line between adult education of a remedial nature and that which is designed to help people cope with their existing and changing condition. For instance, a course in English may be seen as remedial when offered to new immigrants, but, if it is a course called "Communication Arts," offered for, and taken by, anglophones who find themselves lacking skill in simple report writing in their work, it may be seen as learning to cope with changing job needs. In other words, adult education activities of a coping sort are those programs that help people to deal with conditions of life arising out of personal problems such as family breakdown, death and dying, lack of assertiveness or interpersonal communication skills; out of some role change, such as from shop-floor worker to foreman, from single person to parent, from housewife to second income earner; out of changes in the state of knowledge and technologies in one's profession, and pressures in one's profession or place of work or one's family to keep upgrading oneself. The kinds of programs at this place in the continuum include continuing professional education programs, most business-oriented programs, and applied behavioral science programs about basic human relations, coping with stress, self-assertiveness, and parenting.

Again, the line between "coping" programs and "personal

development" programs is not clear-cut. In fact, there is an element of personal growth in most of the programs referred to above. The difference conceptually can be related to Maslow's hierarchy of personal needs (1968:chap. 3); remedial learning is at the level of meeting basic physiological and economic needs; learning directed at coping is at the level of meeting needs for economic, social, and psychological security; learning directed at personal development is at the level of meeting needs for esteem and self-actualization — of stretching oneself beyond what is adequate for survival and social acceptance. In terms of observable adult education activities, such programs are again in the field of applied behavioral sciences, on subjects such as self-awareness, life planning, creativeness, explorations of consciousness, in the arts and humanities, and in certain outdoor and field programs.

As with the transition between each of the previous stages in the continuum, that between personal development and social development is not clean and abrupt. For instance, the movement of consciousness-raising among women is aimed at both individual self-knowledge and growth, and changes in existing social relationships and structures. Social development in this context is taken to mean the development, in a positive and nurturing way, of social institutions, and in changes in the relationships among them, and between them and individuals in the society. It is also taken to refer to society in the way that it is conventionally perceived, as identified with local, regional, and/or national entities. Here the perspective is outward from the individual into the environment. The kinds of programs included in this category are those involving, in terms of content, communal issues, and in terms of mode, activities where the learners are initiators and participants. Some of the terms used for this kind of activity are community education, community development, *animation sociale* and *animation communautaire*.

Crowfoot and Chesler use the term "counter-cultural development" to describe a perspective that stresses social organization as building and rebuilding a new social life-style with more regard to symbolism, myth, and the inner identity of cultures, going beyond present social and political identifications. They suggest such writers and sources as Buber, Fromm, and the Bible as expositors of this perspective. The difficulty with counter-cultural is that its meaning in the terms suggested above, at an ideological level, can be confused with its use to denote dropping out of society as investigated by

Musgrove, a leading educational sociologist in England (1974:9). This study traces not the extent of that kind of counter-cultural behavior among the populations of Alberta and Quebec, but the extent to which adult education in the two provinces invites people to question and challenge existing social, economic, and political ideas and institutions.

This end of the continuum reflects the ideas not only of the writers mentioned by Crowfoot and Chesler, but the more popular works of Reich (1970) and Roszak (1968). There is a growing awareness of the importance of cultural identities, as expressed in the 1979 Club of Rome report, "No Limits To Learning" (Botkin et al., 1979:113–17). There is an element of spiritual seeking, represented in such "new age" ventures as the Findhorn Community in Scotland (Thompson, 1974:chap. 7), and a concern for planetary crises and solutions found in, for example, cross-cultural learning centres.

In Figure 2 the continuum from remedial to social development is extended beyond that point as a dotted line to indicate the tentative and precarious nature of the counter-cultural perspective in contemporary adult education endeavors. It also suggests this type of adult education as being of a different dimension, an intimation that it takes us outside the paradigm into which the others fit. This matter is discussed further in Chapter 12.

Figure 2 is proposed as a measure to make comparisons of adult education in the provinces of Alberta and Quebec. The next section of this chapter suggests an ordering of the elements and forces that influence the pattern of adult education.

Influencing Factors*

Another writer in the field of comparative education, C.A. Anderson (1961–62), suggests that there are two broad approaches to comparative studies in education: one restricted to the collection and compari-

* The framework set out in this chapter is adapted from a previous article by the author: "Comparative Studies in Lifelong Education," *Journal of the International Congress of University Continuing Education*, vol. XII, no. 1, 1973.

sons of purely educational data, and one where the traits of the educational system are related to other features of society. He goes on to cite Kandel's definition of comparative education as an analysis of forces that cause differences in educational systems. This second approach will be used in this study.

The dominant and conventional view held in the sociology of education is in the Durkheim tradition, that education is a means through which society arouses and develops in a child "a certain number of physical, intellectual and moral states which are demanded of him by both the political society as a whole and the special milieu for which he is especially destined" (Durkheim, 1966:42). This is given an institutional cast by educational sociologists Brooker and Gottlieb (1964:79) in their proposition that "no educational institution is external to the society and therefore no educational institution can exert influences for change beyond those implied in its accepted function." And Mills and Gerth (1964:251–52) take the idea further by suggesting that the political, economic, religious, military, and kinship orders impose certain goals and structures in the educational sphere.

These views refer to the formal system of primary, secondary, and post-secondary education. They have been questioned by some in recent years, in the sense that though this state of affairs predominates in schools, the process of learning even there has the potential to be – and should be – subversive of the controlling educational values and practices. (Postman and Weingartner, 1969; Holt, 1972). Whether they can be extended to include education provided to adults through the formal institutions in that system is one of the questions to bear in mind as this study proceeds. Earlier references to counter-cultural development indicate an assumption that somewhere in the range of adult education activities there may be some that at least question the goals and structures imposed by political and other orders. One of the features that adult educationists claim distinguishes adult education from education in the earlier years is a sense of independence, maturity, and questioning on the part of adult learners. Despite this assumption, however, it seems excessively audacious to claim that adult education is not influenced by the dominant social and political ideas and structures of the society in which it takes place. These two elements correspond to what Holmes calls the normative pattern and the institutional pattern; he suggests that these two factors, with a third he calls static elements (climate, terrain, and so on), are what influence education (1958).

There are two other sets of factors that are generally taken to influence the course of adult education. A central tenet of commonly held principles in the field is that adult education must start with the needs of the learners (London, 1960; Kidd, 1973:chap. 10;Wiltshire, 1973). One of the basic skills taught in courses in adult education is needs assessment. Program planning is held to begin and revolve around it, and the literature of adult education is full of explanations, criticisms, and modifications of various models and techniques of needs assessment—questionnaires, interviews, sample surveys, self surveys, demographic studies, statistical analyses, market analyses, and so forth. It is, therefore, reasonable to suggest perceptions of needs as another force influencing the course of adult education.

The fourth major set of such influences may be considered under the term, resources. This, again, is in line with a common thrust of adult education literature (Knowles, 1960:part III; Verner and Booth, 1964), and is a particular application of a wider sociological acknowledgement of the importance of facilities in providing opportunities for social change (Parsons, 1964:90).

So these four sets of forces influence the course of adult education: social philosophy; social structure; needs; and resources. Before proceeding to examine adult education in Alberta and Quebec in terms of these four elements, we need to define each one more clearly and to suggest their interrelationships.

Social Philosophy

Kandel uses the term "national ethos" to describe what a nation considers essential to its security and stability, and he suggests that education is provided primarily in the national interest (1959). That term begins to lead us in the right direction, but it is still too broad to use as a tool. President Nyerere uses the term "national ethic" (1967:6). In the "Arusha Declaration" and "T.A.N.U.'s Policy on Socialism and Self-Reliance" he outlines the broad goals in Tanzania, a democratic socialist country, for the formation and maintenance of co-operative organizatrions (T.A.N.U., 1967). In his statement, on *Education for Self-Reliance* (1967) Nyerere then goes on to write more specifically of the role and organization of education in the newly-independent country: "Our education must inculcate a sense of commitment to the total community. . . . it must counteract the temptation to intellectual arrogance" (Ibid.: 7). Here is an example of a clearly identifiable statement of social policy as a guide to action. Nyerere refers to democratic socialism as a distinguishing feature of Tanzania, and one of his aims as equal opportunity to all men and women irrespective of race, religion, or status. Writing about educational systems, Anderson (1961-62) suggests two types: a status-selective or élitist system, and an equalitarian mass system; these seem to reflect broad political philosophy in the sense that an equalitarian education system is more likely than an élitist one to reflect the Tanzanian national ethic as proclaimed by President Nyerere.

Not everywhere are such guidelines so easily identifiable as in Tanzania. They are sometimes found in presidential speeches, speeches from the throne, political manifestos, or development plans, or they are only implicit in social and political structures and behavior, being the sum of ideas and goals inherent in the behavior of the people and groups who exercise power and enjoy authority in that country. There is, therefore, an important interrelationship between social philosophy and social structure. In countries or states, as in organizations, the goals as officially declared are sometimes not in fact those pursued. Organization theory refers to this as goal displacement (Etzioni, 1964:10-12). Derbyshire describes, with reference to the adult education system in the U.S., how the realization of what is held to be a common set of values—progress, freedom, equality— is still outside the experience of many Americans (1966). In terms of basic education, Cicourel and Kitsuse trace the effect of the American school as a social institution in reinforcing social differentiation rather than equality (1963).

In this study, while we will seek explicit expressions of social philosophy in Alberta and Quebec and examine the extent to which they appear to be reflected in adult education processes, we will at the same time try to be aware of discrepancies between declared philosphy and the way that institutions are structured and related.

Social Structure

Social structure is the complex of existing institutions and their roles in shaping the lives of the people. It includes political, social, economic, religious, cultural, recreational, and educational institutions. In all of these categories there are both formal and informal organizations, so that we can construct a simple schema as outlined in Figure 3.

In the category of formal political institutions are included political parties as well as government ministries, departments, and agencies, including the Ministry of Education, while formal educational institutions include school-boards, *commissions scolaires*, colleges, and universities, which are directly and exclusively concerned with providing education. This is where a distinction commonly occurs between adult education and early education in the formal education system. Normally the latter is concerned almost exclusively with the Ministry of Education and the formal educational institutions. Adult education, however, is the concern of various government departments and other agencies, many of a voluntary nature, outside the formal educational field. Economic institutions, such as industrial and commercial enterprises and labor unions, are of interest not only because of the shape they give to society, and the demands they make on it for certain knowledge, attitudes, and skills, but also because of what they may be doing to provide for these demands. Likewise, cultural and recreational institutions, such as ethnic associations, music and drama groups, sports federations, and outdoor and wildlife

Figure 3
_____

Social Institutions

	Pol.	Soc.	Econ.	Rel.	Cult.	Rec.	Educ.
Formal							
Informal							

groups, create awareness and make certain demands for learning, but also provide opportunities for learning.

This constitutes a very wide and complex field, and to place realistic bounds on this particular study, our main focus will be on the government institutions, as they reflect government policy, and their relationships with the main providers of those "organized educational processes" referred to in the UNESCO definition (*see* Chapter 2), whether those providers are educational or other kinds of institutions. The focus will be on formal institutions and relationships rather than the countless informal groupings, which by their nature are difficult to identify.

Needs

Earlier reference has been made to Kandel's suggestion that education is provided primarily in the national interest. It appears to be what writers like Booker and Gottlieb, and Mills and Gerth, are also suggesting. In other words, the needs education seeks to meet are imposed on the system from outside it; students are taught according to curricula decided and formulated as a result of interpretations of national—or in this case, provincial—purposes.

Adult educationists claim that adult education is distinguished by being geared to the needs of the learners or potential learners. In keeping with such a view it is not valid to presuppose any particular pattern or categories of needs before they have been identified, but from general experience, there appear to be certain categories that are useful to bear in mind in looking at adult education in any region. They can be grouped as social, cultural, political, economical, psychological, and educational needs.

Social needs are those that arise from social changes such as movements of populations from rural to urban life; from changing family relationships such as the decline of the extended family and the emergence of the nuclear family; and from a larger number of older people spending more years in retirement. Cultural needs might well be classified with social needs; they arise especially out of the tensions between groups of people who identify themselves with different cultures. To what extent is an effort being made, for instance, to foster the continuance of traditional customs of different ethnic groups? To what extent is such an effort being demanded by such groups? On the other hand, to what extent is the emphasis on molding people from different cultures into a homogeneous culture, as was the aim of so much adult education in the United States in the early decades of the century?

Political needs are needs for education and training so that people can take a greater part in government at national, regional, and local levels. They are expressed in the demands of people for more participation in decision-making at these levels.

Economic needs include both social and personal needs. They relate to education and training for occupations; labor and management training; training and re-training in the light of changing technology; vocational upgrading; and consumer education to help people make more rational choices in the face of advertising and general marketing strategies of producers and distributors.

Psychological needs are those of the individual in coping with disorientation and alienation brought about by all these other changes. They include, these days, and in some societies, needs arising out of what has been called "existential neurosis"—coping with the meaning of existence.

Finally, educational needs are included particularly with remedial adult education, for the needs of adults depend on what kind of education was available to them as children. Adult literacy programs and adult education of a developmental type are given a higher priority in most developing countries with a legacy of poor educational provision in the colonial past than in more developed countries with a wide base of education. The history of working-class adult education in Britain, in the fire and energy of the Workers Education Association in the early years of this century when secondary, and even elementary, education were limited, also illustrates this point.

Resources

The question of resources for adult education is related to those of the other three elements. First, the extent to which resources are made available for adult education depends to some extent on the status of adult education in the general social philosophy—and whether government sees it as a high priority for government funds or as a matter for private enterprise. Second, the existence of and attitudes within certain institutions, religious and cultural for example, affect the availability of such resources as buildings and support facilities. Third, resources are in some sense the obverse of needs; if, for example, there is a shortage of resources in the shape of qualified instructors, then one of the needs of the adult education system is more training for such instructors.

We can regard resources in three ways: human, material, and organizational.

By human resources is meant on the one hand the numbers and skills of people who can help others to learn, whether such people are teachers within the formal system, or trainers in other fields, or community members with various abilities. To get comparable statistics on the numbers and levels of training of teachers in the formal system is a formidable enough task, but to obtain similar information about trainers in other fields such as industry and other government services can be even more difficult and daunting. For instance, in Alberta there are at least ten provincial ministries that offer some form of education, of a sequential and organized kind, through the services of people with a whole variety of skills and titles from teachers to public health nurses to "human resource development consultants."

Material resources can be further classified under three subheadings: financial, physical, and natural. Financial resources would embrace such elements as the gross national product and its distribution, total tax potential, and actual tax revenues available to government, funds made available through private channels, and individual income levels. Physical resources are mainly buildings and communication facilities. As with human resources, it is often very difficult to obtain clear information about financial and physical resources: in the first case, finance, because of a frequent reluctance on the part of governments and other public concerns to reveal detailed figures; and in the second case, physical facilities, because of the wide variety of such facilities from schools to church halls to the shade of a clump of trees in summer. Our definition of material resources also includes natural geographical resources such as the climate and distances between communities. For instance, it is not possible to discuss the development of folk high schools without taking into account the fallow winter period in rural Scandinavia and in some areas of western Canada where modified forms of folk high schools existed in the 1920s and the 1930s. It is not possible to study and compare literacy programs in arctic Canada and central Canada without taking into account climatic conditions and the accommodation facilities available for meetings.

Finally, organizational resources represent the amalgamated effort of human resources, including such elements as the presence of a tradition of voluntary work. They also reflect the social philosophy and social structure of the society, for example, tendencies toward centralized control or local autonomy, toward government or voluntary effort.

Certain considerations indicate that the relationship between the four influencing factors— social philosophy, social structures, needs, and resources— can be seen as one in which needs have a dominant place. The first of such considerations is the commonly held convention among adult educationists and writers in the field that the adult education process starts with the needs of the learner. This has been referred to above, with reference to a sample of texts from the literature in the field. Such a proposition finds its main justification in the history of adult education in western Europe and North America, where its roots are strongest and where voluntarism, that is, free and voluntary commitment on the part of the learner, was a feature of early adult education developments. People came as volunteers to learning, and the providers were mainly voluntary organizations such as the Workers' Education Association, Y.M.C.A., Women's Institute, and public-spirited academics. This feature of adult education has received renewed support in recent years among those who abhor a movement toward what is called mandatory continuing education and who reaffirm the essentially voluntary nature of adult participation in learning. It is exemplified by the efforts of the National Alliance for Voluntary Learning in the United States, and the 1979 Task Force on Voluntary Learning of the Adult Education Association (A.E.A./U.S.A. Task Force, 1980).

The trend against which this effort is directed is indicative of a reality increasingly evident in adult education: the programs and policies lying behind those programs are based not so much on needs felt

by learners and potential learners as on needs ascribed by the authorities who provide the resources for the programs—by those who
shape social philosophy and the institutional structures that implement that philosophy. Houle has drawn attention to this important
distinction between felt and ascribed needs (1972:233).

The second consideration that points to the primacy of the needs
of the learner in the total adult education picture is that through the
democratic process the needs of the people should be reflected in the
formulation of the dominant social philosophy from which institutional structures are created and resources are, in turn, available to
meet those needs. This consideration does not, however, seem to be
able to controvert the reality that the democratic process is insuffi-
ciently perfect to ensure the fulfilment of the needs of minorities, by
whatever characteristic those minorities are identified: socio-economic status, age, race, geographic location, and so forth.

In these circumstances, the guiding hypothesis of this study, as expressed in Chapter 1, can be carried a step further and made broader.
Not only is it proposed that adult education in Quebec is more
socially oriented than in Alberta, but that the pattern of adult education in different regions is influenced primarily by the dominant
social philosophy, or ideology, in each region. Diagramatically, the
relationship is expressed in Figure 4.

Figure 4
_____

Forces Influencing Adult Education

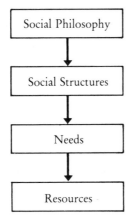

In light of this interpretation, the bulk of this study consists of an analysis of the social philosophies and principal institutional structures in the two provinces. In the course of this analysis some indication of ascribed needs and the allocation of resources to meet those needs will emerge. The final section of the study, Part IV, translates those indications into more quantitative terms, and discusses some conclusions from those allocations.

References

A.E.A./U.S.A. Task Force on Voluntary Learning. 1980. *Report.* Washington, D.C.: Adult Education Association.

Anderson, C.A. 1961–1962. "Methodology of Comparative Education." *International Review of Education,* vol. 7.

Botkin, J.W., Elmandjia, M., and Malitza, M. 1979. *No Limits to Learning.* Oxford: Pergamon Press.

Brooker, W.B. and Gottlieb, D. 1964. *A Sociology of Education.* New York: American Book Co.

Cicourel, A.V. and Kitsuse, J.L. 1963. *The Educational Decision-Makers.* New York: Bobbs Merrill.

Coombs, Philip H., Prosser, Roy C., and Ahmed, Manzoor. 1973. *New Paths of Learning for Rural Children and Youths.* New York: International Council for Educational Development.

Crowfoot, J.E. and Chesler, M.A. 1974. "Contemporary Perspectives on Planned Social Change: A Comparison." *Journal of Applied Behavioral Science,* vol. 10, no. 3.

Derbyshire, R.L. 1966. "The Sociology of Exclusion: Implications for Teaching Adults." *Adult Education* (U.S.), vol. VII, no. 1.

Durkheim, E. 1966. *Education et Sociologie.* Paris: Presses Universitaires de France.

Etzioni, A. 1964. *Modern Organizations.* Englewood Cliffs, N.J.: Prentice-Hall.

Freire, P. 1972. *Pedagogy of the Oppressed.* New York: Herder and Herder.

Holmes, B. 1958. "The Problem Approach in Comparative Education: Some Methodological Considerations." *Comparative Education Review,* vol. 2, no. 1.

Holt, J. 1972. *Freedom and Beyond.* New York: Dell.

Houle, C. 1972. *The Design of Education.* San Francisco: Jossey-Bass.

Kandel, I.L. 1959. "The Methodology of Comparative Education." *International Review of Education,* vol. 5.

Kidd, J.R. 1973. *How Adults Learn.* New York: Association Press.

King, E.J. 1957. "Education for Adults Today: An International Survey." *International Review of Education,* vol. 3.

Knowles, M.S., ed. 1960. *Handbook of Adult Education in the United States.* Chicago: Adult Education Association of the U.S.A.

London, Jack. 1960. "Program Development and Adult Education." In *Handbook of Adult Education in the United States,* ed. M.S. Knowles. Chicago: Adult Education Association of the U.S.A.

Maslow, A.H. 1968. *Toward a Psychology of Being.* New York: Van Nostrand Reinhold.

Miller, H.L. 1964. *Teaching and Learning in Adult Education.* New York: Macmillan.

Mills, C. Wright, and Gerth, Hans. 1964. *Character and Social Structure.* New York: Harbinger Books.

Musgrove, Frank. 1974. *Ecstasy and Holiness.* London: Metheun.

Nyerere, J. 1967. *Education for Self-Reliance.* Dar-es-Salaam, Tanganyika: Government Printer.

Parsons, T. 1964. "A Functional Theory of Change." In *Social Change,* ed. A. Etzioni. New York: Basic Books.

Participatory Research Group. 1978. *Working Papers 1, 3, 4.* Toronto: International Council for Adult Education.

Postman, N. and Weingartner, C. 1969. *Teaching as a Subversive Activity.* New York: Delacorte.

Powell, J.W. and Benne, K. 1960. "Philosophies of Adult Education." In *Handbook of Adult Education in the United States,* ed. M.S. Knowles. Chicago: Adult Education Association of the U.S.A.

Reich, C. 1970. *The Greening of America.* New York: Bantam Books.

Roszak, T. 1968. *The Making of a Counter Culture.* New York: Anchor/Doubleday.

Statistics Canada. 1978. *1976 Census of Canada,* cat. 92–827. Ottawa: Ministry of Supply and Services.

Tanzanian African National Union (T.A.N.U.). 1967. *Arusha Declaration and TANU's Policy on Socialism and Self-Reliance.* Dar-es-Salaam, Tanganyika: TANU Publicity Section.

Thompson, W.L. 1974. *Passages About Earth.* New York: Harper and Row.

Verner, C. and Booth, A. 1964. *Adult Education.* New York: The Centre for Applied Research in Education.

Wiltshire, H.C. 1973. "The Concepts of Learning and Need in Adult Education." *Studies in Adult Eduction,* vol. 5.

Part II

Social Philosophies and Government Structures

Introduction

Part II contains the main body of the comparative analysis of the situations in the two provinces in accordance with the schema set out in Figure 4 at the end of Chapter 3. The emphasis in the schema is on social philosophy and social structures. It was suggested, in the process of defining those two terms, that they are closely linked; institutions, their roles, and their relationships tend to reflect policy based on underlying social philosophies, and where the philosophy is not explicitly articulated in official texts or interpretations of those texts, it can often be inferred from the roles and actions of government and other major institutions.

Because this is not primarily a work of political or social philosophy, the search is directed particularly at those statements that appear to have a bearing on the development of adult education policy and practice in the two provinces. Before studying the conditions in the two provinces separately, it is necessary to note aspects of what might be seen as a broader national social philosophy that affects conditions in the provinces, particularly as they relate to education.

In the light of the political realities of the mid-nineteenth century and previous Canadian history, the British North America Act included an assumption that education was closely tied to deeply held social, religious, and political traditions, and that in Canada there were two main sources of such traditions: French Canada, predominantly Roman Catholic, and English Canada, predominantly Protestant. These were the two main components of the new country, and they were each protective of their linguistic and cultural heritage, so in the founding legislation, education was ruled to be a matter within the exclusive jurisdiction of the provincial governments (Government of Canada, 1970:sec. 93). This affected the legislative rights not only of predominantly French and Roman Catholic Quebec, where education was firmly in the grip of the church, but all the other provinces as they became parts of the Dominion. Hence, insofar as adult education is provided by or through institutions of education such as schools, colleges, and universities, and is recognized by rewarding formal certificates, diplomas, and degrees to students, it will tend to reflect policies and practices in the different provinces. There will, of course, be a number of common features in adult education across the country, since many of the learning needs of adults are likely to be similar: the need for vocational upgrading, the desire for personal and interpersonal skills, and certain cultural (art, literature, and music for example) and intellectual interests.

On the other hand, there are two matters related to adult education that have been judged to fall within the jurisdiction of the federal government, and therefore tend to introduce common features into certain policies and practices in the provinces. First, in terms of both the B.N.A. Act, 1867, and the new Constitution Act, 1981, the responsibility for "Indians and land reserved for Indians" is expressly and exclusively placed within the federal jurisdiction (Ibid.: sec. 91), including the education of Indians. Secondly, the section of the B.N.A. Act, 1867, and the Constitution Act, 1981 (sec. 92), listing matters that fall exclusively to the provincial governments and section 93 relating to education do not make manpower training the exclusive preserve of the provincial governments. In recent decades, as manpower development has been seen to be closely linked with general economic development, there have been increasing incursions into this field by the federal government, mainly as a provider of funding to buy certain types of training from provincial institutions. During the course of this study, the influence of these legal responsibilities on adult education practices in the two provinces will be traced.

There is one other element common to both provinces, outside the constitutional one, which exerts similar influences on policy-making, and that is the relative change of the society from agricultural to industrial, from rural to urban. In Alberta, the number of persons over fifteen years of age in farming occupations declined from 141,052 in 1941 to 88,347 in 1971, while in Quebec the change was from 249,933 in 1941 to 83,143 in 1971. On the other hand, the numbers of people over fifteen years of age occupied in craft and production process work increased in Alberta from 70,836 in 1941 to 187,370 in 1971, while in Quebec the equivalent rise in the same period was from 309,738 to 588,370. By 1976 the total population in Alberta of 1.8 million was divided into 1.4 million living in urban areas (78 percent) and 400,000 in rural areas (22 percent), while in Quebec, out of a total 6.2 million people, 4.9 million, or 79 percent, lived in urban areas and 1.3 million, or 21 percent, lived in rural areas. In both provinces, over half the population lived in two urban centres: Edmonton and Calgary in Alberta, and Montreal and Quebec City in Quebec (Statistics Canada, 1974:vol. 3, part 2).

4

Social Philosophies
and Broad Policies

Quebec

In the years before the early 1960s, the dominant agent of political socialization in Quebec was the Roman Catholic church (Bernard, 1977:80). Bernard points out that the church influenced social and political attitudes in three respects: it engendered a sense of absolutism among people, and restrained the tendency toward a pluralism of views that existed in the rest of Canada where there were a number of co-existent religious faiths; it engendered a feeling of dependence and resignation in the face of inequalities; and it underlined the traditional nationalism of French Canada. With respect to the latter of these, for instance, the schools in Quebec, which were in effect annexes of the church, had a classical, confessional curriculum that glorified the great deeds of the French regime in Canada from 1608 to 1760, whereas the history and manuals in the rest of Canada emphasized the period after 1760 (Ibid.:84).

In more recent years, however, the church's dominance has been vastly weakened in general. Bernard quotes a 1971 study showing that in the Hochelaga-Maisonneuve district, 77 percent of the population no longer went to mass on Sundays (Ibid.:82). The dominance of religion has likewise been eliminated in the education system. Over the last fifteen years or so, because of the introduction of more foreign texts and of a new class of lay teachers of a more materialistic persuasion, Bernard suggests that the schools have become a strong agent of differentiation between the values held by the older and newer generations (Ibid.:86).

But both Bernard and Dion (1976), possibly the two leading analysts of the socio-political scene in Quebec, point out that as one ideology or system of ideas and judgements rises and becomes dominant, it does not entirely eclipse existing ideologies. For example, conservatism has remained a factor in Quebec, while nationalism was revived and flourished at a later point in time with the rise of the Parti Québécois. These changes in ideology over the last few decades form a complex picture within which we must place a study of adult education in Quebec.

Dion points out that emancipation from the bonds of a tradition that had been corrupted by the Union Nationale government began during the Duplessis regime. There was a revulsion against the self-serving behaviors and attitudes of both political and church leaders. Journals such as *Le Devoir* and *Cité Libre* attacked the regime at the level of ideas, while abortive political groups such as the Union des Forces Démocratiques appeared in the 1950s (Dion, 1976:5). Leaders of the quiet revolution such as Trudeau, Pelletier, and Lévèsque came to the fore in Quebec political life in those years. It is, however, the election of the Liberal government of Lesage in 1960 that is popularly taken to mark the beginning of that revolution. This government embarked on a number of reforms to strengthen the economy, to loosen the grip of the church in matters of social welfare and education, and to support the cultural aspirations of the Quebecois: the establishment of a health insurance system, and of the Parent Commission on Education (which led to the formation of the Ministry of Education in 1964), the establishment of an Economic Planning Council, a Ministry of Cultural Affairs, and an Office of the French Language (Parti Libéral, 1973:28).

An indication of his future government's policy was given by Lesage in 1959. He said that "The *first problem* [his italics] which confronts us....is education," and "This concern extends to *all* [his

italics] levels of teaching, without preference for one over the others."
And some of his underlying thinking is revealed in his statement that

> What is necessary is an education system responding to the
> needs of an *industrial civilization* [my italics]. Only then will
> enough of us be able to raise ourselves, through our own com-
> petence, to the higher levels of the management and administra-
> tion of our economy, so that we shall no longer feel the humili-
> ation of being servants in our own house. (Lesage, 1959:31–32)

Here are revealed two themes central to the formulation of Quebec
policies in the succeeding years: a sense of ethnic identity and nationalism, and an awareness of the implications of the move from a primarily rural agricultural society to an urban industrial one. By relating this to education, and making references to renovation of the
system at all levels, Lesage indicates that adult education was not being ignored.

Nevertheless, in those early days of the quiet revolution the
dominant ideology of the new government and its broad goals were
still not advanced. The question of defining the goals in terms of a
basic ideology was, in Dion's view in 1961, the most serious problem
facing the new regime (Dion, 1976:9). He suggested that the government could no longer be a simple afterthought of capitalism, as were
its predecessors, and he questioned its ability and will to give birth to
a new society. He stressed the difference between political ideologies
and electoral slogans, and suggested that there was a tendency to con-
fuse ideological approaches with political choices. It was necessary to
search beyond such Liberal slogans as *"Maîtres chez nous"* and *"Politique de grandeur"* for a political ideology from which would arise a
new society. Dion used the term "ideology" to describe "a more or
less elaborate system of representations reflecting group interests and
aimed at promoting action" (1976:12). Writing in 1966, he perceived
that the current ideologies in the province had, during the 1950s and
early 1960s, seemed to cluster in two main constellations: "conservatism" and "progressivism"; "the clerico-political conservatism" of
the church/state amalgam that had typified the Duplessis regime was
in contest with the "challenge of progress" of the new regime. There
were still elements of the former to be reckoned with, and the bitter

debates around Bill 60 in 1964—the legislation to set up a government
Ministry of Education and, in effect, to take over from the church—
was a strong indication of this.

The most serious consequences of the conservatist regime lay in

> Quebec's economic occupation by alien industry, business and
> finance, non-French in language and culture; and in the develop-
> ment among French Canadians of a political culture strikingly
> similar to that of colonized people: the rise of *rois nègres*,
> kinglets who bow to the will of economic rulers while publicly
> treating them with consummate contempt; the invention of in-
> stitutional mechanisms aimed at preventing the emergence of an
> enlightened and free public opinion; the development of elec-
> toral methods designed to ensure popular support for govern-
> ments whose social, economic and cultural measures systema-
> tically go against the basic interests of the people. (Dion,
> 1976:16)

The absence of such a basic ideology as Dion suggested was needed,
ensured that many of these consequences continued to flow in the
years after the election of the Liberal government in 1960 and the
subsequent Union Nationale and Liberal administrations. Thorburn,
in his foreword to Dion (1976), indicates that the secularization of the
education system and the crash program of economic development
started by the Lesage government benefitted the middle class most of
all. There was, during this period, the rapid industrialization of the
Quebec economy and the rise of the urban, wage-earning class as a
vast counterpoint to the middle- and upper-class élites—French- as
well as English-speaking. Thorburn goes on to suggest that these internal happenings, in conjunction with a general weakening of legitimate authority and the decline in religion and tradition in the western
world, prepared the way for the separatism and social democracy of
the Parti Québécois, whose electoral strength grew in the early 1970s
until the party became the government in 1976. Dion would bid us
remember that the conservatist-progressive contestation is not entirely resolved by such an event and is likely to remain an element in
Quebec life, and in the pronouncements and actions of the Parti
Québécois (P.Q.) government, where the dominant social philoso-

phy colors current developments, we shall see that this is so. These pronouncements, except in the clear P.Q. choice of a separate, sovereign Quebec, are only the culmination of a process of reform, and an expression of Quebecois identity that started in earlier years. This view is reinforced by the P.Q. Minister of Education, Jacques-Yves Morin, who, in his introduction to the 1977 Green Paper on Primary and Secondary Education, points out that the undertaking to change and renew the educational system of Quebec started fifteen years before, at the time of the quiet revolution (Ministère de l'Education, 1977). This Green Paper is a suitable place to look for an expression of social philosophy in Quebec as it affects adult education at the present time, even though it addresses itself to primary and secondary education. The document was produced by the P.Q. government, shortly after its election to office in 1976, as a response to public expressions of disillusionment with the quality of education in the new system: the depersonalization of learning in the big new *polyvalent* schools, the "teaching factories," the quality of teaching, lack of evaluation, and so on. In the same introduction, Morin reaffirms that "Every worthy education policy presupposes a philosophy of life and of the nature of man," and he goes on to say that such a philosophy will be found between the lines of this document. What in effect appears is a viewpoint which, in the words of one critic, is a mixture of "Judeo-Christianism, liberalism and personalism" (Lucier, 1968:29). It is the sort of mixture of individualist and collectivist aims discussed with reference to adult education in Chapter 1, with the balance coming down rather more heavily on the side of the development of the individual: "the cultural and political tradition of Quebec places the person at the heart of education.... the flowering of man's personality in the realms of knowledge, will and feeling —as well as the acquisition of autonomy, of a sense of responsibility, of commitment, and of moral values" (Ministère de l'Education, 1977: paras. 1.78–1.88). The claim that the cultural and political tradition of Quebec emphasizes the person is questioned by another critic, Jasmin (1978:72), who makes two points: that it smacks of the Catholic tradition of Quebec, by now weakened; and that it contrasts with the Parent Report's orientation toward the social aims of education and toward a community-based pedagogy. A general feeling among one group of commentators on the Green Paper is that it fails, in fact, to relate to the guiding philosophy of the reforms begun in the early 1960s, and to set out overall objectives for Quebec's educational development for the future (C.A.D.R.E., 1968). It pronounces generalities that are not new—dating from Aristotle and appearing through history— and that do not address the present and future condition of Quebec.

The Minister of Education, in his introduction, indicates that this is the first of a number of studies of important aspects of education in the province, including adult education. The latter may lead us to a more particular understanding of the guiding philosophy in that field. In the meantime, the government has published another document to provide such a philosophy in the broader context of cultural development. *La Politique Québécoise du Développement Culturel* is a two-volume White Paper on the basis and purpose of the cultural development of the province— or rather, *le pays*, the country. The first volume gives a general perspective and pursues the question "What culture?" and the second volume deals with the three dimensions of such a policy: lifestyle (*genres de vie*), cultural creativity, (*création*), and education. And at the beginning of Volume Two the claim is made:

> culture is a *pedagogy*, an education.... human beings are not boxed in to an endless succession of reflexes and habits. They are ceaselessly growing, exceeding themselves. It would be ridiculous to confuse this pedagogical element of culture with the programs in the schools, for these are only one instrument among others. But it is important, to a government which invests considerable resources in education, to evaluate the part teaching plays in a larger pedagogy, to see its place among the many different resources from which citizens should benefit in their self-chosen paths of growth and fulfillment....(Ministre d'Etat, 1978:153)

There, if anywhere is at least a hint of a philosophy of lifelong education.

Throughout this White Paper there are clear indications of the underlying purposes the Parti Québécois government gives to education as part of cultural development. They start with the notion of Quebec and its place in the world. Going back to the quiet revolution, the White Paper states that it was at first a cultural mutation, a mutation by which earlier governments sought cultural sovereignty. Here is the first basic theme: the re-emergence in clear terms of the strain of nationalism that is a part of French Canadian history. There is an acknowledgement by the P.Q. of its antecedent nature, but it is the P.Q. government that sharpens it into an uncompromising keystone of policy underlying its future actions with the equating of Quebec with *la patrie,* "ce pays."

The second theme that underlies Quebec's social philosophy as it affects education relates to socio-economic conditions, and it has a number of aspects. The first of these is articulated in the earlier quotation from Lesage about the need to build up local management and administrative skills so that francophone Quebecois can assume more power in economic affairs. This is an extention of the theme of nationalism, and it is taken up with added vigor and expanded in the White Paper on cultural development. Referring back to the quiet revolution, it underlines some of its actions and consequences:

> Quebec is aware that it is urbanized and industrialized, that it must renounce its old sources of security, throw off its tutelage. It places in question its principal institutions and structures, launches itself into planning and research, boldy innovates in educational planning, takes in hand its social and health services, nationalizes electricity, inserts a state presence into the private sector of the economy. (Ministre d'Etat, 1978;5)

But that was not enough. The political will faltered and the movement slowed down: "It is necessary to resume the march toward autonomy and auto-determination at the point where it had stopped." It was the duty of the state to establish true social justice, and if existing power relationships and inequalities made this impossible or difficult, it behoved the state, the principle guardian of the collective welfare, to redress the balance and bring help to the weakest people. This was what democracy and humanism meant (Ibid.: 6). Here was a strong expression of social democracy, a response to Dion's call referred to earlier, that the government should not be a simple afterthought of capitalism.

With this goes a feeling for the masses. "It is probable that our perspectives on development in Quebec since the 1960s have been

formed mostly by the ideas of the bourgeoisie and middle classes"
(Ibid.: 110). Both culture and economy can oppress and exploit social
classes, and what can be called the people's culture (*culture populaire*)
is the ill-defined totality of the way of life resulting from such exploitation; it is a culture of class (Ibid.: 112). From a more left-wing
perspective, there is a strong awareness of "les classes défavorisés"
(Lafleur, 1975). The White Paper refers to such "Leftist" movements
(108) in such a way as to indicate that its authors would not choose to
be identified with the latter, but the tenor of its case permits the
reader to see ideas that are in common with some of those of democratic socialism.

Quebecois attitudes toward business are, as Dion points out, am-
biguous, to say the least (1976:65), and some of that ambiguity appears
in the White Paper. On the one hand, a great many francophone
Quebecois have a negative, rejecting attitude toward business in its
capitalistic form, but on the other hand, they are up against the apparent necessity to tolerate it, at least to some extent, for the sake of
the advancement of their economy. There is also by now a new bourgeoisie that has joined to the older middle-class élite and conservative
rural people. It is a situation that is reflected by certain tensions within
the governing party itself, and causes it to proceed with some caution
in both its democratic socialism, or what Dion calls "social democratic nationalism" (1976:142–43), and its move toward greater sovereignty. Nevertheless, Dion indicates that since the quiet revolution
there has been a stronger tide of socialist ideas flowing in the province, along with separatism. And, as distinct from liberalism, which
talks of improved conditions for the individual to educate himself, to
work, and so on, socialism talks of "community enhancement" (Ibid.:
151). In the White Paper, there are statements such as "We are thinking particularly of all those who, in most diverse associations and
movements, fight for the conquest of the 'quality of life'" (Ministre
d'Etat, 1978:151).

So there is a chord that includes the notes of ethnic identity;
political, cultural, economic, and social-democratic nationalism;
under-priviledged classes (mainly francophones); and an awareness of
group and community. But there are also other notes, of cautious
conservatism and liberalism at the one end and Marxist socialism at the
other, and from time to time it may be that one of these notes dom-
inates. Seeking a set of policies in its particular fields of responsibility,

the government constantly cocks an ear to the dominant sound.

One of these sounds, which comes steadily from the socialist end of the gamut, is critical of the purposes of much of the existing adult education in the province. This is typified by a closely-reasoned analysis of Multi-Média by Lafleur (1975). Multi-Média was instituted in 1971 as an experimental program aimed at helping less priviledged people to remedy their lack of educational opportunities. It involved the media of radio and television and other distance learning techniques, some group animation, and self-directed learning. Despite its apparent orientation toward working people and *défavorisés*, it was atttacked from the outset by some observers for a number of reasons.

Lafleur argued that in its objectives, techniques, and administrative structures, it was individualistic in its emphasis–"une idéologie de l'éducation qui est *particulière*"– and that it only benefitted those who already had enough education to be able to cope with the tools it used. In other words, it did not really redress the fundamental inequalities of the times. Lafleur was arguing from the point of view of what Dion calls socialist nationalism, as distinct from the liberal, and even conservative, nationalism which characterized the Bourassa Liberal regime. He was writing under the title "The *Collective* [my italics] Cultural Development of the Under-Priviledged Classes," testing Multi-Média–and by extension, much of adult education in Quebec–against the urgent needs of the *milieux populaires,* the world of the masses. He represented a view that adult eucation in Quebec at that time was a kind of cultural invasion on the part of the favored "higher" social classes, against the "lower" classes.

Groulx (1977) pursued the argument with the criticism that the basic principles of Multi-Média were conservative; they expressly eschewed socio-political involvement and changes in socio-political structures, holding that change must come from within each individual. These criticisms are reminiscent of those made about the Samuel Smiles's philosophy of "self-help" in Victorian Britain– the criticism that self-help merely helped some individuals to rise in the class hierarchy, leaving the causes of social inequality unaffected. It was a middle-class solution of simply making over the whole of society in its own image (Harrison, 1961:39).

Multi-Média came to an end in June, 1978, and its main features

were taken over by a new program of citizen education set up by the
P.Q. government, which will be discussed in a later chapter. This
note is meant only to draw attention to the interest in and debate
about the broad purposes of adult education in Quebec, which arises
out of the range of political orientations present in the province.

The White Paper suggests right from the beginning that such a
cultural policy embraces the educational domain. Planning cultural
change requires a rationalization of the educational system and
process to that end—and the reorganization of the system over the
preceding years was meant to meet that requirement. The establishment of a government Ministry of Education in 1964 had been recommended by the Parent Commission because "A master plan is needed,
an orientation needed to serve a common good....a job which
properly belongs to the political authorities (Commission Royale,
1964:vol. 2;79). The White Paper recalls that sentiment in pointing
out that the ministry was formed because the legislature of that time
intended that henceforth education in Quebec would be the responsibility of the government in the last resort. But the White Paper states
that it is necessary to go further than the Parent Commission, which
considered primarily the formal education system in a fairly conventional way. The Ministry of Education must be more than a ministry
of schools, colleges, and universities; even if for some time it had been
forced to put its main effort into those institutions, it is not to be limited to a restrictive concept of schooling. The schools, colleges, and
universities have to be persuaded to extend themselves beyond
narrow teaching programs and to seek means of introducing themselves into the broader life of society. They must develop relationships with other institutions, which, while not being primarily
education agencies, can assume such a role by extending learning
opportunities. The time has come, in other words, for both consoli-
dating and intensifying this process. (Ministre d'Etat, 1978:413–14).
Two strategies to be involved are: while retaining the concept and
practice of decentralization through school-boards and other institutions, there must be a recognition of the role of correcting a
disequilibrium of opportunity between different regions; and there
must not be merely a recognition of, but an accent on, and support
for, lifelong education (Ibid.: chap XX).

Alberta

Just as in Quebec there are elements of earlier conservative nationalism that continued through the quiet revolution and of liberal
nationalism that continued through the early years of the P.Q. government, so in Alberta there are elements of older social and political
ideologies and practices in the Progressive Conservative regime of
today. As in Quebec it is therefore necessary to begin by looking
back some years to trace some of the earlier factors influencing social
and political attitudes in the province.

One factor was the much more varied ethnic composition of the
settler-population that came to the West in the late nineteenth and
early twentieth centuries, and which is still a marked feature of the
society. In 1921, 46 percent of Albertans had been born outside Canada, compared with only 8 percent of Quebecers (Dominion Bureau
of Statistics, 1924). And the origins of both those born in Alberta and
those who immigrated were much more diverse than in Quebec.
Table 1 shows the distribution of the populations of Alberta and Quebec in 1921 and 1971 according to the main countries of origin. It
illustrates how, in Alberta, it was unlikely that a strong nationalistic
focus, of the kind existing in Quebec, would be a factor influencing
educational policy at whatever level. In fact, it illustrates how the support for multiculturalism could become a feature of government policy in Alberta. The large component of British origin in Alberta was
not nearly as dominant as the French component in Quebec, and the
remainder was both larger and more evenly spread among half a
dozen or so other ethnic groups. It is interesting that in 1921, people of
Ukrainian origin were not deemed to be a large enough component
to be separately distinguished, whereas by 1971 they amounted in Alberta to 135,510 persons, 8.3 percent of the total, and exceeded only by
people of German origin.

This dispersal of ethnic origins among Albertans was complemented in another regard, sharply distinguishing the two provinces
and indicating how much less focused the social picture is in Alberta.
Alberta has had an exceptional history of religious nonconformity
(Mann, 1955). From the early years there was a substantial immigration of people belonging to what Mann, writing as a scholar of religion, defines as sects—institutions of social and religious protest—in-

Table 1
_____

Alberta and Quebec: Main Population Origins

Origin	Alberta				Quebec			
	1921 Total	%	1971 Total	%	1921 Total	%	1971 Total	%
Britain	351,820	59.8	761,665	46.8	357,108	15.1	640,042	10.6
France	30,913	5.2	94,665	5.8	1,889,277	82.5	4,759,360	79.0
Germany	35,333	6.0	231,010	14.2	4,668	0.2	53,870	0.9
Poland	7,172	1.2	44,425	2.7	3,264	0.14	23,975	0.4
Scandinavia	44,545	7.6	98,430	6.0	2,219	0.09	8,825	0.1
N. American Indian	14,557	2.5	44,540	2.7	11,566	0.5	32,840	0.5
Other European (Ukrainian)	69,103	12.0	135,510	8.3	7,346	0.3	20,330	0.3
Total	588,454		1,627,875		2,361,199		6,027,765	

Note: This does not mean place of birth, but origin as claimed by respondents, irrespective of place of birth.

Sources: Dominion Bureau of Statistics. 1924. *Census of Canada, 1921.* Vol. 1. Ottawa: King's Printer.
Statistics Canada. 1974. *Census of Canada, 1971.* Catalogue 92-774 (SP-4). Ottawa: Queen's Printer.

cluding the Apostolic Faith Mission, Salvation Army, and German Baptist Church of North America. In 1946 the number of persons belonging to over thirty such sects, all of which are more or less fundamentalist, was about 35 percent of the actual combined strength of all the regular Protestant communions (Mann, 1955:30–31). Here again was a wide dispersal of belief structures, on top of the ethnic mix. Moreover, since the sects incorporated a spirit of protest, they represented at the same time both a high level of individualism and nonconformity, and a feeling for tight communion against the surrounding environment. In his account of the genesis and progress of the Social Credit party, Barr, one of the "young Turks" of the party in the late 1960s, indicates that many Albertans had come from the United States with strong ideas about temperance, women's rights, and radical social philosophy (1974:14). In 1921, Alberta's population of 588,454 included 99,879 persons born in the U.S.—the largest absolute number of all the provinces. This in itself makes an interesting mixture of attitudes that appears to be a feature of Alberta life: on the one hand a strong sense of individualism and nonconformity, and on the other hand a strain of social consciousness and conscience.

This is a part of the demographic background that enables us to understand some of the dominant social philosophies that have produced political and social policies in Alberta, which in turn have resulted in certain structures and practices of adult education.

If a diversity of ethnic and religious backgrounds in Alberta dispersed energies and loyalties and failed to bring about the nationalistic sentiments characteristic of Roman Catholic francophone Quebec, one factor did focus those energies: distrust of eastern government, its economic policies, industrial biases, and political parties. Alberta was primarily agricultural. Even up to the beginning of World War II, half the population lived on farms, and as late as 1976 almost a quarter of the population was rural. According to Macpherson, one of Canada's leading political economists, Alberta's economy was, in effect, quasi-colonial, dependent on and affected by eastern interests (1953:6). This led to a feeling represented by H.W. Wood, president of the United Farmers of Alberta (U.F.A.) from 1916 to 1931, of the exploitation of the mass by the few (Ibid.: 34). Wood saw the farmers of Alberta as a class, and it made sense for them to be organized, not as a political party, but as a social movement of protest against eastern business and government. It was as such that the U.F.A. was voted into office in the province in 1921 and stayed in office until 1935. Wood also held that whereas competition was the true law of animal life, co-operation was the true law of human life. Democracy was seen as a non-exploitative, just, co-operative social and political order (Ibid.: 48). During the whole of the twenties and early thirties, Alberta politics showed aspects of this type of agrarian populism and co-operativism. The U.F.A. initiated the Alberta Wheat Pool and United Grain Growers, two co-operative agencies that played a part not only in grain marketing but in education among farmers. Macpherson points out another interesting effect of these co-operative interests; they effectively cut across the religious and cultural differences that existed in the localities where the co-operatives functioned (Ibid.:56).

On a broader scale the movement as a whole had a formative influence in socialist thinking and practice on the Prairies. Some of its leaders, particularly William Irvine, were active in the formation of the Co-operative Commonwealth Federation (C.C.F.), in Regina in 1932—a party that formed the government of Saskatchewan for many years and was the forerunner of the New Democratic Party (N.D.P.). In Alberta, however, the movement as represented by the U.F.A. government had, by the 1930s, become conservative and ineffectual in dealing with the problems of the Great Depression (Ibid.:149). There was a resurgence of interest in socialism toward the end of World War II, and the C.C.F. contested the general election of 1944 with what appeared to be a threat to the Social Credit government of the day. But though the Social Credit lost some of its radical members to the C.C.F., it gained more from the growing business community, which by that time could see that Manning's regime was not a threat, but in fact the best protection against the growing strength of the C.C.F. (Ibid.: 206-9). The Socred government was returned with a larger majority than ever before.

This era is recent enough that many people, some of whom have since become town dwellers, were a part of it and were affected by it, carrying some of its ideals into the post-war years. As Dion says in respect of Quebec, manifestations of this sort do not entirely disappear as new conditions and ideas come to predominance; they remain a part of the social and political fabric. The political theory expounded by Wood and Irvine on behalf of the U.F.A., which was based on a rejection of political parties and the advocacy of group representation in a smaller governing body rather than expensive and ineffectual periodic general elections to fill Parliament, did not ever become even the practice of the movement while it was in power, let alone leave a legacy of aspiration for the future, but elements in the mood of co-operation of that period of Alberta's short history appear not to have been entirely extinguished. An important institution in Alberta life, the Farmers Union of Alberta, now known as Unifarm, is a lineal descendant from the U.F.A.

At the time of its rise in 1934 and 1935, the Social Credit movement profited from a split in the U.F.A. between two factions: the monetary reformists and the agrarian socialists. The former were wooed by the Social Credit, leaving the latter to continue as a trace in Alberta life (Barr, 1974: 66). Social Credit rule straddled the era of agricultural dominance and the later era of oil wealth, urbanization, and the rising influence of both small and big business. The pattern during that time reflected the oscillation between radicalism and conservatism referred to by Macpherson as a characteristic of the petit-bourgeois nature of Alberta society. The Social Credit movement began in Alberta as a protest against depressive economic conditions and the inability of the provincial and federal governments to do much about them. Its rise was a demonstration of radicalism not so much in terms of a movement away from individualistic conservative social values toward a more socialistic regime, as in terms of a desire for a change in the system of government, over which the people could somehow have more direct control, and the fruits of which they could more directly enjoy. And as in the case of the U.F.A. earlier, once the movement became the government, radicalism gave way to conservatism, so that by 1944 Manning was able to present his party (as it had in fact become) as a solid free enterprise government, organized and run on orthodox parliamentary and cabinet lines.

The basic tone of the Manning era from the 1940's to mid-1960s was balanced budgets and cautious reforms. In post-war years it was an era of increased prosperity as a result of the huge oil discoveries, increased consumption, increasing American influence, and hardly a diminution of the Alberta self-image as a frontier, individualist society. Though the government was opposed to socialism and the welfare state, there was in fact a reformist tinge to it (Barr, 1974:130), and there were also some features of government control that tainted the purity of a free enterprise image: the government-run quasi-bank system of the Alberta Treasury Board, the monopoly of the Alberta Liquor Control Board, and the Alberta Government Telephones. It was in the mid-sixties that Manning, as Socred leader, began a more reflective searching into the humanist reform roots of the movement, and directed the formulation of fresh policies. In 1967 he published a White Paper on Human Resource Development, "to provide an initial synthesis of governmental thinking and pertinent research findings, in the form of new concepts and policies for the future" (Manning, 1967:13). This document provides a statement of the main features of the philosophy of the Socred government in the last few years of its life up to the advent of a Progressive Conservative government in 1971.

"All government policies and administrative action should," the White Paper intones, "be based on certain fundamental principles and values pertaining to the proper governing of men and nations" (Ibid.: 18). Central to this thinking is that the individual human being is of supreme value and importance, and the government must therefore help to provide an environment in which human beings can be free and creative.

The use of the term "human resources" paralleled to "physical resources" appears to have a somewhat utilitarian, factors-of-production ring about it, as if the ultimate motives of the authors were economic rather than humanistic. The expression of one of the basic principles and values as "a free enterprise economy, in which all individuals have maximum opportunity to participate, will be regarded as more desirable than a state regimented economy," reveals a lack of appreciation of the gradations of political economics, and in fact a convenient or unconscious overlooking of some of the state-control features of the provincial political economy referred to above, the Treasury Board and Alberta Liquor Board, for example. It comprises, possibly for the dramatic effect of hyperbole, a simplistic contrast of two conditions at different ends of a continuum. This concern to show a briskness of individualistic thought and not the fuzziness of liberal socialism may have been an endeavor to be in tune with what was perceived to be the dominant individualistic view of the people of Alberta, or it may have been a strategy to reassure those who were seen to hold such views, as in the statement, "Only by stressing the development of the individual can there emerge a society the characteristics of which will be determined, not by state planners, but by free and creative individuals themselves" (Ibid.: 26). The introduction of the term "state planners" as the antithesis of creative individuals is a witness and guarantee of the proper thinking of the government standing behind the document. It must be remembered that this was a political document, put out by a leader at a time when his party had been in power for over thirty years, when its image was one of being somewhat stale and flabby, and at a time when there were signs of a resurgence of a Conservative party. So the White Paper hoped to strike a note in tune with generally conservative public sentiment in the province: "Alberta should avoid the error of those who define their utopia in collectivistic and socialistic terms and who are then committed to the implementation of coercive measures in order to force individuals into some prescribed mold" (Ibid.: 25). Such a statement of philosophy was not, however, just a ploy in the game of catching the current mood of the people and matching the views of a threatening Conservative party. It reflects the attachment to independence and individualism in the history of the province since white settlement began.

In the White Paper there is also a recognition of the increased materialism that occurred with the growth of Alberta's oil wealth and general economic prosperity. It has been suggested above that the document is basically economic in its thrust. It set out in a general way to ensure a good economic climate, and in particular to ensure the efficient use of the resources and government processes of the province—i.e. to ensure accountability—which was a concept becoming very popular at that time. It used such language as "the functionality of social capital projects," and "a functionality index to make possible scientific evaluation of the operational efficiency of such facilities as schools, hospitals and public buildings." The government would remove barriers and hindrances to the generation of industrial capital in Alberta, and would do everything in its power to maintain a political climate responsive to private enterprise and investment capital. Recognizing the place of oil in the affluence of the province, the government promised a warm welcome and freedom from the threat of nationalization to the outside enterprises responsible for petroleum exploration and development. In other words, as distinct from the sentiment of cultural, political, and economic nationalism, which was gaining ground in Quebec, Alberta was accepting and depending openly on the increased control of its economic life by outside private investors, in the interests of high living standards and prosperity in the province. Any manifestation of nationalism, or its equivalent in provincial terms, was directed, in the traditional western way, against big government in central Canada. This was to be carried further by the Progressive Conservative government of Peter Lougheed in following years.

At the same time, there was evidence of a feeling for the more tender aspects of humanity, harkening back to the social values of western frontier life when things had not been so good and people helped one another. There was reference to the "willingness to help" that was at the roots of the humanitarian tradition of "western hospitality," and to the "social concern derived from Christian principles." From the years of the Great Depression there came that "consciousness of human welfare as a function of economic development" and it was in this respect that the Manning White Paper gave the impetus to a wide range of government policies and actual effort in the field of human development. The document makes the important point that by this time the province's wealth was such as to make the acceptance of this challenge financially feasible (Ibid.: 25). The principal structures and programs to come about as a result will be discussed in the following chapters, but the general direction of such effort was toward increases in education institutions and programs, community development programs, preventive social services, and research facilities and programs in applied social sciences. In fact, such proposals went so far in the direction of government support of human resource development that some important Socred cabinet figures were against the program, and it was only Manning's prestige that drove it through.

One of the results of this surge was the Educational Planning Commission under Dr. Walter Worth, which began work in 1969. An interesting feature of its establishment was that it was given a very broad mandate to "inquire into current social and economic trends within the province to determine the nature of Alberta's society during the next two decades" as a context for establishing "bases for the priority judgments of Government with respect to the course of public education in Alberta in the next decade"—public education including adult education programs (Commission on Educational Planning, 1972). And in the letter and spirit of that mandate the commission made futures studies and oriented some of its central propositions to those perspectives. Their report suggested four basic ideals for future educational planning: a futures perspective; lifelong learning; faith in participatory planning; and development of socially sensitive, autonomous individuals (Ibid.: 37).

In this report, the interests of the individual are balanced with those of society, and a concept of involvement in social decision-making emerges. The Commission saw two broad alternative kinds of society in the future: a second-phase industrial society, which in the main continued the existing forms and values of conformity, hierarchical structures, competition and competitive relations, and economic and technological advance, and a person-centred society, which marked a break from past trends and reflected the values of individualism, self-fulfilment, service to others, interdependence, co-operation, and collaborative relations. The commission appeared to opt for the second as a basis for future educational planning, though it suggested that the educational system must be designed to help Albertans make that choice themselves. Conversion to a person-centred society would necessitate basic shifts in current ways of thought and action. The government to which the Worth Commission eventually reported in 1972 was not a Social Credit one, but a Progressive Conservative one, which in 1971 had broken the reign of Social Credit after thirty-six years. The values the Conservatives represented were not different from those of the Socreds in terms of individualism, economic advancement, and functional welfarism. Among the guideposts published by the Tory convention in 1966 were:

> –the provincial government should not just preach free enterprise but also promote it by creating a supportive atmosphere (for business).
> –the greatest challenge to the Province was to administer welfare in relation to need without detracting from human dignity (Barr, 1974:217).

In 1971 the P.C. election manifesto sounded the same note: protection of individual rights against ingrown and autocratic bureaucracy, and a government climate favorable to free enterprise. It made interesting concessions to the traditional Alberta penchant for anti-centralism by proposing a return to local government, "a reversal of the trend to bigness in government and in business," and support for Alberta's smaller communities. It claimed "a recognition that agriculture is a basic industry of the province and that the general prosperity was significantly dependent on it." With regard to education, the party advocated "eduction to train people not just for jobs but to improve the quality of their lives." However, this broad and generous recognition of the liberal and social role of education was not reflected in the manifesto's reference to adult education, which was exclusively to economic purposes and manpower development (Progressive Conservative Party, 1971). By 1975 the Tory platform made only passing reference to education, and that was confined to education from kindergarten to grade twelve. The emphasis of the party's interest is now on such matters as the management of the Heritage Trust Fund, the huge amount of money accruing to government from oil royalties, Alberta's economic and financial position, and Syncrude and oil sands research.

In the 1972 P.C. manifesto there had been an undertaking to "implement *valid* [my italics] recommendations of the Worth Commission." It is difficult to trace, from the government's own pronouncements, how, in fact, it views the basic analysis and propositions of the Worth Commisson. In presenting the report to the Legislature in November 1972, the Minister of Advanced Education merely quoted a selection of comments and criticisms made by some bodies such as the universities: "a mishmash of catch phrases and a piecemeal conglomeration of educational management ideas" from the University of Alberta, and "a botch job to a degree altogether remarkable" from the University of Calgary. In May 1973 the minister tabled responses from the Department of Advanced Education, which related to certain particular recommendations in the report. For instance, the commission's proposal that the Department of Advanced Education (which had been established in May 1972) should have two divisions—higher education and further education—was rejected by the department (the current structure will be discussed in a later chapter). Only in May 1978 do we find an oblique reference to the broader philosophical base of the commission's propositions when Premier Lougheed said in the Legislature, "I reread that document and I came out with a concern with the underlying philosophy that was there. I wondered whether that philosophy was reflective of the public policy point of view of the elected legislators of Alberta" (Alberta Hansard, 11 May 1978).

Lougheed's comment was made during a debate on a statement, "The Goals of Basic Education for Alberta," which was adopted by the House on 15 May 1978. We can infer from this statement and its adoption that not only for basic education but with respect to education as a whole, the underlying philosophy of the government in the late 1970s emphasized the development of the abilities of the individual to fulfil his personal aspirations, "while making a positive contribution to society."

From Social Philosophy to Institutional Structure

This discussion of the dominant strains in the social philosophies of the two provinces will have intimated some of the main features we might expect to see in the social structures, and which might influence adult education.

In Quebec the importance and influence of religious institutions, particularly the Roman Catholic church, are seen to have diminished significantly over the last twenty years; the church lost the dominance it had held in basic education for centuries, and its influence over the learning needs and aspirations of adults diminished as people moved from traditionally inclined rural areas to the urban centres. Moreover, since formal avenues of adult education are a recent development, they have reflected from the beginning the more secular aims of a society emerging from the quiet revolution. These aims have to do with what Lesage wrote about in 1959 – the need to train Quebecers to take their place in the economic leadership of the province, and the concommitant need to assert a cultural national identity. In institutional terms the responsibility for meeting these aims could be expected to devolve to a great extent on the political structures, because they were basically political aims. The political structures comprised chiefly political parties. So in Quebec, the sway in fortunes and influence of the four main parties, Liberal, Union Nationale, Social Credit, and Parti Québécois, over the last couple of decades has had an important influence over nuances in adult education policy. All have had a common commitment to some degree of education for cultural and national identity, and to economically oriented training. We have seen, however, that the Liberal party tended to retain a certain attachment to the historical socio-economic pattern, in which there was a broad coincidence between management, *anglophonie,* and foreign control on the one hand, and labor, *francophonie,* and auto-determination on the other. Hence came the feeling expressed by Thorburn that the educational and economic policies of the Lesage government benefitted the middle classes most of all (Thorburn, 1976:xiii). The Parti Québécois, on the other hand, has accentuated the nationalistic and cultural aspects of development. It might be said that the Social Credit party in particular most clearly represents those elements in the society which have to do with conservatism and older petit bourgeois and rural values.

This has tended to produce a set of economic influences that are mutually antagonistic and that make different demands in terms of adult eduction, that is, management and professional development on the one side and labor and labor education on the other. Furthermore, the tendency in the political sphere has been toward creating a countervailing francophone cultural thrust against the dominant anglophone economic thrust. The two elements have sought to meet their educational needs through different resources. The needs of the predominantly anglophone, managerial sector in terms of professional and management education have been met in the main by anglophone institutions. On the labor side, the growing francophone working class has identified itself more with francophone trade unions and community organizations. And because of the coincidence of this division with that of nationalism, such organizations have tended to be more or less politically militant, with some representing the socialist strain in Quebec life to which Dion has pointed (1976).

With this strengthening of nationalism in the last twenty years or so, and the growing emphasis by all main parties on the assertion of a stronger (in some cases, separate) Quebec identity in economic as well as cultural and political terms, the most important structural relationships in respect of adult education developments are those in the political realm, the relationships between the ruling political party and the various sectors of society. These relationships are realized through the instruments of government, the departments of government administration that carry out party policies, including the educational institutions in the formal sense. We shall therefore concentrate most of our analysis on these relationships, and trace how they work out in terms of adult education practices in the provinces.

In Alberta the picture is somewhat different. We have seen that rather than a cultural nationalism, there is a strong multi-cultural flavor to the society. Instead of one dominant religious institution, there is a pluralism—and even a plethora—of various institutions and sects. But while some of the more fundamentalist sects assert a strong claim to determining their own educational path, particularly for

their children, none of them is sufficiently strong to exert a significant influence on the general pattern of adult education. There is, as
in Quebec, a divison between Catholic school-boards and Protestant
school-boards, but while in the basic education curricula there is an
interest in a certain degree of religious and moral education, this does
not appear to have a significant influence as far as adult programs are
concerned. On the other hand, among the various ethnic groups
there are some such as the Ukrainians, who claim and achieve some
influence in the basic eduction of their children, and who make certain demands in terms of support for cultural forms of adult education. In terms of education of a formal kind, there is the fairly high
demand for French language instruction from non-French-speaking
Albertans, but this is a function of support for bilingualism in the
national context; it comes from no particular social group or institution, and is directed mainly at the formal educational institutions.

The political structure in Alberta appears to be the dominant one
in relation to adult education, as in Quebec, but whereas in Quebec in
the last decade or so there has been an increasing tension between the
political structure and the dominant economic structure, in Alberta
the interests of the two have tended to have more in common with
each other. There has, since the U.F.A. government of the 1920s, been
a strong identification of the government with what was perceived to
be the dominant economic group. In the U.F.A. days it was the farmers; in Social Credit days it began by being the farmers and petit
bourgeois, and in both cases the common enemy was big business, or
eastern business. As the oil boom diminished the relative importance
of agriculture and increased the presence and influence of big and
small business, the ruling political party – first Socred and then particularly Progressive Conservative – accepted those influences. As we
have seen, even in Socred's later years, Manning emphasized the need
to create and maintain favorable conditions for industrial and commerical development. Agriculture, however, retained an influence
that was recognized and accepted by Lougheed in his 1971 Manifesto.

In contrast with the situation in Quebec, where the trade unions
were able to reflect and benefit by a coincidence of economic and social and cultural interests, in Alberta workers do not have such a con-
solidated interest. The political climate and political establishment are

not a common cause, and there is no condition of poverty, economic depression, or ethnic identity that gives an urgency and an emotional strength to their collective needs.

Whereas in Quebec much energy, in various forms, is devoted by government to supporting adult education that is, in a sense, anti-establishment —or at any rate against the old establishment— in Alberta there is a more *laissez-faire* government approach, which results from an implicit acceptance of the influences in the community, because such influences coincide, in turn, with the generally individualistic, capitalistic, (small-scale or large-scale) philosophy of the government. One manifestation of this coincidence may be the historical fact that from the advent of the U.F.A. government in 1921 to the reign of the Progressive Conservative government in the 1970s, each government has been elected with such an overwhelming majority as to constitute a one-party government.

In both provinces from different standpoints, it is fair to say that the institutions linked to government by jurisdiction and/or funding have a major influence on the pattern of adult education. As we move from the realm of social philosophy to social structure, we are interested in the ways in which the first is translated, or fails to be translated, into institutions and networks of institutions, which play a role in adult education, either as their primary, or as a secondary, responsibility.

It has been pointed out earlier that a good deal of adult education is carried out by a variety of agencies whose nature and multiplicity make them difficult to trace and discuss, such as church groups, in-service training in business, and clubs. This study will not attempt to cover the whole field including such enterprises as these, but will concentrate on two sets of institutions. The first will be government units—ministries and departments— and the relationships that exist between such units themselves and between them and the principal agencies that provide adult education and depend to a greater or lesser degree on government direction and funding. The second set of institutions will be those that are relatively independent of government direction, having to do with particular groups in society, such as organizations of native people, labor and agricultural unions, and provincial adult education associations. We will look at adult education from their point of view, their own internal efforts, and their relationships with government. Chapters 5 and 6 will cover government units, and Chapters 7 to 10 in Part III will cover the others.

References

Barr, J. 1974. *The Dynasty*. Toronto: McClelland and Stewart.

Bernard, A. 1977. *La Politique Au Canada et Au Quebec.* 2d ed. Montreal: Les Presses d'Université du Québec.

Centre d'Animation, de Développement et de Recherche en Education (C.A.D.R.E.). 1978. *Prospectives.* vol. 14, no. 1–2.

Commission on Educational Planning. 1972. *A Choice of Futures.* Edmonton: Queen's Printer.

Commission Royale d'Enguête Sur l'Enseignement. 1963–65. *Rapport.* Quebec: Editeur Officiel.

Dion, L. 1976. *The Unfinished Revolution.* Montreal: McGill-Queens University Press.

Dominion Bureau of Statistics. 1924. *Census of Canada, 1921.* vol. 1. Ottawa: King's Printer.

Government of Canada. 1970. *British North America Act.* Revised Statutes of Canada. Ottawa: Queen's Printer.

Groulx, L.H.J. 1977. "Multi-Media. Ideologie progressiste au conservative?" *Revue des Science de l'Education.* vol. III, no. 2.

Harrison, J.F.C. 1961. *Learning and Living: 1790–1960.* Toronto: University of Toronto Press.

Jasmin, B. 1978. "Réflexions Sur Le Livre Vert." *Prospectives,* vol. 14, no. 1–2.

Lafleur, Guy. 1975. *La Promotion Culturelle Collective des Classes Défavorisées.* Montreal: Institute Canadien d'Education des Adultes.

Lesage, J. 1959. *Lesage S'Engage.* Montreal: Les Editions Politiques du Québec.

Lucier, P. 1978. "L'Ecole et Les Valeurs." *Prospectives.* vol. 14, no. 1–2.

Macpherson, C.B. 1953. *Democracy in Alberta.* Toronto: University of Toronto Press.

Mann, W.E. 1955. *Sect, Cult, and Church in Alberta.* Toronto: University of Toronto Press.

Manning, E.C. 1967. *A White Paper on Human Resource Development.* Edmonton: Queen's Printer.

Ministère de l'Education. 1977. *L'Enseignement Primairie et Secondaire Au Québec.* Quebec: Editeur Officiel.

——. 1972. *L'Education des Adultes au Québec.* Quebec: Editeur Officiel.

Ministre d'Etat au Développement Culturel. 1978. *La Politique Québécoise du Développement Culturel.* Quebec: Editeur Officiel.

Parti Libéral du Québec. 1973. *Le Québec C'est Ton Affaire!* Montreal: Editions du Jour.

Progressive Conservative Party. 1971. *Now: New Directions for Alberta in the Seventies.* Edmonton: Progressive Conservative Party.

Statistics Canada 1974. *Census of Canada, 1971.* Ottawa: Queen's Printer.

Thorburn, H. 1976. Foreword to Dion, L. *The Unfinished Revolution.* Montreal: McGill-Queens University Press.

5

Government and Government-Linked Structures in Alberta

The present structure of government departments insofar as it affects adult education in Alberta dates, in the main, from 1972, when the Department of Advanced Education was established. Previously the Department of Education was the only one directly responsible for all education at all levels, with a Universities Commission and a Colleges Commission intervening between those actual institutions and the government. While adult education had in fact been offered for many years by the universities, colleges, institutes of technology, and local school-boards (particularly the Calgary Board of Education), the first explicit recognition of the growing importance of this kind of education was the appointment within the Department of Education in 1971 of a Co-ordinator of Continuing Education. The co-ordinator's role was not intended to impose on the institutions and agencies in the field a form of government dictated co-ordination of adult education activities, but there was by that time some concern in the government, and among some agencies, about the overlapping activities of various government-funded institutions, and the appointment was a reflection of such concern.

Outside the Department of Education there were a number of

other departments which were, and had been for many years, very active in adult education, such as the departments of agriculture, labor, social development, youth, health and the provincial secretary. The Department of Youth had been formed in 1966 as part of Manning's review of human development policies referred to in Chapter 4. Another organizational feature of that late Manning period, which had some influence on aspects of adult education outside the formal education system, was the Human Resources Development Authority (H.R.D.A.), a co-ordinating body at ministerial level, responsible for a wide area of government intervention in and funding for human resource development. Indeed, that era saw a number of imaginative government ventures in social types of adult education. Under the aegis of the H.R.D.A., a Community Development Service was set up to "facilitate human resources development among underprivileged people and underdeveloped communities," which were mainly native Indian and Metis (Manning, 1967:73). Under the new Department of Youth there was formed the Alberta Service Corps, a volunteer social action organization for university students to work with poor and disadvantaged people. Under the Department of Social Development, a Preventive Social Service was established in 1967 to work with municipal authorities in all aspects of preventive social work— daycare facilities, senior citizen activities, family life education, and so on. Along with H.R.D.A. a Human Resources Research Council was established to initiate studies designed to increase "the functionality of people engaged in human resources development" (Ibid.: 71).

Of these ventures, some did not survive the Manning government. The Human Resources Development Authority never appeared to have a sure base between the contending ministries and departments; along with the Research Council it was finally eliminated in 1972 under the Progressive Conservative government. The Community Development Service was always a thorn in the flesh of the political and economic establishments, and was phased out in the early 1970s. It is possible that these retrenchments would have taken place even if the Socred government had continued in office, but the prompt action taken by the new Tory government in the early 1970s was in accordance with its image of being a businesslike, efficiency-oriented administration guided by principles of individualism and restricted government intervention in social affairs. To some of the workers in the field, the impact came as a shift to a more technocratic and less people-oriented approach to human development services.

The general picture at the beginning of the 1970s was painted in this way by the Lifelong Education Task Force of the Commission on Educational Planning:

> What, in fact, appears is that there is at present no discernible pattern. There are many different agencies conducting their efforts in many different ways with less rather than more liaison, cooperation of effort, or mutual recognition. Adult education subsystems within larger institutions (i.e. universities) operate with little impact on or interest from the main parts of such institutions. At government level there are a number of ministerial portfolios which cover some aspect of (adult) education in the province. With regard to the co-ordination of the work of all these departments, this would appear to be one of the terms of reference of the Human Resources Development Authority, but we are not clear about the extent to which co-ordination is in fact carried out between departments. (Lifelong Education Task Force, 1971)

The Task Force went on to recommend, on the assumption of the continuance of the one Department of Education, the establishment of a Commission on Lifelong Education, parallel to the Universities and Colleges Commissions, with the responsibility for overseeing the total picture of lifelong education, for working toward obtaining co-operation between all educational agencies at regional and provincial levels, and for bringing to the attention of the executive body of government matters in which the concept of lifelong education was affected by decisions and developments in other fields—economic, social, and political.

Departments of Education and Advanced Education and Manpower

Before the Commission on Educational Planning—to which the task force reported and made its recommendations—issued its final report, the government split the educational portfolio by creating the Department of Advanced Education, which was responsible for higher education, university, college, and institute of technology affairs, and also what was called further education, or adult education (*see* Chapter 2). The universities and colleges commissions were disbanded. There seem to have been two or three main reasons for such a move. First, the leaders of the new Progressive Conservative government felt that the educational enterprise in its entirety had become so large that one minister could not relate sufficiently well to all its parts; expenditure in that part of the system dealing with full-time students in post-secondary education institutions was very high and significant in itself. And there was also a feeling that such enormous expenditures should not be so much under the influence of small bodies of appointed commissioners working at arm's length from the government. There is little evidence that consideration of the importance of adult education played any significant part in the creation of the new structure, and it has already been noted, in Chapter 4, that a Worth Commission recommendation that the new department have two main divisions—higher education and further education—was rejected in principle by the new department in a document tabled in the Legislature in May 1972.

The educational institutions initially coming under the jurisdiction of the Department of Advanced Education comprised four universities, the Banff Centre, six community colleges, four regional (formerly agricultural) colleges, two institutes of technology, four Alberta vocational centres, a network of community vocational centres in the Slave Lake area, and the Alberta Petroleum Industry Training Centre, all of which provided, to some degree, adult education programs to the public. The Alberta vocational centres offer short-term training programs, while the community vocational centres offer basic upgrading and life skill courses. The relationships between these institutions and the department indicate interesting signs of movement in government thinking over the last few years. Initially, only the universities and six colleges (called public colleges) operated under their own boards of governors; policies and priorities with regard to their adult education and extension work were matters for internal institutional decision-making, subject only to the ultimate control the government exercised in overall funding. The Banff Centre had a peculiar status because it had a council, but was only about half-way toward the autonomy of a university. The others were called Provincial Administered Institutions, and came directly under the department to the extent that for adult education, as well as other functions, policy and programming were directly controlled by the department. In 1978 the four regional colleges, which by now had a wider role than purely agricultural and vocational, were also made public colleges administered by boards of governors responsible for planning and programming. In 1981 the two institutes of technology were also given their own boards of governors. The Banff Centre also acquired the same status. So, while the government has delegated planning and policy-making functions to the institutions involved in the broad range of general non-vocational adult education, and given them a broader community role, it retains control over the vocational training centres. This is not to say that the latter do not offer any general interest adult education programs. The Alberta vocational centres, particularly in Grouard and Lac La Biche, where there are no other similar institutions, offer a range of general interest programs in response to local demands. The two institutes of technology retain some such programs, a carry-over from an earlier time when they and the universities were dominant agencies in the field.

The government has passed over to the non-vocational post-secondary institutions the mandate to respond to local adult education demands of a general nature as they perceive those demands. This seems to be in line with general government philosophy, and diminishes the role of government in influencing general adult education in particular directions.

Government retention of control over vocational training, however, reflects the perception that these institutions are linked to manpower and economic development policy, and thus should be more amenable to direct government decision-making. Moreover, manpower training has become the ground for negotiation between provincial and federal governments, whereby the latter provides funding for provincial institutions and industries to offer programs to meet national manpower needs. Presumably, partly in recognition of this close link between manpower needs and the educational and training resources of the province, in 1975 the Manpower Services Division of the Department of Labor was hived off and combined with Advanced

Education to form the Department of Advanced Education and Manpower. This meant that now one department was responsible, not only for manpower training through the institutes of technology, Alberta vocational centres, colleges, and private trade schools, but also for the administration of such matters as apprenticeship and trade certification legislation. There had long been an overlap in the jurisdiction and activities of the Department of Advanced Education through its vocational training institutions, and those of the manpower training division of the Department of Labor, and this had caused some interdepartmental friction. Premier Lougheed's solution was to bring the two under one department.

Within the Department of Advanced Education and Manpower there are four main divisions: program services, administrative services, manpower services, and field services. Three of these have a role with respect to adult education, outlined as follows.

In the Program Services Division, whose general responsibility is for the actual programs offered in the province, there are six directorates: campus (or university) programs, college programs, technical and vocational programs, further education services, health and social service programs, and learning systems. Further education is concerned with providing partial funding for non-vocational, non-credit adult education courses (the equivalent of éducation populaire in Quebec) offered by all the public agencies such as universities, colleges and school-boards, and by volunteer (but not commercial) agencies such as the Y.M.C.A. and Women's Institute; and with promoting and assisting local further education councils throughout the province, which are discussed in more detail later in this chapter. Responsibility for the promotion, funding, and monitoring of vocational courses given in the teaching institutions lies with the directorate of technical and vocational programs. Courses for people in health and social services, such as nurses, social workers, and ambulance drivers, come under the directorate of health and social service programs. This division works in conjunction with agencies such as the institutes of technology or colleges, which conduct the above courses, and with other government departments and divisions. The programs themselves are the concern of these administrative divisions, and not the operations of the agencies providing them. It is not unlikely, however, that the operations of these institutions are indirectly influenced by the source and volume of funding for their programs.

Broadly speaking, adult education programming is influenced by the characteristics of these programming directorates themselves. They have a mixture of institution-based and purpose- or function-based jurisdictions. The directorates of campus, college, and technical and vocational programs see the world through the eyes of the universities, colleges, and technical and vocational centres respectively, and when their staffs become aware of certain potential or identified needs for education and/or training, they see them in terms of the roles of the institutions rather than in terms of the group of people in whom the need is seen to exist. In other words, the surveying and administering to the needs of particular vocational or social groups is seen as a matter for the educational institutions themselves. Insofar as the programs that might emerge in this way attract government funds, for example, through manpower training arrangements, or insofar as the client group is able to meet the costs, the institution will be prepared to proceed. But insofar as these conditions are not met, this is likely not to happen, and the group in question will not be served.

This arrangement of depending on institutional initiatives seems consistent with the *laissez-faire* tendency in the province. It has some advantages. It places the initiative for programming nearer to the source of needs, and provides some flexibility. On the other hand, it keeps the source of the funds, the government, at arm's length from the source of needs, so that the government's reference group becomes not the people, but the intervening institutions, and the government's direct awareness of the people's needs is diminished.

The exception to this pattern is the directorate of health and social services programs—a function-based jurisdiction. The formation of this directorate seems to have arisen in a pragmatic way, out of the fact that nursing and social work training were being provided in more than one type of institution. Nurses were being trained in universities and hospital schools with some increasing involvement on the part of colleges, so it became a matter of rationalizing and coordinating the roles of the various agencies in this particular field of training. A similar need arose from the training of social workers at different levels in the universities and colleges. In other words, these problems spanned more than one type of institution and directorate.

There are a number of other fields, such as local government administration, personnel management, and real estate, where the training
appears to cut across the institutional boundaries, and which do not
appear to be amenable to rationalization under the present division of
programming jurisdictions, so that competitive program marketing
results.

The directorate of learning systems is a service unit to the other
directorates, concerned with program design and evaluation.

Manpower services has three roles in respect of adult education.
First, it negotiates agreements with the federal government with respect to the Canada Manpower Training Program and the Canada
Manpower Industrial Training Program; such programs, insofar as
they are to be provided by the institutions, that is, the institutes of
technology, the Alberta vocational centres, and so forth, are then
handled by the directorate of technical and vocational programs referred to above, while in respect of programs provided by industry, the
Manpower services division retains direct administrative responsibility and works in conjunction with industries. Second, this division
administers short-term, *ad hoc* employment programs such as the Student Temporary Employment Program (STEP), and third, it administers the operation of eleven Alberta Career Centres in various
localities in the province. These are centres open to all adults for
testing and counselling in matters of career and career training.

The field services division is the arm of the Department of
Advanced Education and Manpower that administers the Alberta
vocational centres, community vocational centres, and the Alberta
Petroleum Industry Training Centre in Edmonton, and also oversees
the operations of private trade schools.

The provision of adult education in the province is spread over a
large number and variety of public institutions, from universities to
small rural community vocational centres, all of which are subject to
a greater or lesser degree of influence by the Department of Advanced
Education and Manpower. The universitites and public colleges exercise considerable autonomy in defining their own priorities and their
role with regard to adult education. Until 1976–77 the three universities other than Athabasca University were influenced to a greater
degree than at present in that besides their normal operating budget,
which until then had been tied to full-time student enrolments, they

shared an additional Public Service Grant from the government, some of which was allocated directly toward the operation of the departments or faculties of extension or continuing education. This separate appropriation has since been absorbed into the general budgets of the universities, and the effects of this are not yet clear.

What the description of the department indicates is that not only is the actual provision of adult education spread over many agencies, but that the internal responsibility for adult education matters is spread among many sub-units of the department. It may be circumstances of this sort that pursuaded the minister to establish an Advisory Committee on Further Education, initially representing various institutional interests and the general public, and appointed by the minister to keep him in touch with the field. On the other hand, the *raison d'être* for this advisory committee may be quite otherwise, since a number of other such committees were appointed in respect of such matters as university affairs, technical training, and native education. These are referred to below and illustrated in Figure 5, which shows the extent of the involvement of other departments in this field, and some of the linkages between tham all.

The closest structural links are between the departments of Advanced Education and Manpower and of Education. The latter department is responsible and provides funding for extension credit programs, evening, day time, and summer courses for adults in high school subjects. These programs are held in schools run by school-boards in various centres, mainly Calgary and Edmonton, and in Alberta vocational centres, since many adults are taking such courses as a requirement for entering vocational programs. For this purpose, Alberta vocational centres are registered under the Department of Education as high schools, and are therefore linked to the school system. Second, some school-boards offer non-credit extension programs, which attract grants from the Department of Advanced Education and Manpower, through the directorate of further education services. In other words, the division of responsibilities between the departments of Education and Advanced Education and Manpower is based not on students' ages but on the Department of Education's mandate to provide formal education from kindergarten to grade twelve to persons of any age. All other education for adults falls under the Department of Advanced Education and Manpower. Third, the Corres-

Figure 5

Alberta Government Structures

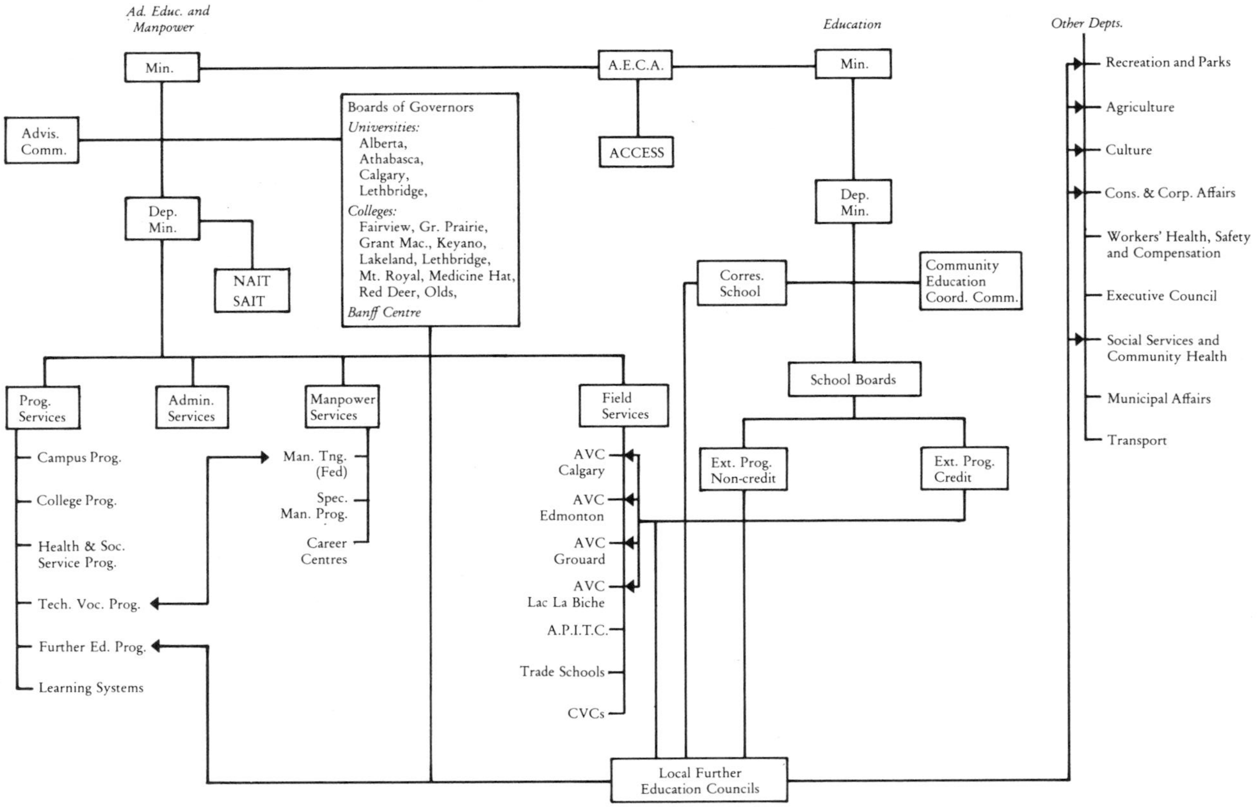

Ad. Educ. and Manpower

Advis. Comm.

Min.

Dep. Min.

NAIT SAIT

Boards of Governors

Universities: Alberta, Athabasca, Calgary, Lethbridge,

Colleges: Fairview, Gr. Prairie, Grant Mac., Keyano, Lakeland, Lethbridge, Mt. Royal, Medicine Hat, Red Deer, Olds,

Banff Centre

Prog. Services

Admin. Services

Manpower Services

Campus Prog.

College Prog.

Health & Soc. Service Prog.

Tech. Voc. Prog.

Further Ed. Prog.

Learning Systems

Man. Tng. (Fed)

Spec. Man. Prog.

Career Centres

Education

Min.

Dep. Min.

A.E.C.A.

ACCESS

Community Education Coord. Comm.

Corres. School

School Boards

Ext. Prog. Credit

Ext. Prog. Non-credit

Field Services

AVC Calgary

AVC Edmonton

AVC Grouard

AVC Lac La Biche

A.P.I.T.C.

Trade Schools

CVCs

Local Further Education Councils

Other Depts.

Recreation and Parks

Agriculture

Culture

Cons. & Corp. Affairs

Workers' Health, Safety and Compensation

Executive Council

Social Services and Community Health

Municipal Affairs

Transport

pondence School offers a service to adults throughout the province who are interested in school-level studies. These are services and linkages at the operating and administrative level. Other linkages exist at the policy and planning level, through the Alberta Education Communications Authority and the Community Education Co-ordinating Committee, both of which are discussed in more detail below.

Other Government Departments

Figure 5 also lists the other principal government departments involved in some aspect of adult education. Of these, the Department of Agriculture has the longest standing and most probably the most extensive role. This educational role was accepted and described in the department's first annual report in 1905, when the department worked with local agricultural societies in spreading knowledge of farming matters. The role has been pursued since then through the agricultural colleges—three of which were started in 1912—and through district officials (Boulet, 1977:a). The colleges have, as indicated above, been absorbed into the provincial college system under the Department of Advanced Education and Manpower. Extension officials from the Department of Agriculture have been in the field since 1916, and by 1975 there were ninety district agriculturalists and assistants, and sixty-one district home economists and assistants, part of whose role was education, not only among rural people, but also in some of the urban centres (Boulet, 1977:b). An extension branch was formed in 1938 with the following objectives: to co-operate with other extension agencies, to distribute information pertaining to agriculture and home economics, to help form community organizations through which extension workers might reach the country people, to assist in every way to develop local leaders. Extension field work is grouped in six regions under Regional Directors responsible for all departmental business in their region. Co-operation with other extension agencies has been pursued for many years through working with the University of Alberta, the Rural Education and Development Association (which will be disucssed further in Chapter 7), wheat pools, and the Canadian Department of Agriculture.

In the Department of Workers' Health, Safety and Compensation, the Research and Education Branch has twelve education officers in three centres—Calgary, Edmonton, and Lethbridge—whose function is to organize courses, seminars, and presentations for industry in such matters as accident control, safety, working in confined spaces, and industrial health. They use the resources of other departments where appropriate, and they work with the formal post-secondary education institutions by indicating needs requiring longer term industrial educational programs. In 1978–79 the branch made 442 presentations to a total of ten thousand persons. The branch is funded from contributions to government by the Workmen's Compensation Board, which in turn is financed from assessments on employers in the province. This branch is also concerned with education in labor relations, but since the initiative in this regard is seen to rest with the trade unions, it provides resource persons and financial assistance only if approached. More is said about this type of activity in Chapter 7.

The Department of Consumer and Corporate Affairs has two adult education functions. The Consumer Education Branch provides formal courses to adult groups in subjects related to a knowledge of the marketplace, and common consumer problems. These courses are generally given through college continuing education divisions in the large centres, and in conjunction with local further education councils in smaller centres. They also provide such courses and workshops on demand to particular groups. Besides this, the branch prepares and distributes teaching packages that can be used by other government departments and officials, such as public health nurses and district home economists. Some of these packages have been requested by and sold to organizations in other countries. This branch has, with the Alberta Education Communications Corporation ACCESS, produced an eighteen-part T.V. series, "The Complete Consumer," for use in post-secondary institutions and local councils. Besides the branch head office staff in Edmonton, there are three regional consumer specialists in Calgary, Edmonton, and Lethbridge, with a prospect of other regional representatives in Red Deer, Peace River, and Fort McMurray in the near future.

The second important education function performed by the Department of Consumer and Corporate Affairs is a family financial counselling service. This provides people with individual counselling on the prevention of and remedies to debt problems, and the service is available through all six of the department's regional offices. The staff of this branch also prepare and present information on money management and household budgeting for community groups, for courses in preparation for marriage, and for the news media.

In the Department of Recreation and Parks, the main adult education thrust is through the Recreation Division, which in turn has three branches. The planning branch is concerned mainly with broad divisional planning, but it does from time to time hold workshops in local communities in regard to the planning of recreational facilities. The field service branch is responsible for activity in the communities through twenty-five regional offices staffed by professional recreation consultants. These consultants conduct workshops in various aspects of recreation administration, staffed variously by themselves, local resources, officials from other departments or from the third branch in this division: the recreation programs branch.

Within this branch the community education services section works with local recreation boards in small centres and recreation departments in the municipalities in such matters as leadership training, inter-agency co-operation, the joint use of school facilities for adult activities, how to conduct effective meetings, and group problem-solving. It is responsible for working with the Department of Education and local school-boards under a program called Project Co-operation, in which funds are made available to encourage the use of school facilities for community purposes. This is mentioned again below in the discussion of community education. Three other sections in the recreation programs branch also have certain adult education responsibilities. The section on recreation for special groups works with such groups as handicapped persons, pre-school associations, and senior citizens, in arranging recreational programs geared to their special interests. It also works with other government departments such as the senior citizens branch of the Department of Social Services and Community Health, and associations such as the Alberta Council on Aging. The outdoor recreation section holds workshops and clinics for recreation leaders, and runs an outdoor training centre in the Rockies, while the sports and fitness section helps sports associations in organizational matters and the preparation of officials and coaches.

The parks division of this department conducts less extensive but nevertheless important activities in adult education in the form of a guiding and interpretation program on nature and history in the provincial parks.

The Department of Culture has a Cultural Development Division that provides adult education programs or assistance to individuals in the visual arts and crafts, the performing arts, and film and literary arts. It is responsible for supporting the province's public library services, and it operates the two largest public auditoria in the province, the Northern and Southern Jubilee Auditoriums in Edmonton and Calgary, which are the venues of symphony concerts, opera, rock concerts, and, in fact, the whole range of the performing arts. The Cultural Development Division also supports and stimulates ethnic groups interested in contributing to the multicultural nature of the province's heritage. The purpose of the division is "to promote, encourage and co-ordinate the orderly cultural development of Alberta to ensure that cultural development becomes an enriching reality in the lives of the people of the province." (Alberta Culture, 1978). This department most clearly reflects the ethnic diversity of the population of the province, and the political influence attached to these groups in their demands on government resources. Over four hundred ethnocultural organizations in the province are registered with the department. Among the types of financial assistance provided to such groups is a language support program, under which small subventions, on a per student basis, are made to language schools operated outside school hours by such organizations.

An important objective of this department has been not only to support professional activities and high level performances in centres large enough to sustain them, but to help build a broad provincial base, at a grass roots level, of skills in and appreciation of the arts. Residential summer schools are held annually for practitioners in the smaller centres of Drumheller (for drama) and Camrose (for music). The department provides financial and consultative assistance to communities planning to bring performing artists into their areas, and runs training and leadership programs for local instructors in arts and crafts and periodic workshops and demonstrations by the department's staff of professional consultants. In these outlying programs the central administration is served by a staff of field representatives based in five smaller centres. It also participates, with the Department of Recreation and Parks, in a program for partially funding the erection of major cultural and recreational facilities, and for the formulation of recreational master plans, in smaller centres. In other words, this department sees its role not simply as a provider of funds, which carries the danger of creating dependency on the part of local communities, but as providing incentives for sustained local effort in this field.

The Department of Social Services and Community Health is, in effect, two separate departments, each with a deputy minister, under one chief deputy minister, and has a wide range of adult education functions. In respect of two of the most important of these, it has a funding and support role rather than directly providing educational services. First are its relations with rural health units, of which there are twenty-seven in the province, besides the two boards of health in Calgary and Edmonton. The health units come under boards made up of local people appointed by the government, while the boards in the two large cities come under the city governments. The provincial government provides full funding for the rural health units and advisory and consultative services through local offices of the Department of Social Services and Community Health. The role of these units is meant to be primarily preventive, so a range of educational material and educational programs is made available in subjects such as nutrition, family life education, family planning, sanitation, environmental control, maternal and child health, and mental health. Second, the preventive social service boards, locally appointed boards with their own staffs under a director employed by the board, have a responsibility extending over the whole range of social services from day care to senior citizens. They were set up under the Preventive Social Service Act, introduced by the Social Credit government in 1967, as part of the wave of what in the North American and particularly Albertan context was very progressive social legislation. Again, the emphasis is on prevention rather than welfare, and depending on the energy of the local board and the director, a great deal of social education has been carried out under this service throughout the province. The local boards and directors are advised and supported by consultants from the Department of Social Services and Community Health. In

April 1981, the name of this branch was changed to Family and Community Support Services.

In the department there is a senior citizens branch, which, again, is primarily concerned with supporting educational programs rather than providing a direct service. It provides information to all senior citizen centres; it underwrites the cost of educational programs conducted by other agencies, such as the University Extension Departments; it sponsors a few regional workshops for professional and volunteer workers in senior citizen centres; and it provides grants to professionals and semi-professionals working with senior citizens who wish to improve their knowledge and skills by attending formal programs offered by educational institutions.

The fourth principal adult education function of this department is carried out through the Division of Rehabilitation Services, and these services fall under two main heads: services for the handicapped, and vocational rehabilitation. The first of these comprises a variety of services designed to help handicapped persons "achieve their highest potential and prepare as many as possible for gainful employment" (Alberta Social Services and Community Health, 1978). This division helps fund activities centres, where severely handicapped persons can learn skills necessary for independent living, recreation, communication, and inter-personal relations; vocational training centres, which provide handicapped persons with work skills in a typical business atmosphere; vocational rehabilitation centres, which train persons in new marketable skills after some form of disablement; and sheltered employment centres for those who will be unable to meet the requirements of employment elsewhere. These training services are provided by twenty-five different agencies throughout the province, offering about fourteen hundred places for handicapped persons.

The other thrust of the Division of Rehabilitation Services is through its Employment Opportunities Program, which offers training for employment and placement advice to adults who at the time are employable but are not employed, and who have registered with a Canada Manpower Centre but have not benefitted from its services. This program is complementary to the Canada Manpower Service, which is the primary agency for employment training and placement in the country. Some forty-three placement officers under this program, working in a number of places across the province, provide clients with advice and direction in respect of pre-employment counselling and training, job training or re-training, and family support services. The actual training itself takes place in one of the public or private trade schools operating in this field.

As an offshoot of this program, the provincial government has established under the Division of Rehabilitation Services, the Opportunity Corps, which operates in five areas in northern Alberta, centred on Slave Lake. This program is funded on a cost-sharing basis by the Alberta government and the federal Department of Regional Economic Expansion. The purpose is to teach basic life skills to the predominantly native population in that area through short-term employment, community work projects, and special workshops, and to encourage communities to identify and meet their needs through self-help as a group. It is therefore directed at both personal and social development. Since its inauguration in 1970 the program has completed over five hundred project contracts such as constructing or renovating day care centres, playgrounds, community halls, and senior citizen centres, and by the end of 1976 it had handled over eleven hundred trainees; half remained permanently employed and many others went on to further education and training.

The Opportunity Corps Program is one of a number of government services directed primarily at native people and administered by more than one department of the government. In the Department of Municipal Affairs there is an administrative unit called the Land Tenure Secretariat, which works with people in unincorporated areas, crown lands that have no local government identification such as county or municipal district. The jurisdiction of the Land Tenure Secretariat extends in principle to all of what is called the Green Area, that is provincial public lands, which cover about two-thirds of the province, but in fact its work so far extends only to fifteen communities in three Improvement Districts in the northern part of the province. The role of the secretariat is to help people in those communities form land tenure committees and to work toward becoming recognized communities with land ownership rights for its members, and therefore a firmer economic base. The secretariat sponsors and sometimes conducts workshops in these communities in matters such as community organization, group decision-making, community procedures, aspects of law, and the role and functions of government departments. The secretariat initiated a course in civics for the native people in these northern communities, which is now taught through the Alberta vocational centres and community vocational centres in the area. The work of the secretariat is funded equally by the provincial government and the federal Department of Regional Economic Expansion.

Finally, the Department of Native Affairs has the role of monitoring all programs offered by other departments for native people, and of bringing to the attention of the Department of Advanced Education and Manpower the educational needs that can be met through the community vocational centres. It keeps abreast of developments in such areas as Cold Lake, where large new oil exploitation industries were being planned, and where training for local native people was desirable so that they can participate in such developments. For this purpose it works with the Departments of Labor and Advanced Education and Manpower, and with Native Outreach, an organization run by native people to help improve the training and placement of their own people.

The Department of Transportation has an apprenticeship system for its employees, though the formal part of the training is provided through the Northern Alberta Institute of Technology.

The Executive Council has formal financial responsibility for a number of adult education programs of different kinds, in that the latter are funded through government estimates of expenditure under its control. Native affairs expenditure, for instance, is a sub-vote under Executive Council, as is the expenditure on ACCESS, referred to below. Until April 1979, the expenditure for occupational health and safety education was also voted through Executive Council, but since then it has come under a new Department of Workers' Health, Safety and Compensation. The Women's Bureau, coming directly under the Executive Council, provides some leadership and funding in programming for women.

Educational Communications

The final element in Alberta, as shown in Figure 5, is the organization of a media network for educational purposes. One of the main recommendations of the Worth Report on educational planning was that an Alberta Communications Centre for Educational Systems and Services (ACCESS) be established immediately as a Crown Corporation with a mandate to develop the province's educational communica-tions services (1972:266-69). Educational television organizations and facilities in Edmonton and Calgary and an educational radio station financed by Alberta Government Telephones already existed, and the proposal was to bring these together as the nucleus of a province-wide system to provide existing institutions with broadcast capabilities, to promote the production of educational materials, and to serve outlying areas of the province. The Alberta Education Communications Authority at the ministerial level was responsible for overseeing developments in this field. Another related recommendation of the Worth Commission was that there be established an institution to carry lifelong education by a variety of distance learning methods to persons out of reach of the conventional post-secondary institutions by reasons of geography, occupational or family priorities, or lack of academic prerequisites for university entrance. The report called this kind of open university the Alberta Academy.

Three institutions have developed as a result. First, the proposal for ACCESS was realized in the establishment of the Alberta Education Communications Corporation, which retains popularly the title of ACCESS, and which has a mandate to produce radio programs of an educational and "enrichment" nature for broadcast through its radio station, C.K.U.A., and similar television and film programs for broadcast through commercial or community channels or as video or film packages for use by groups and institutions. The adult education responsibilities of ACCESS have been set out by the body having legal jurisdiction over it, the Alberta Education Communications Authority, which comprises the ministers of Education and of Advanced Education and Manpower, and has a full-time director. Until 1978 this latter body was served by a Program Policy Advisory Committee, selected and appointed by the authority itself and, in general terms, representative of various educational interests in the province. This committee recommended policy guidelines and procedures, which provide that the proportion of the total ACCESS programming devoted to adult education is 25 percent (early childhood programming is given 20 percent, basic education is given 40 percent, and higher education is given 15 percent).

The relations between the authority and the corporation provide an interesting illustration of the balance between the provincial jurisdiction over education and the federal jurisdiction over communications. The corporation was established by the Alberta Education Communications Corporation Act of 1973, which provides that "subject to any directions made by the provincial authority (it may) produce, acquire, sell, lease, distribute, exhibit or otherwise deal in programs and materials of an educational nature whether for use in broadcasting or otherwise." The use of the term "directions" might be interpreted to mean that the corporation and its broadcasting services were subject to government control, and this would bring the latter up against the Canadian Radio and Television Commission, the federal agency authorized to licence broadcasting stations in Canada. In fact C.K.U.A., formerly under Alberta Government Telephones and now under ACCESS, has at its licence hearings in recent years been obliged to demonstrate clearly that it is not an instrument available to the provincial government for politically oriented broadcasts which would contravene the C.R.T.C. licencing requirements. The corporation was able to use this argument in resisting what were formulated and recommended as "directives" by the Program Policy Advisory Committee to the two ministers who constitute the authority. The term "directions" was then softened to "guidelines."

The corporation's resistance to such directives appears not to have been entirely based on this legal provision, but to arise partly from *amour propre*. The board of the corporation is appointed by government and its members have the same general representative character as did the members of the Program Policy Advisory Committee. The board therefore saw itself as being, in a sense, judged by another group of persons with no more knowledge or widom than themselves. The perception of this writer, as a member of the advisory committee for a period, was that the committee's members, in turn, were never quite sure what was required of them, and some felt the uneasy possibility of being used both as a foil to the board of the corporation and as a token nod toward the principle of citizen participation, which was in vogue at that time. For whatever reasons, the Program Policy Advisory Committee no longer exists.

The third institution in the educational communications network is Athabasca University. In the time of expectations of rising student enrolments of the late 1960s, this university was planned by the Socred government as a fourth, campus-based provincial university. Before this plan advanced very far, university enrolments began to level off, and a new, Progressive Conservative government came to power with promises to review all capital projects, so plans for a new campus were shelved. But the push for some kind of institution along the lines of the Worth Report's Alberta Academy still existed, and in 1972 a new Athabasca University was created to undertake a pilot project on the design and delivery of multi-media university-level courses to off-campus students (Daniel and Smith, 1979: 63–74). By 1975 the government was sufficiently convinced of the usefulness of the venture to agree to its continuance, and in 1978 a new Order-in-Council made the new university official and permanent.

Athabasca University is a part of the educational communications network only insofar as it is an educational institution using various media and distance-learning capabilities. It is a fully autonomous university like the others in the province, awarding its own undergraduate degrees and offering a variety of other programs, some in conjunction with other institutions. It co-operates with ACCESS, and is a member of a number of cable television consortia in the delivery of some of its courses.

Cable television is a part of the educational communications system that lies outside the institutional framework discussed so far, but it is important as a service element to those institutions. The consortia just referred to are groups of institutions, including, in different combinations in the different centres, universities, institutes, colleges, and some of the school-boards in Edmonton, Calgary, Grande Prairie, and Lethbridge. They are provided with an educational channnel by the cable television companies, under an obligation placed upon the companies by the C.R.T.C. The strength and effectiveness of these consortia has varied, and the enterprise has yet to make a significant impact, though it appears to offer some potential. There exists an association of these consortia at the provincial level, which brings together representatives of each consortium from time to time to discuss common issues and problems. One of the perennial issues is the question of the availability, suitability, and cost of materials and programs produced by ACCESS. Alongside this kind of enterprise is the community channel, also provided by each cable television company. This has a looser connection with education institutions, though

from time to time some of them use this channel for information purposes, and even for more structured programs.

Co-ordinating Machinery

It has been indicated above that at least since the early 1970s there has
been concern about co-ordination, or the lack of it, between the
various agencies in the field, some of them under the same government departments and some under different departments, and between relatively autonomous agencies such as universities and
colleges. The quotation from the report of the Lifelong Education
Task Force referred to earlier indicates that in the early 1970s there
was little evidence of the co-ordination of programming provided by
the various government departments offering adult education. There
is still no formal machinery for such co-ordination, apart from the
Community Education Co-ordinating Committee, which is described below, and liaison between departments in respect of their
adult education responsibilities appears to be on a personal and informal basis. We have seen that particularly in relation to adult education among native people in the northern part of the province, there
is fairly good interdepartmental co-operation and a number of departments use the facilities of the Alberta and community vocational
centres. There appears to be a fuzzy line between the responsibilities
of different departments in some aspects of training, for example,
leadership training and community organization training, and an
overlap is left to be sorted out at the local level between field officers.
It is, in fact, at the local level that most organizational effort toward
co-ordination has been directed.

One of the functions of the offices of co-ordinator, established in
1971, and the Director of Further Education Services, which absorbed
this responsibility into the Department of Advanced Education in
1972, has been to encourage and help the formation of a network of
local further education councils in as many centres as possible
throughout the province. Such a prototype council had been formed
in Edmonton in 1969 on a voluntary basis between a number of the

principal agencies in the city, and this provided a model for the encouragement of other councils in other centres. The idea was that in each town or rural centre the agencies offering programs of a non-credit non-vocational nature should be represented on a council whose purpose would be to see that all the adult education demands expressed by the local people were met without undue duplication, either by local agencies or by inviting in agencies from elsewhere. In the large cities such a council typically includes representatives of the colleges, universities, Alberta vocational centres, government departments, school-boards, city parks and recreation departments, the library, and voluntary associations such as the Y.W.C.A. and Y.M.C.A., and family life education associations. The size of the councils in the two big cities has been so large that it has, as yet, been difficult to arrange for the representation of citizens at large. The basis on which such general representation should rest has also been difficult to resolve. In the rural areas the council will, typically, include the district agriculturalist, the district home economist, the local recreation director, the school superintendent, the preventive social services director, a public health nurse, the local community art club, and perhaps one or two private citizens representing no particular organization.

This movement was given impetus in the mid-1970s with the promulgation of the Department of Advanced Education and Manpower's *Further Education Policy Guidelines and Procedures.* This document sets out a policy of financial assistance for non-credit adult education programs. First, it provides a system of grants in respect of each hour of instruction of approved non-credit programming. The responsibility for approving most of the courses for grant purposes has been passed by government to the local councils. The result of this laudable intention to thus decentralize authority for grant approval has been to divert energies of local councils away from coordination and co-operative programming toward the activity of preparing and approving course proposals to maximize grant receipts. Further consequences of the grants policy are discussed in Chapter 11.

Second, the policy document provides a grant of $7,000 (increased to $10,000 in 1981–82), or 15 percent of the total amount paid in instructional grants, to a school-board that undertakes to handle the administration and leadership of the local council, plus further small grants for travel and advertising. In smaller centres, the $7,000-administrative grant has been used to employ part-time co-ordinators. Though the intention of the policy was to encourage the co-ordination of programs offered by the various existing agencies in the area, and not to set up another programming agency, in many centres the local co-ordinator has become practically a full-time programmer, and the focus and generator of local effort. In some cases this has alienated some of the existing agencies. Nevertheless, the establishment and work of these councils, which at the beginning of 1979 numbered 83 in all parts of the province, appears to have had a great influence in increasing non-credit adult education, particularly in smaller centres. Furthermore, there is by now some evidence that although the demands initially tended to be for recreational courses— macramé, cake-making, basketry—they are now becoming more sophisticated and show a rising level of educational aspirations. Whether as a result of the work of the councils or not, there has been a marked increase in recent years in the number of non-credit general interest courses offered in the province, for which grants are paid, as shown in Table 2.

Still questionable is whether or not these councils have achieved much co-operation between agencies in program planning and rationalization, particularly in the larger centres. The constituent members of the councils are more or less autonomous, and there are no sanctions against ignoring efforts to obtain co-ordination of program-

Table 2
_____

Courses and Participants in Non-Credit
Adult Education: Alberta

	1975–76	1976–77	1977–78
No. of Courses	9,700	12,000	12,500
No. of Participants	148,000	165,600	180,400

Source: Directorate of Further Education, Department of Advanced Education and Manpower.

ming. Historically, a number of agencies such as university extension divisions and school-boards carry some of the programming they had built up before other agencies existed—agencies that may now be more appropriate for some of that programming. Here a characteristic of Alberta's individualistic, competitive economic and social philosophy is manifest. Since most extension operations of the educational institutions depend on course fees for their operating revenue, there is a strong tendency toward forceful marketing according to the economic model, which does not lend itself to co-operative planning.

Community Education

Nonetheless, despite this qualification, the local further educational councils are meant to—and they partially do—achieve some measure of co-ordination of programming at the local level. There is no equivalent structure in the provincial government that brings together all the main departments involved. One interdepartmental committee, the Community Education Co-ordinating Committee, has the particular mandate to develop a policy for recommendation to government in respect of community education, and to co-ordinate initiatives that occur in the meantime. The committee has four departments: Education (which provides the chairman); Advanced Education and Manpower; Recreation and Parks; and Culture. A full-time senior consultant acts as executive director to the committee.

There has been formal interest in community education and community schools in Alberta since the early 1970s. Under the Social Credit government, it was intended to establish fifty community schools in the province. In 1971, however, the Progressive Conservative government agreed to the establishment of only three such schools as a pilot project for three years. After 1975 two of these—in St. Paul in the northeast and Pincher Creek in the southwest—continued as community schools. In addition, the Department of Recreation and Parks provides funds to school jurisdictions (sixty-five cents per head of population of the town or city in question) for developing areas of the schools for adult evening classes or for other appropriate purposes such as the employment of a community school co-ordinator. This funding is provided under the program called Project Co-operation, mentioned earlier in the description of the work of the Department of Recreation and Parks. The aim of the co-ordinating committee is to foster the development of schools consciously oriented to the total community in terms of the curriculum, the style of teaching, the use of community resources, and the attitudes of the school staffs. The committee has produced a proposal under which a school-board may apply to have one or more of its schools designated as a community school, provided it undertakes a commitment to lifelong learning, a life-centred curriculum, co-operation with other agencies, a suitable modification of facilities, and the use of community processes and facilities. As a community school, it receives up to $50,000 per year to implement the concept and practice of community education. This proposal had been approved by the Deputy Ministers of the four departments concerned prior to the 1979 provincial election.

Here there is a movement toward a measure of co-ordination at the government level, and of co-operative adult education programming at the community level. If many more schools are open for adult programs, there could be a significant increase in adult education activity all over the province. The question of whether that activity will spread to embrace the fuller concept of community education, the engagement of people throughout the community in the enterprise of learning and social change, still remains. If this does not happen, the emphasis on adult education in the schools will tend to rest in the middle part of the continuum shown in Figure 2 in Chapter 2.

Consortia

In 1980 there appeared another institution that had some degree of a co-ordinating role in education for adults at a local level. As a means of partially meeting demands for the establishment of new community colleges in various regions of the province not already served, the government responded by initiating the formation of consortia of existing post-secondary institutions in a position to serve the regions. The function of these institutions is to offer credit courses, both degree and diploma level, in the defined region of the consortium. By 1981 five such consortia were in operation or in advanced stages of organization in different parts of the province. Features of this institution are: a government-appointed board of representatives of the serving institutions; an advisory group of local residents; the appointment of a director; and an annual administrative budget of $275,000. There is no operating budget; the costs for programs are met by the offering agencies. In the early stages of the development of the consortia, it was not clear how far the local boards and directors would move into the field of non-credit adult education programming, and thus possibly impinge on the work of Local Further Education Councils. The generous funding for administration, in comparison with that for Local Further Education Councils, appears to indicate an emphasis on credit and occupationally oriented education and training rather than socio-cultural education.

Summary

The picture that emerges from this survey is a diversity of institutions offering a diversity of adult education programs. These offerings are most plentiful in the five or six larger urban centres, where there are a number of agencies such as universities, colleges, institutes of technology, vocational centres, and school-boards. Also, larger centres have numerous private and voluntary agencies, between whose jurisdictions and programs there is little interdependency and therefore a potential for overlapping. On the other hand, similar programs may attract different client groups to different institutions. There is machinery for liaison and co-operation at the local level, through local councils of further education, but it is not clear how well such councils co-operate.

The role of government departments that provide adult education programs appears to be relatively more significant in smaller centres and rural areas, whether the programs are offered directly or through agencies such as colleges, Alberta vocational centres, or community vocational centres. While some programming, such as that related to native people, maintains some co-ordination of departmental effort, the potential for overlapping appears in some types of programming offered by various departments. This is mitigated by informal and personal contacts between officials. The development of distance learning facilities, particularly through Athabasca University at the post-secondary level, helps to fill some of the gaps not filled by agencies that operate in fixed facilities. A number of other institutions are in the process of examining the possibilities of using more distance learning techniques.

The overall impression is not so much one of a system or network; the parts are not linked in such a way that changes of practice by one part affects the others to some degree. A clear change of policy by a government department such as Advanced Education and Manpower—for instance, in the funding of educational institutions— could affect the operations of the parent institutions, the universities or colleges that depend on such funding. But within the framework of existing policy, because most of the actual programming of these adult education units is funded by student fees, each has a high degree of independence, both from government and within their parent institutions.

Funding also governs the type and range of student these adult education units can and do serve. Insofar as the programming of these agencies is governed by the demands of the educational market-place, there will be needs they cannot meet and purposes they cannot pursue. And if other institutions, whether they be government agencies or not, are unavailable or unprepared to follow those purposes, there will be biases in the pattern of adult education one way or another. From this analysis, it appears that whatever limitations there are on the scope of institutional adult education, the services of some government departments appear to be designed to meet needs—generally of a social nature—of groups unable to benefit from the formal institutions. This question will be pursued further in the discussion on needs and resources in Chapter 7.

References

Alberta Culture. 1978. Cultural Development Division Booklet. Mimeographed. Edmonton: Department of Culture.

Alberta Social Services and Community Health. 1978. *Vocational Training for the Handicapped.* Edmonton: Department of Social Services and Community Health.

Boulet, G.C. 1977. Some Aspects and Origins of Educational Programs for Alberta Farmers and Their Families. Mimeographed. Edmonton: Alberta Agriculture.

———. 1977. Alberta Agriculture Extension Services. Mimeographed. Edmonton: Alberta Agriculture.

Commission on Educational Planning. 1972. *A Choice of Futures.* Edmonton: Queen's Printer.

Daniel, J.S. and Smith, W.A.S. 1979. "Opening Open Universities: the Canadian Experience." *Canadian Journal of Higher Education,* vol ix, no. 2.

Lifelong Education Task Force. 1971. Interim Proposals. Mimeographed. Edmonton: Commission on Educational Planning.

Manning, E.C. 1967. A White Paper on Human Resources Development. Edmonton: Queen's Printer.

6

Government and Government-Linked Structures in Quebec

For a picture of the structure of government and government-linked institutions in Quebec as it exists today, it is helpful to go back to the Parent Commission, whose report came out in a series of volumes between 1963 and 1966 (Royal Commission, 1963–66). This commission made a number of recommendations for the creation or reconstruction of various institutions, thus laying down a general pattern of development up to the present time. To understand the significance of those recommendations and their results, it is worth a brief look at the general situation that existed beforehand. From the green youth of western Canadian life, it seems almost incredible that the institutions that shaped educational policy and practice in Quebec up to the 1960s were basically those that had been established in the mid-nineteenth century. In 1841 a Superintendent of Public Instruction was appointed for Lower Canada, and this official remained as Minister of Education until the mid-twentieth century. In 1957 a Department of Public Instruction was set up, with control over the accounts of local school commissions, normal schools, and the certification of teachers, but the really effective machinery of educational policy-making emerged in 1859, in the form of a Council of Public Instruction, which had authority to direct the province's school systems. The strong religious characteristics of Quebec society were underlined in 1869 by the establishment of two separate committees, one Roman Catholic and the other Protestant. From then on the two systems worked more or less independently, and the two committees were virtually their own Ministries of Education. The council and the two committees were appointed under arrangements set out by the government, and the Roman Catholic and the Protestant elements were roughly representative of the population split in the province; for instance, in the first council in 1859 there were eleven Roman Catholics and four Protestants. From 1875 the Superintendent of Public Instruction, who came to have the rank of minister but without such a title or a seat in the Quebec Legislature, was ex-officio President of the Council of Public Instruction and the two committees, but he could vote only in the committee of the religious denomination to which he belonged.

From 1908, when the Council of Public Instruction last met, until the early 1960s, real authority lay with the Superintendent of Public Instruction and the two denominational, or confessional, committees. By 1961 a set of strongly entrenched institutions had existed for many decades: at the local level, strong, elected school commissions identified as Roman Catholic or Protestant (with the former dominant); two central committees controlling the funding and general policies of these commissions; and a Superintendent of Public Instruction. And though the Education Act of 1941 established a Department of Education and continued the existence of what was now called the Council of Education, the real authority continued with the superintendent and the two committees. The effect was that at all levels, from primary school to university, the Protestant, predominantly Anglophone, education system and the Roman Catholic, predominantly Francophone, system developed their own separate regimes of study, examinations, and advancement of students from primary to higher education.

The Education Act of 1941 provided that the governance of the systems by the two committees was subject to "orders and instructions" of the cabinet, but in fact the cabinet's role in respect of education was marginal. In 1960 the link with cabinet was through the Minister of

Youth, but this appears to have been a matter of form. Some tightening of the minister's jurisdiction was made in 1961, when he was given more authority over the finances of school commissions, including (in this case with the Minister of Municipal Affairs) their ability to borrow money.

There were a number of other ministries that had jurisdiction over aspects of education. The Minister of Youth governed the operations of "specialized schools," the institutes of technology, trade schools, and other occupationally oriented schools. The Ministry of Family and Social Welfare controlled the schooling of children placed in institutions for shelter and protection. The Minister of Labor was responsible for apprenticeship; the Minister of Agriculture was responsible for dairy and agricultural schools; and the Ministers of Game and Fisheries and Lands and Forests were responsible for the vocational training of fishermen, game wardens, and forest rangers.

The mainstream of education in Quebec was controlled not by government but by the leaders of the two main religious groups, the Roman Catholics vastly dominating. (Jews, a relatively small group, were included in the Protestant school jurisdiction, except that in Montreal in later years there was a Jewish Committee.) In other words, the social, economic, and ethnic divisions in Quebec were carried over into, and in turn supported by, the educational system (Royal Commission, 1963: chapter 1).

Against this background, the Parent Commission made some sweeping recommendations. In the light of its view that the aim of education was to prepare every citizen to earn his or her living through useful work and to fulfil his or her social responsibilities sensibly, it found that the existing private initiatives were not adequate or appropriate; this must be a responsibility of the state:"A master plan is needed, an orientation to serve a common good—a job which properly belongs to the political authorities"(Ibid., part 1:74).

The main recommendations of the Parent Commission that concern this study were: that a Ministry of Education be established by merging the Department of Education with the Ministry of Youth; that all teaching services then connected with other departments or ministries be placed under the jurisdiction of the Ministry of Education; and that a new Superior Council of Education take the place of the former Council, not with executive responsibilities but advisory ones. "Its very first function will be to assure a channel of communication between the general public and the government" (Ibid.: 107).

Advisory Councils—Quebec and Alberta

Before going into the details of the structure of the Ministry of Education, it is useful to compare briefly the role and structures of the one advisory Superior Council of Education in Quebec with the six Advisory Committees to the Minister of Advanced Education and Manpower in Alberta. The Quebec Council was set up by a separate act of the Legislature in 1964. It has a membership of twenty-four persons, of whom at least sixteen must be Roman Catholics, four Protestants and one from neither of these two faiths. The carry-over of the former religious perspectives in education is reflected in this membership, and in the retention of two confessional committees tied to the council. The Catholic Committee has an equal representation of church hierarchy, parents, and educators, and while the two latter types of representatives are appointed by the Lieutenant-Governor in Council, the church representatives are appointed by the Assembly of Catholic Bishops. All members of the Protestant Committee, representing churches, parents, and educators, are appointed by the Lieutenant-Governor in Council. These two committees can make regulations concerning religious and moral education, for which they must approve material and programs.

The duties and powers of the council are to advise the minister on regulations submitted to him and on other matters he refers to the council, and to prepare an annual report, which the minister must table in the Legislature. The council can initiate and sponsor research projects and solicit opinions and evidence, and can submit recommendations to government on any educational matters. It is served by a permanent staff of over thirty officials, including over ten professional workers, and by five commissions concerned with the various sectors of education, one being the Commission for Adult Education. Each of these is chaired by a member of the Superior Council, and has nine or ten members from various interest groups outside the council.

In the first Superior Council, two members appear to have brought an adult education perspective: Fernand Jolicoeur, Director of Education Services for the Confederation of National Trade Unions, and Jean-Marie Couet, Secretary of the Federation of Catholic Farmers, which was and is involved in rural adult education. This kind of representation appears to have continued through the life of the council. Among the opinions and recommendations submitted to the ministers over the years, a number have related to adult education, for example, concerning the training of adult educators, the roles of the school-boards and Multi-Média, and opportunities for less privileged groups.

In Alberta, as indicated in Chapter 5, the Minister's Advisory Committee on Further Education is one of six such committees, the others covering university affairs, college affairs, student affairs, the education of native peoples, and technical and vocational education. The members of all these committees are appointed by the minister, and the chairman of each is selected from among the members by the minister. Under the Department of Advanced Education Act of 1972, the minister is given the power to establish "such Boards, Committees or Councils as he considers necessary or desirable...." The duties and powers of the Alberta Advisory Committee on Further Education as originally set out were: to facilitate citizen, client, and professional participation in policy development; to ensure representation of special needs and interest; to give Advanced Education continuing access to knowledge and expertise in the province; and "to advise specifically on issues affecting planned adult educational experiences designed to be integrated on a recurring basis" (Alberta Advanced Education). To these ends the committee may recommend the initiation of studies or procedures. Originally, the membership was to consist of eight members appointed at large, and two members of Local Further Education Councils, two members of the Alberta Association for Continuing Education, one faculty member each from a university, a public or regional college, and a technical institute or vocational centre. Each of the six advisory committees is assigned an executive secretary from the staff of the Department of Advanced Education and Manpower.

Originally the Advisory Committee was intended explicitly to provide professional as well as citizen participation in policy-making, and the designated membership took account of this intention. Over the intervening years the minister, within his powers and without consultation with the institutions concerned, has changed the purposes and terms of reference of the committee to refer only to the facilitation of citizen participation, and has changed its composition to omit the provision for representation from any specific associations or groups. The associations and institutions themselves—certainly the Alberta Association for Continuing Education—did not, in early 1979, appear to have been apprised of this change in philosophy regarding the purpose and functioning of these public advisory committees.

In terms of status, role, and functioning, there are important differences between the Superior Council in Quebec and the Advisory Committees in Alberta. First, the Quebec Council is established under its own act, and the conditions of its existence, composition, and role, and any changes in these, therefore require the agreement of the Legislature. It also reports to the Legislature insofar as its annual report must be tabled by the minister, and is therefore open for debate. In Alberta the Advisory Committees' composition, role and resources are determined, and can be altered, at the discretion of the minister. A number of such changes have, in fact, been made unilaterally by the minister. The committee reports only to the minister as an internal departmental matter. Moreover, while the Quebec Superior Council has, by statute, a duty to engage in studies and make recommendations with the help of a full-time professional staff, the Alberta committee may only recommend the initiation of studies, and has no staff. Significantly, in Alberta the committee's representations, recommendations, and opinions (when it has time to muster them) go no further than the minister, and Legislature is not informed. One of the advantages of a parliamentary democracy is claimed to be the potential watch-dog role of the Legislature in respect of the activities of the Executive; this role is fulfilled in Quebec but not in Alberta in this regard. However, in the Alberta Legislature, referred to in Chapter 4, historically—and certainly currently—the Executive is neither obliged nor inclined to pay much attention to the opinions of either a miniscule opposition or a more than somewhat docile following of back-benchers; even if the formal legal status and role of the Alberta committees were put on a par with the Quebec Superior Council, it would have little real significance. Here the differences in the two provinces are not in details of legality and administration, but in broad patterns of political philosophy and reality.

Quebec Ministry of Education

As part of the general design of the Parent Commission, three working committees were set up to study different aspects of the broad picture: adult education, leisure, and physical education and sports. They were established by the Ministry of Youth, which already supported education populaire and leisure services. The Adult Education Committee was chaired by Claude Ryan, who has more recently become leader of the Liberal party. The Ryan Committee found that there was already a great deal of adult education in the province. Various government departments were actively training in agriculture, the professions, co-operatives, French and English language, sol-fa, leisure activities, and fine art; many private organizations were in the business; and six universities were offering a B.A. for adults through a mixture of evening, day, and summer courses, and by correspondence. The committee stated that there was a problem of persuading professors—except at Sir George Williams University in Montreal— to teach evening courses for adults. The committee suggested that a plan was required to co-ordinate the work of the many agencies in the field, first within each category of government, private, and formal education agencies, and then between those categories. It called on government to compile an inventory of the programs being offered, to study the publicity being used in order to prevent false advertising, and to standardize terminology, such as the word "certificate" (Comité d'Etude, 1963:24). The committee also found that despite this wide variety of agencies already in the field, there was a serious problem of social participation and a lack of training for leadership in organizations and community associations, through which people developed and grew in terms of both career and leisure (Ibid.: 13). It went on to stress this need for *éducation communautaire des adultes,* and suggested that while the responsibility for adult education directed at individual learning and fulfilment should lie with a Ministry of Education, community-oriented adult education should come under some other ministry or an agency such as the Economic Development Council; in other words, there should be co-ordination between planners in education and in the realm of economic development.

The Parent Commission endorsed the principal recommendations of the Ryan Committee, except for the division of individual-oriented and community-oriented adult education between the Ministry of Education and others. It appears to have made a distinction between the teaching of adults (*enseignement aux adultes*) and continuing education (éducation permanente). In its main recommendation relating the the establishment of a Ministry of Education, it suggests that the services of the ministry be grouped in three divisions, each with a director-general: Divisions of Instruction, Administration, and Planning. The Division of Instruction would include services related to the teaching of adults and inspections and examinations, while the Division of Administration would include a Service of Teaching Institutions for Adults. The French text of the report is more precise than the English in making this distinction, which is a feature of the Quebec situation. The English version refers in general terms to adult education and to the Adult Education Service within the Division of Administration, while the French text makes it clear that the latter is a service responsible not for the teaching process but for administering the teaching institutions for adults (Commission Royale, 1963: Tome I, 98 and 103-4).

In discussing the wider concept of continuing education or éducation permanente the report distinguishes in the following manner: adult education signifies a specific response to the particular needs and tastes of adults, through certain courses and similar experiences; continuing education, on the other hand, is a general educational service that not only makes such specific responses, but encourages people and opens up in them a concern for, and habit of, study during adulthood. Continuing education is a framework, a way of looking at the process of learning as a lifelong one, and it seeks to create the conditions to make that possible (Ibid., 1964: vol. II, 327). The government and some of the institutions, particularly the universities, are still trying to cope with this distinction, which has both supporters and detractors among adult educationists in the province. There has been, and still is, continuing debate about its actual implications in organizational and educational terms.

The Parent Report went on to recommend the establishment of a continuing education service (*Service de l'Education Permanente*) in the Ministry of Education with the following responsibilities: to formulate study programs; to offer guidance to agencies in areas where the service itself did not operate (which seems to indicate that the commission saw this government department as a providing agency, among others); to arrange courses for adults throughout the province by correspondence, radio and television in collaboration with formal education institutions; and to help organizations concerned with educational, cultural, and leisure activities (Ibid., 1964: vol. II, 334–45). It recommended that the responsibility for continung education at the various levels—elementary and secondary, pre-university and vocational, and university—be the responsibility of school-boards, colleges, and universities respectively. Finally, it recommended that the Ministry of Education, with the universities, undertake the inventory recommended by the Ryan Committee and that it should undertake the necessary research for improving adult teaching methods, organize training courses for adult teachers, and help and co-ordinate private initiatives in the field.

The recommendation regarding the inventory of adult education agencies will be discussed in Chapter 11. Here we will follow through from the commission's recommendations regarding the structure of the ministry. First, under the minister are two Ministers of State, one for Post-Secondary Education—which shows a regard for the particular importance of this level of Education—and the other for the High Commission on Youth, Leisure, and Sport. This latter position is a carry-over, in reverse, from the pre-1964 situation; in other words, while education had previously come formally under the Minister of Youth, now the responsibility for youth and leisure activities lies with the Ministry of Education. The objectives of the High Commission are: to formulate global policy for government intervention in the field of leisure; to contribute to the improvement of the quality of life of citizens by the promotion of outdoor and socio-cultural activities; to assist the personal and social growth of individuals through leisure education; and to assure accessibility to leisure activities for all Quebecois. Under an assistant director-general, the High Commission has three services: sports, regional and outdoor development, and socio-cultural activities (Ministère de l'Education, 1978:23). It has three regional offices, at Montreal, Rimouski, and Trois-Rivières. Its program for the development of socio-cultural activities provides for assistance to municipalities to employ social animators and to establish sociocultural centres; it works with local organizations in the development of art, literature, and science; it sponsors travel programs for adults to enable them to discover their main cities; it helps in the organization of festivals and popular fêtes; and it consults generally with public and private organizations on the development of socio-cultural activities in the province.

One interesting feature of the ministry is that though the Parent Commission made no such recommendation, the ministry includes, under two associate deputy ministers, Services of Catholic Instruction and of Protestant Instruction, thus again emphasizing the religious perspectives of education in the province.

At the next level downward in the bureaucracy, there are three assistant deputy ministers, one for planning, one for elementary and secondary education, and the third for post-secondary education. And under the latter are three directorates-general: higher education, college education, and adult education. When the ministry came into being with these directorates-general in 1964, the third was in fact, called the Directorate-General of Continuing Education and not Adult Education, according to the distinctions discussed above. The change in name was made in 1972, and reasons for doing so are interesting. In the intervening eight years there was a feeling that the concept of continuing education (éducation permanente), while expressing a worthy philosophy, was diverting energy from the practical business of meeting the specific needs of adults. There was some resentment about the influence of the French adult educationist Bertrand Schwartz on the Parent Commisson, Schwartz being one of the chief proponents of the concept of éducation permanente. Many leading adult educationists in Quebec had trained in, and they tended to adhere to, the more pragmatic tradition of Canadian and American adult education. In 1972 the Liberal Party Congress of Quebec passed a resolution that in the light of the general weakness of the Directorate-General of Continuing Education, which "spends 80% of its time defending its existence," and in the light of a "a complete lack of planning and inter-intra-ministerial co-ordination," a strong Directorate of *Adult* Education be formed to look after the totality of adult education in the province. (Parti Libéral, 1973). The responsibility for éducation permanente was to lie henceforth with the ministry as a whole and all its institutions.

Today the Directorate-General of Adult Education takes responsibility for assuring "to all Quebec adults learning opportunities allowing them to achieve their full potential economically, socially, and culturally, and to share actively in the planning and the development of Quebec society" (Ministère de l'Education, 1978:69). Toward the achievement of that long-term end, it has the following sub-objectives: to offer a range of activities and projects for economic, social, and cultural development according to the needs of individuals and of the collectivity;* to provide educational services which are accessible to the whole adult population of a given milieu or region; to meet with adults from under-privileged groups and to provide them with the means of meeting their needs for education at the social, cultural, and economic levels; to promote, encourage, support, and co-ordinate any educational project responding to the needs of adults and meeting the objective of collective development and advancement; to provide a methodology of learning appropriate to adults, applied in various teaching techniques; to help teaching personnel in the decentralized regions to increase their competence and develop a real "adult pedagogy"; to provide technical and financial assistance to certain organizations that share a responsibility for adult education; to assure the co-ordination of training centres administered by decentralized authorities and by non-government organizations interested in adult education; to engage in and promote research for resolving various problems in adult education; and to bring about a strategy for responding to problems in relation to orientation, information, and encouragement that occur in adult education and training.

---

* In Quebec there appears a tendency recently to prefer the terms "collectivity" and "collectivities" rather than "community," which is said to have an anglophone and somewhat fuzzy connotation.

So, within the Ministry of Education there are two main units more or less responsible for adult education. The Direction Générale d'Education des Adultes (D.G.E.A.) has the responsibilities set out above, and a High Commission for Youth, Leisure, and Sport, has also been described briefly. The universities under the Direction Générale d'Education Supérieure (D.G.E.S.) have, like the universities in Alberta, responsibility for their own adult education policies and practices. The colleges or CEGEPs are more closely tied into the formal network of pre-university education than in Alberta, and their adult education programs are more closely planned and supervised by the government. One of the main reasons for their establishment, besides meeting community education needs and training people directly for certain occupations, was to provide a transitional phase between school and university. They are more integral to the formal education process than is the case with the colleges in Alberta. Some of the latter offer university transfer courses in addition to community-oriented continuing education and some occupational training, but they do not link with the formal pre-university system of Alberta in the ways that the CEGEPs do in Quebec. In one sense the latter are more comparable with the Alberta vocational centres, which offer high school courses to adults and in that respect are supervised by the Alberta Department of Education.

Figure 6 shows the principal administrative units within the Ministry of Education that have some connection with adult education, directly or indirectly. It shows how, under the Assistant Deputy Minister for Post-Secondary Education, the direct responsibility for work in adult education is focused on the D.G.E.A., apart from the High Commission for Youth, Leisure, and Sport. The D.G.E.A. is responsible for the school-boards and the CEGEPs only insofar as they offer programs for adults, whether these programs are related to general education or high school upgrading, vocational training, or popular adult education. In other words, the D.G.E.A. has the same jurisdiction that in Alberta is spread over a number of administrative units of the Department of Advanced Education and Manpower and the Department of Education. Moreover, Figure 6 shows that the government, through the D.G.E.A., has direct contact with and involvement in the adult education activities of a wide range of other organ-

Figure 6

Interlinking Government Structures: Quebec

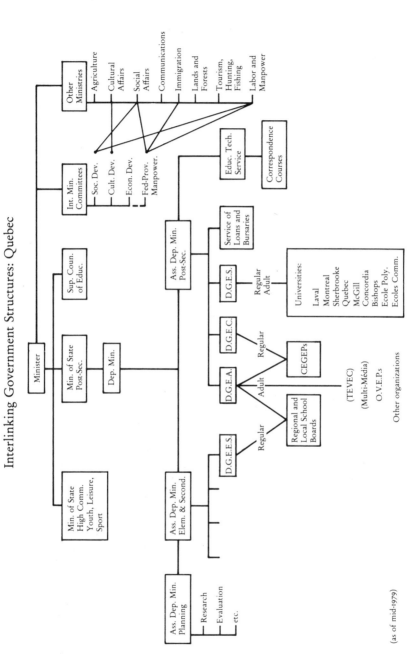

(as of mid-1979)

izations and institutions. Most of these are referred to as Organismes Volontaires d'Education Populaire (O.V.E.P.s), which include such organizations as trade unions, the Association of Women's Education and Social Action, and the Co-operative Association of Family Economy. They are mainly province-wide bodies with education and social action roles. This service works mainly through the central offices of such organizations, which compile global programs for their participating branches for submission to the government on an annual basis. "Other organizations" listed in the diagram, with which the D.G.E.A. deals directly, are institutions such as the prisons, armed forces, Canadian National Railways, and Chambers of Commerce. Figure 6 also shows a direct connection between D.G.E.A. and two other enterprises—TEVEC and Multi-Média. These are placed in brackets in the diagram because in effect they no longer exist. TEVEC was an experimental project in the use of television as a strategy and means of mass education; it offered courses in French and arithmetic, and was conducted between 1967 and 1969 in the Saguenay-Lac St. Jean region. Following this experiment in 1972 the ministry established a wider-based program, still of an experimental nature intended particularly to help disadvantaged groups (les défavorisés) under the name of Multi-Média. It involved the use of media and the participation of students in a self-learning process. As indicated in Chapter 4, there was some criticism of this program, particularly from persons and groups who saw a need for strategies and programs that have a social purpose. The mode and learning outcomes of Multi-Média were individualistic. Moreover, so the criticism went, the Multi-Média program, involving as it did self-learning, was not appropriate for those who were virtually illiterate and needed help the most; it simply helped people who were already capable of using the conventional tools of education and personal development. Whether as a result of such criticism or not, the P.Q. government terminated Multi-Média in 1978, and inaugurated in its place a new program of citizen education. The purpose of the new program was to address problems that arise in the relationship with environment, enabling the students to participate in making decisions that affect themselves, and helping them to face and be responsible for their future as seen in social terms (D.G.E.A., 1978:6).

As part of this thrust, a service called Services Educatifs d'Aide

Personelle et d'Animation Communautaire (S.E.A.P.A.C.) was set up for adult education aimed at both personal and collective, or social, development. It operates through regional school-boards, as distinct from the O.V.E.P.s, which are operated directly by the D.G.E.A.

Figure 7 shows the internal structure of the D.G.E.A. First, there is a divison between the responsibility for education related to work and for education related to citizenship. Within the former field, the responsibility is divided between full-time general or academic education for upgrading, pre-employment training, professional education, training-on-the-job or at the work-place, and counselling. Within the

Figure 7

Two Main Program Areas of the D.G.E.A. (Quebec)

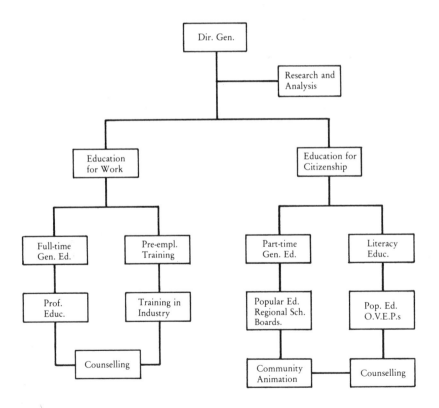

latter field the responsibility is divided between part-time general or academic education, literacy education, popular adult education through school-boards (S.E.A.P.A.C.), popular adult education through voluntary organizations (O.V.E.P.), community animation and the support of community development, and counselling. The broad term of socio-cultural education is given to all adult education other than academic upgrading and vocational and professional education.

Outside the D.G.E.A., but linked to the Assistant Deputy Minister for Post-Secondary Education, is a unit responsible for different types of educational technology such as correspondence education and other learning techniques. The French terminology, which refers to processes of teaching, can be translated into educational technology. Between 1976 and 1978 this service dealt with about 25,000 students by correspondence and produced twelve new correspondence courses besides films, audiotapes, and videotapes. Under this office comes the service for correspondence courses, which is based in Montreal. Correspondence courses are for adults unable to take advantage of the facilities of CEGEPs or school-boards, and the courses provide either a college credit or a certificate of studies in general education or vocational training. In the year 1977–78, ninety-five courses were offered. The service for educational technology in 1978–79, included the diversification of the production of teaching materials, updating correspondence courses, and working with libraries and other learning resource centres to stimulate the use of written and audio-visual learning materials (Ministère de l'Education, 1979).

Figure 6 also shows the position of the Assistant Deputy Minister for Planning, alongside the other two Assistant Deputy Ministers for Elementary and Secondary Education and Post-Secondary Education. This planning division is responsible for research, evaluation, and information over the whole jurisdiction of the Ministry of Education.

Whereas in Alberta the internal structure of the Department of Advanced Education and Manpower is oriented, to a significant degree, to the various types of institutions, making these institutions the focus of planning, administration, and financing, and leaving them the responsibility to respond to adult education needs according to their own resources and priorities, in Quebec the internal structure of the D.G.E.A. is oriented more to types of educational service, and to the responsibility of government in respect of these services. The direct influence of government can be brought to bear through the connections between the D.G.E.A. and the O.V.E.P.s, and further influence can be exercised through the system of financing for some of the programs of the regional school-boards. For instance, those services offered as éducation populaire by school-boards, which are seen to have social importance by the government, are partially funded by government, thus making them much cheaper than the other self-financing courses. In addition, a regional school-board's adult education service can obtain special funding, for example, through S.E.A.P.A.C., for particular socially significant programs such as in the operation and management of co-operatives and credit unions. The Ministry of Education has a network of eleven regional offices, but the main role of these offices is principally in elementary and secondary education. Their role in adult education is focused on vocational and professional training, both in the education institutions and in industry.

Other Ministries

Just as in the case of Alberta, a number of government ministries other than the Ministry of Education are engaged in some form of adult education in Quebec, and are listed in Figure 6.

In mid-1979, a study tracing the responsibilities of and linkages between various ministries revealed a complex maze of jurisdictions. Relating to the subject of professional adult education alone, the Superior Council of Education referred to "the administrative jungle of the program of professional training for adults" (Conseil Supérieur de l'Education, 1978). For the field as a whole, the complexity is extended and deepened, and is described by Lassonde in 1978 (writing as an official within the ministry), who provides part of an examination of post-secondary education in Quebec with the view to redefining the policy of the Ministry of Education. In other words, the ministry is aware of the complexity of the system that confronts prospective learners (and researchers) and is continuously re-examining its policies and practices.

This expenditure of energy in discussion, self-examination, and redefinition of roles appears to be a feature of Quebec political life in the late 1970s. The concern is not restricted to the ministries themselves; at the Annual Congress of the Parti Québécois in June 1979, a resolution was passed that a global policy be adopted to meet the learning needs of adults in the province, including more flexible admission procedures, the recognition of experience other than formal education for accreditation purposes, and paid educational leave. Behind this statement there appears to lie a deeper and more significant political concern that adult education should have as its primary ideal not so much an economic, manpower-development bias, as a cultural one. At the ministerial level in the P.Q. government, there are some interesting tensions between proponents of these biases. The stress put on the central place of culture and cultural activity in education in the Ministry of Cultural Affairs' 1978 White Paper may signify a bid by that minister to stake a claim against the monopoly, or dominance, of the Minister of Education in policy-making in this field. But according to some of the persons interviewed in the course of this study, such a contention appears to be subordinated to another, broader one: a joint concern on the parts of the Ministers of Education and Cultural Affairs to exert the dominance of their influence in adult education over that of the Ministers of Labor and, to a lesser extent, Social Affairs. A cultural emphasis against a utilitarian one is the basis of the conflict.

Ministry of Labor and Manpower

The ministry closest to the Ministry of Education in adult education matters is that of Labor and Manpower. We have seen that the main division of functions of the Directorate-General of Adult Education is between technical and professional education on the one hand, and citizen education on the other, and it is in respect of the first of these that the two ministries are closely linked. First, there is a federal provincial committee whose membership includes the federal Minister of Labor and Immigration and the Quebec Ministers of Labor and Manpower, Education, Immigration, Social Affairs, and Intergovernmental Affairs; the chairmanship of this committee alternates between the federal and the provincial Ministers of Labor. Under this ministerial committee there is a federal-provincial team of officials whose role is to monitor and administer the agreed policy on technical and professional training in institutions and in industry. Within the Quebec Ministry of Labor and Manpower the Director-General of Manpower has a Service of Technical Training, whose direct responsibility is the ongoing co-ordination of the work of this ministry with the federal government and with the Ministry of Education. There appears to be some fuzziness of responsibilities between the Ministries of Labor and of Education. The actual negotiation with the federal government on manpower training course requirements is done by the D.G.E.A. of the Ministry of Education, with the Ministry of Labor acting as a liaison, in regard to such matters as needs assessment and evaluation. In the matter of needs assessment, there is a feeling in the Ministry of Education that the Ministry of Labor's approach is too *ad hoc* and present-oriented, whereas what is needed is a longer-term view, taking into account the developing picture in the province. So in 1979, discussions and negotiations took place between the two ministers with a view to clarifying areas of responsibility and roles at both the provincial and regional levels.

There are eleven administrative regions, and the field staff of each in the two ministries are expected to work together to carry out the joint policy. Regional Commissions of Professional Training in both ministries, representing various trades and enterprises, are responsible for co-ordinating training in institutions. These commissions adhere to the Ministry of Labor. The general rule is that apart from training in industry itself, the actual instruction, whether full-time or part-time, is given through educational institutions such as the colleges and polyvalent high schools (Ministère du Travail et de la Main-d'Oeuvre, 1977–78).

One interesting feature of the situation is that in the reports of the Quebec Ministry of Education there is little reference to these mechanisms for liaison and shared responsibility with the Ministry of Labor and Manpower. In the general presentation of the Directorate-General of Adult Education in 1978 there is a full description of the services of the Directorate-General in technical and vocational training, with no inkling that they are linked with or affected by the role and functions of the Ministry of Labor and Manpower. There is a short footnote connecting them to the Canada manpower training programs (D.G.E.A., 1978:14). The impression given by the document is one of autonomous responsibility on the part of the Ministry of Education. The description and explanation of the interdepartmental linkages and shared responsibilities are contained in the annual report of the Ministry of Labor and Manpower (1977–78), which leaves a clear impression that this ministry has the primary responsibility and leadership in this field. In these circumstances, one can conjecture about the degree of collaboration that actually exists between the staffs of the two ministries at all levels, and about the need for the discussion and negotiations referred to above. In Alberta the union of the two aspects of adult education under one ministry appears to be a recognition of the existence of dissonances between approaches in the two different ministries.

Another unit of the Ministry of Labor and Manpower, called the Service of Local Initiatives, has a responsibility to ensure that all federal government make-work projects do not conflict with the priorities and policies of the Quebec government. Federal programs such as Canada Works (formerly Local Initiatives Program), Jeunesse Canada au Travail, and New Horizons, a program for senior citizens, come under the eye of this service, which is governed by an interdepartmental committee representing all Quebec ministries.

A third unit of this ministry, the Directorate-General of Safety, offers courses and conferences for employers and workers on safety matters in the same way as the Research and Education Branch of the Department of Labor in Alberta.

Some significant contrasts between Quebec and Alberta are revealed in this short account. Whereas in Alberta the whole of the manpower training function has passed directly to the Department of Advanced Education and Manpower, in Quebec it remains separate from education, in the Ministry of Labor and Manpower, with liaison and co-operation through interdepartmental committees. According to the Superior Council of Education in Quebec, this liaison is not satisfactory. The Alberta system appears to suit the administrative need better. At the level of philosophy, however, in Alberta the joint responsibilities of education and manpower training within the Department of Advanced Education and Manpower appears to indicate a strong identification of education at the post-secondary and adult level with the economic aspect of development. The danger of such an identification is expressed by the Quebec Superior Council of Education. The resulting education is subject to "the exigencies of the labor market and is not in the interests of the total development of the person. It puts candidates for Canada manpower training in a category apart, and subverts the objectives of adult education and, in the long run, of lifelong learning" (Conseil Supérieur de l'Education, 1978:11–12). This appears to be the situation in Quebec, but whereas in that province the issue is being debated in the light of broader purposes and with a view to change, in Alberta such questioning is not evident. In Quebec manpower training is seen in a wider context of the needs of all sectors of the society as represented by other ministries of the government. In both provinces there seems to be a consistency between the characteristics of the dominant social philosophy, as discussed in Chapter 4, and this relationship between manpower development and other aspects of life. In Alberta the emphasis is on economic, material advancement, and so education at the post-secondary and adult level is closely identified with manpower development, and vice versa. This is the clear message given by a senior Alberta government official to a conference of adult educationists in the province in 1976 (Mansfield, 1977). In Quebec the emphasis is on the consonance of economic and social development with cultural development, all of which are focused on a common end of national identity and sovereignty. This is reinforced by the role of the Service of Local Initiatives, which closely monitors, from Quebec's point of view, the federal local initiatives programs. This is an example of Quebec's strong concern or suspicion that federal initiatives might divert this focus.

The other Quebec ministry with an educational function, like that of Labor and Manpower, tied to federal government functions and funding, is the Ministry of Immigration. The province's interest in the integration of immigrants into its life and culture is another reflection of its concern with identity in a way not felt in Alberta. The ministry has a Directorate-General of Adaptation, in which there is a Division of Adult Education. The main need centres around Montreal, and to some extent Quebec City, where most immigrants are settled, and where Centres d'Orientation et de Formation des

Immigrants (C.O.F.I.) have been established. These are wholly funded by Federal Manpower and Immigration. The C.O.F.I.s are involved mainly in teaching French and English as second languages. They are not the only centres for such instruction, some being provided as well by regional school-boards and the Y.M.C.A. (Ministère de l'Immigration, 1973-74).

The Ministry of Tourism, Hunting, and Fisheries has direct links with the Ministry of Education in that it is responsible for training personnel for the hotel, restaurant, and tourist industry. An important part of this responsibility is fulfilled through courses conducted in institutions coming under the Ministry of Education—courses that come under the rubric of éducation permanente. These courses are designed to retrain persons from other occupations for work in hotels and restaurants. Some are held in places other than the main urban centres (*cours itinérants*), and others are offered in collaboration with the Catholic School Board of Montreal. The central training location for this field is the Institute of Tourism and Hotel Management in Montreal, where initial and in-service training are offered, part-time and full-time.

The other principal education activity of this ministry is instruction on hunting and proper handling of firearms. Ten instructors, in nine administrative regions (two of the instructors are in Montreal), offer such training to specific groups and to the public at large, and presentations are made at conferences and public events (Ministère du Tourisme, de la Chasse et de la Pêche, 1973-74). This type of training is paralleled in Alberta by courses of the same kind offered by the Department of Public Lands and Wildlife.

There are three other ministries involved in education and training directed at some particular role or activity. They are the Ministries of Agriculture, Lands, and Forests, and Municipal Affairs, and with regard to agricultural training, there is a joint committee of the Ministry of Education and the Ministry of Agriculture, which meets four times a year and appears to work well. The Ministry of Agriculture has an Assistant Deputy Minister of Research, Instruction, and Administration, with a Directorate-General of Research and Instruction. These government offices are served by the Council for Research and Agricultural Services of Quebec, which have a co-ordinating role in this field. The main government sources of adult training are two Institutes of Agricultural Technology, at La Pocatière and Ste-Hyacinthe, which, in addition to full-time professional courses, offer a range of part-time programs for producing farmers – typically, courses of thirty hours' duration on various aspects of agriculture. The legal responsibility for the operation of these institutes lies with the Ministry of Education. There are also shorter courses for upgrading people's knowledge and skills in such subjects as dairying, horticulture, and agricultural mechanics, and correspondence courses are offered in subjects such as business organization.

As a general service to the public, staff from these institutes work with agricultural societies and with the media in popular education. There is also collaboration between government staff and the universities, particularly Macdonald College at McGill University, and the Faculty of Agricultural and Food Sciences at Laval University (Ministère de l'Agriculture, 1974–75).

The Ministry of Lands and Forests performs an educational role in various ways. Under its reforestation program it runs short courses for nurserymen from a number of its forestry stations, and courses for forest workers at some of the CEGEPs. For the general public it runs a popular education program, similar to those in Alberta, through four interpretation centres, where visitors to parks are provided with presentations and written and visual materials that interpret the natural characteristics of the respective areas. Finally, the ministry provides some funding for education programs offered by non-government organizations such as the Quebec Forestry Association (Ministère de la Terre et des Forêts, 1976).

The educational role of the Ministry of Municipal Affairs is a narrow one, and relates to the problem of fire control and prevention. Besides offering on-going training for people working in that field, it engages in public education on the subject, through printed materials distributed to households and through short public T.V. presentations (Ministère des Affaires Municipales, 1975–76).

There are three ministries besides the Ministry of Education, that play major roles in adult education for the general public in the province, through structured programs of counselling and formal instruction, through non-formal programs or learning experiences offered outside formal education institutions and not for any formal qualifications, and/or through informal education or the creation of opportunities for learning as a part of the flow of life. In general, the last of these three categories of adult education is outside the scope of this study, because it is so ill-defined and includes a multitude of groups and associations of people that are difficult to identify. In view of the strong and deliberate effort of the Quebec government in creating a whole cultural milieu, however, and in view of the visibility of this effort, we must and can take some notice of it. It can be contrasted with the less forceful or less pervasive efforts of the Alberta government in cultural matters directly and in public education and enlightenment through the media indirectly. The difference in scale between such efforts in the two provinces constitutes one important point of contrast. The three ministries in question in Quebec are Social Affairs, Cultural Affairs, and Communications.

The Ministry of Social Affairs in Quebec is the nearest equivalent to the Department of Social Services and Community Health in Alberta, and there are some similarities between them insofar as adult education is concerned. For instance, in Quebec, as in Alberta, there are local health units (seventy-five in all), which, being concerned with prevention more than treatment, are active in promoting good nutrition, maternity practices, school health, and so on through individual and group instruction. They are, as in Alberta, supported by government funding and consulting services. The services of the ministry itself are provided through four other types of institutions: hospitals, reception centres, social service centres, and local community service centres—all established by provincial law and financed entirely by the government. Both the social service centres and the local community service centres, as their names imply, are involved in social education. The former are oriented to providing individual, private consultation in psycho-social matters, much along the lines of private clinics. (In Alberta the cost of similar services, when provided by consulting psychiatrists, is covered by the provincial Health Care Insurance Plan, but the costs of services provided by consulting private psychologists and social workers is not so covered; a portion of a licensed psychologist's fee may be met by the privately run Alberta Blue Cross Plan.)

The local community service centres (C.L.S.C.) are of particular interest in a study of this nature. A C.L.S.C. is a public establishment providing a range of preventive health and social services and community action, with a holistic and multi-disciplinary approach, for the purposes of improving health and social conditions for individuals and for the collectivity, helping people to take an active part in solving their problems, and in improving their whole milieu from the perspective of community development (Fédération des C.L.S.C., 1976). The accent is on public and group work rather than private and specialized consulting as in the social service centres. Each is run by an administrative council of thirteen persons, five of whom are elected by the client population, subject to guide-lines laid down by the government. Each centre brings together a team of professional workers in the fields of health, social work, and community animation. The latter, in particular, work with local groups who want to have more control over their community life by being able to identify their problems and find solutions to them. (Ministère des Affaires Sociales, 1976–76). The establishment of the C.L.S.C.s has met with some opposition, particularly in larger centres where similar services were already being provided outside the government fold. People's clinics in Montreal, for instance, were working in poor areas and were oriented to the problems of their clients. Professional groups saw these centres as endangering their work. In other words, there has been a tendency toward duplication of services, which has caused some tension. Moreover, the amount of local involvement through the administrative councils has not been as extensive as was hoped (Development Associates, 1975).

In other words, the social service centres and the C.L.S.C.s are examples of the sort of multi-service community centre that has been discussed for many years, but has been tried in relatively few places. The Worth Commission in Alberta flirted with the idea of centres combining social, recreation, and educational (including counselling) services, but nothing along the lines of the Quebec centres has been developed in Alberta. The only agency with any similarity in Alberta has been an experiment in Edmonton called West Ten, which was another manifestation of that burst of progressive activity that happened in the last years of the Socred government. West Ten was initiated by the Edmonton city government as a multi-service community agency comprising ten community leagues on the west side of the city. The emphasis was to be not merely on co-ordination of the delivery of such services by professionals, but community input and a community development approach to local problems. The funding came under the province's Preventive Social Service arrangements, 80 percent from the provincial government and 20 percent from the municipality. The agency appears to have had little community commitment and little support from the city's public school-board, and the perception of the staff of the centre was that the concept did not fit the new image and approach of the more systems- and technocracy-oriented Progressive Conservative government. To the new government, West Ten was, in fact, an administrative anomaly. In any event, in the last few years the organization's funding has been progressively cut, leaving it relatively ineffective. This contrasts with progressively increased funding for C.L.S.C.s in Quebec, to the stage where some receive up to one million dollars per annum.

The educational role of the next two Quebec ministries is more general and pervasive, extending beyond institution-based activities. The Ministry of Cultural Affairs has three principal avenues along which it moves: the sponsorship and publication of books and other print materials, and support for the plastic and the interpretive arts. In these functions it parallels the Department of Culture in Alberta, and while a strong note in the Alberta program is culture diversity, in Quebec it is cultural homogeneity.

With regard to books and other printed materials, the ministry supports three kinds of endeavor: direct support for the creation and diffusion of Quebec literature through help to writers and support for publications and publishers; development of the provincial public library network; and development of the National Library of Quebec as a centre for the preservation of, and accessibility to, Quebec cultural heritage, using various media of popularization such as cultural exhibitions, concerts, art exhibitions, theatre, and cinema. With regard to the plastic arts, the ministry's objectives are the conservation, diffusion, and creation of such arts. It pursues those objectives by helping artists and craftsmen financially, operating two state art galleries and providing financial support for private galleries and art associations; and, through the Director of Educational Services and his staff, organizing conferences, exhibitions, and public encounters with artists, and making audio-visual materials for use by educational institutions.

With regard to the interpretive arts, the ministry gives support in three ways: by training artists in seven music conservatories, two theatre schools, and a number of dance schools; by providing artists with bursaries for initial and subsequent training; and by giving financial and consultative help in festivals and productions and direct financial help to the music industry (Ministère des Affaires Culturelles, 1976-77).

Finally, a brief description of the role of the Ministry of Communications in Quebec as compared to the educational media network in Alberta is useful. The Quebec ministry has a much more comprehensive role. The ministry's responsibility is to formulate and administer a provincial policy for communications – by wire, cable, and radio waves and by electric, electronic, magnetic, electro-magnetic, or optical means. Its purposes are: "to place communication techniques at the disposal of human communications, and to provide the people of Quebec with means for free expression of their identity" (Bureau de la Statistique, 1975-76). Under its jurisdiction are the government's activities in regard to telephones, telecommunications, the government printer, government public relations, and cinema. Realizing the importance of the latter as a mode of social communication and influence, the ministry has a Directorate-General of Cinema responsible for creating an industrial, commerical, and artistic infrastructure on which a Quebec cinema industry may be built.

Part of the ministry's public information function is carried out through the publication of *Guide for Citizens*, a three-hundred page booklet giving comprehensive information on such matters as social affairs, education, labor, housing, justice, the environment, and leisure. There is also a system of information delivery from regional telephone centres of information, to which access is free at any time.

It is in the use of and access to means of television communication that interesting developments have taken place in Quebec (Willet, 1975). There has been experimentation with satellite communications in transmitting health information between Quebec and France, and in creating links between Inuit villages in the North and the centres of population in the South. More will be said about this in Chapter 7. The Office of Radio-Telediffusion of Quebec (O.R.T.Q.) is licensed by the Canadian Radio and Television Commission to transmit educational T.V., and according to Willet, education broadcasting forms the central core of the O.R.T.Q.

Here again is a source of friction between the Quebec and federal governments, in that federal control of communications is seen by the former to be a derogation from its own rightful powers. An important instrument of the O.R.T.Q. is Radio-Quebec, which transmits from two stations, in Montreal and Quebec City, and has an extensive distribution system of tele-cassettes. Radio-Quebec plans to extend its transmissions to eleven new zones. In televison transmission facilities, Radio-Quebec has an advantage over Alberta, where one of the disadvantages suffered by ACCESS is its need to rely on other T.V. transmission services, both broadcast and cable. Both Radio-Quebec and ACCESS (through its radio service, C.K.U.A.) share the problem of distinguishing between strictly educational programming, for which they are licensed by the C.R.T.C., and enrichment programming which brings them into competition with the CBC and commercial stations.

The Radio-Quebec service is complemented by local television and radio co-operatives, exemplified by a local station, C.F.V.O., in the Ottawa region of the province. C.F.V.O. was licensed to broadcast in 1973, and has inspired a number of such local co-operatives in television, radio, and printed communication. Beside this activity in broadcasting, there is a wide network of local community cable operations, most of them in rural centres in small towns of the province. Willet reports thirty-eight community T.V. groups, twenty-two radio groups, and thirteen community print media groups.

These local groups are funded to a large extent by the government (some by the federal government), but they also receive funding from industry; local, regional, and provincial organizations such as the trade unions; and individual supporters. A Development Council for Community Media, a non-profit organization, co-ordinates groups and their projects.

One community cable group at Drummondville serves as an illustration of some of the features of these groups in the province. The Drummondville service (C.D.T.V.) was set up in 1972 by a group of citizens, helped by students in a Youth Perspective Project at the University of Quebec, and by the National Society of Quebecers, to take advantage of the community channel made available by Drummondville Inc. T.V. in terms of the requirements of the C.R.T.C. It comprised a number of elements: members of the public, student activists, a pro-Quebec nationalist organization, and the cable company. The latter provided the technical staff and equipment, while the National Society of Quebecers provided a studio and hired a film director-animator. Funding was provided by the federal Secretary of State through the Local Initiatives Program (L.I.P.), Youth Perspectives, the Company of Young Canadians, the National Society of Quebecers, and the Quebec Ministry of Communications. Relations with the Quebec government were through the Development Council for Community Media, referred to above. A central assembly, held for the general public once a year, elected an administrative committee and a program committee. The membership fee was fifty cents.

The animator was a crucial element in the enterprise, establishing liaison with public groups, handling publicity, and organizing the assemblies. As programming developed, it tended toward social and public issues set out in the interests of working-class and unemployed people, and links were formed with trade unions. In other words, television was seen not as an end in itself but as an instrument of information capable of developing solidarity among some elements of the community. Because of this, a set of tensions and some opposition developed between and among the constituent groups. The cable company did not support the militant political tendencies of the group, and even the National Society of Quebecers, with its nationalist ideology, was not very happy about the kind of militancy demonstrated. "The political élite can show reticence if community T.V. is seen to be defending the interests of the lower classes." (Development Associates, 1975). These tensions may not be characteristic of all such community T.V. groups, but they are not surprising under the fairly fluid and active political and social conditions indicated in Chapter 4, and in a situation where so many relatively new organizational patterns are emerging.

Earlier in this chapter there was a reference to TEVEC and Multi-Média, two ventures of the Ministry of Education. Both have been closed down, and their educational purposes have been assumed in the wider program of citizen education under the D.G.E.A. Another institution that can be considered an important component of the educational communications network is the Télé-Université, established in 1972. It has a function comparable to that of Athabasca University in Alberta. The Télé-Université, with its head office in

Quebec City, is a constituent institution of the University of Quebec, which has ten campuses or units situated in seven centres in southern Quebec. Four main programs are offered: a certificate and a bachelor's degree in teaching mathematics, a certificate in French language teaching, and a certificate in "Man and His Environment." The courses for teachers are being phased out, leaving that function to the campus-based units of the university, but students already in those programs are being carried through to completion. Other courses have been put together in conjunction with other institutions, such as a course on co-operatives in conjunction with the co-operative movement, and a course on aging in conjunction with the Ministry of Social Affairs.

There are some interesting comparisons and contrasts between the Télé-Université and Athabasca University in Alberta. Both use correspondence materials, written and audio, and television and radio. But whereas Athabasca University is restricted to local cable channels, the Télé-Université uses the television transmissions of Radio-Quebec. In Quebec these means are supported by a system of local groups of students working with an animator who is a local part-time employee of the Télé-Université. Such groups meet about once every three weeks. In Alberta the pacing of the learner's progress is carried on through individual telephone links with tutors. This supports the suggestion that there is a generally more individualistic climate in Alberta and a more collectivist one in Quebec.

With regard to the content of the programs, whereas Athabasca University tends toward the development of degree programs, the Télé-Université appears to lay more stress on the development of individual courses as part of a contribution to the general development of popular adult education without too many academic strings attached. The courses in the "Man and His Environment" program, reveal another aspect of the conscious encouragement of Quebecois life and culture, for example, "Publicity in Quebec," "Introduction to the Quebec Economy," "Introduction to Co-operation," "Contemporary History of Quebec," and "The Quebec Heritage." The Athabasca University courses, on the other hand, are more general, for example, "Ancient Roots of the Modern World," "Canadian History," "Modern Consciousness in Literature," and "Psychology Today."

Co-ordination

This account indicates that, as in Alberta, there is a wide range of government agencies offering some sort of adult education in Quebec. There is also evidence that whereas in Alberta a major part of manpower training is planned and conducted by one ministry, Advanced Education and Manpower, and that there is at least a formal departmental co-ordinating mechanism, in Quebec this sector is administered by two ministries, with some evidence of lack of co-ordination. This problem appears to be the subject of evaluation and possible rectification within the Ministry of Education and between the two ministries mainly involved.

In Quebec, there are two forces working toward a degree of co-ordination in adult education of a more general nature. The first is the policy, initially recommended by the Parent Commission, of bringing all responsibility for formal instruction in the insitutions, mainly the colleges and school-boards, under the Ministry of Education. This is shared by the number of CEGEPs—thirty-eight colleges with fifty-two campuses—able to meet local needs over a wide expanse of the province. (They are, however, all in the southern part of the province, leaving the vast north still ill-served.) This policy is supported by large provincial organizations such as the Union des Producteurs Agricoles, which see themselves as taking responsibility for the social and organizational education of their members (*éducation syndicale*) and leaving the technical skill teaching to the educational institutions. The fact that the one ministry is responsible for school-boards in respect of their entire operation gives a more coherent and focused thrust to the part that schools and school jurisdictions can play in adult education. Seventy-six school-boards and regional school-boards have an adult education service, which is overseen by the D.G.E.A. (Ministère de l'Education, 1979). Quebec does not have the equivalent of Alberta's local further education councils, but it appears that in at least some areas the persons who are responsible for school-board adult education services act in a co-ordinating capacity with other community groups.

The fact that the D.G.E.A. has a direct relationship with the voluntary popular education organization (O.V.E.P.s), of which there are 441 throughout the province (Ibid., 1979) also provides a means of overseeing and influencing the total picture of adult education offer-ings in local areas. The real degree of co-ordination will depend on the working relationship between the officials of the S.E.A.P.A.C. and the O.V.E.P. services within the Ministry of Education.

At the higher, policy-making level, the second force toward co-ordination are three top level inter-ministerial committees—super-ministries—on two of which the Minister of Education sits. The first is the Committee for Cultural Development, chaired by the Minister of Cultural Affairs and including the Ministers of Education, Social Affairs, and Financial Institutions and Co-operatives. (The Council for the Status of Women is also represented on this commit-tee). The second is the Committee for Social Development, chaired by the Minister of Social Affairs and including the Ministers of Educa-tion and Labor and Manpower. On the third such super-ministerial committee, Economic development, the Minister of Education is not yet represented.

Again the overall strategies of co-ordination in the two provinces, insofar as they exist, appear to fit with that of the dominant ideolo-gies. In Alberta the main thrust is left to local initiatives, mainly through the local councils, and there is a widespread inclination to leave it to the forces of the educational market-place, in the faith that this will reflect the broader hierarchy of needs in the province. In Quebec there is more government intervention in the process at the administrative and financial levels. The staff of the Directorate-Gen-eral of Adult Education, those directly concerned with the adminis-tration of adult education in the ministry, numbered 205 in 1977–78 (Ibid., 1979), including seventeen senior administrators and ninety-three professional officers. In Alberta the figure for persons doing the equivalent work in the Department of Advanced Education and Man-power in the same year was twenty-two.

Summary

The general picture that emerges from this survey of the structure of government services in adult education, taken together with that revealed in Chapter 4, confirms the suggestion by an O.E.C.D. team studying education policy in Canada that Quebec has established both a general policy and an institutional structure addressed to a broad political philosophy and a conception of the province's future (O.E.C.D., 1976:20,99–100). That conception and philosophy is clearly related to the cultural identity and sovereignty of the people of Quebec, and it is articulated not only in general statements such as the 1978 White Paper on Quebec's policy on cultural development, but also in the mandates of the ministries of Communications, Cultural Affairs, and Education. The structures and mandates of these ministries are clearly geared to allow direct government influence in and support for programs consonant with general government philosophy. Moreover, they are not recent creations of the P.Q. separatist government, but were set up by previous, federally oriented governments. In other words, they are a manifestation not of recently emerged extreme separatism, but of a trend that has developed in the province for some years and is supported even by less radical and nationalistic elements of Quebec society.

One event in 1979 serves as an illustration of this sensitivity to Quebec identity, even on the part of many who are not separatists. In the early part of the year the CBC and the Canadian Association for Adult Education co-operated in producing a national television program called "People Talking Back." It consisted of an initial T.V. broadcast, linking groups of people in centres all across Canada, to discuss problems those people and others saw as being crucial economic, political, cultural, and social issues in Canadian life. Subsequent programs followed and were accompanied by group discussions and phone-in arrangements. Inevitably, one of the issues that could be expected was that of Canadian identity and national unity. In the planning stage of the program, francophone persons and organizations in Quebec, including the francophone counterpart of the C.A.A.E., the Institut Canadien d'Education des Adultes, who were approached about participating in the venture, expressed an unwillingness to become involved, either as sponsors or participants. Nor did the French-language Radio Canada participate. In the cross-country groups appearing on the program, Quebec was represented by an English-speaking group from Montreal.

As in Alberta, in Quebec there is strong federal influence in technical and vocational training, and Quebec shows an even stronger sense of reservation about these federal incursions than demonstrated by Alberta and the other provinces. The division of government jurisdiction in this field between two ministries appears to cause a less smooth-running operation of manpower training than in Alberta, where it is under one ministry. On the other hand, the inclusion of other ministries in aspects of policy-making and practice, and the two super-ministries on which the Minister of Education is represented, indicates that Quebec sees manpower training in a wider social and cultural light than Alberta does.

The evident interest on the part of the Quebec government in influencing, directly supporting, and taking a hand in the provision of a wide range of popular or socio-cultural education gives rise to two consequences. From the perspective of most other Canadian provinces, and certainly of Alberta, one of these consequences is seen as unfortunate. Skewing adult education toward a particular political, social, and cultural viewpoint might be damned by some as the socialization of education. In Alberta the dominant trend might, in contrast, be called the privatization of adult education: "the user pays." The second consequence appears to be the likelihood of and potential for a good deal of overlapping of activities between, for instance, animators working with school-board adult education services, with C.L.S.C.s, with community T.V. groups, with organizations coming under the O.V.E.P. scheme, and so on. An overlap of activities may be a result of increased activity in this whole field in recent years, and may be resolved as co-ordinating machinery is improved; on the other hand, it may get worse as ministries and relatively new ministers survey and become attached to their present territories and powers.

References

Alberta Advanced Education. [n. d.] *Advisory Committees to the Minister*. Edmonton: Alberta Advanced Education.

Bureau de la Statistique. 1975-76. *Annuaire du Quebec.* Quebec: Ministère de l'Industrie et du Commerce.

Comité d'Etude sur l'Education des Adultes. 1967. *Rapport.* Quebec: Ministère de l'Education.

Commission Royal d'Enguête Sur L'Enseignement. 1963-66. *Rapport.* Quebec: Editeur Officiel.

Conseil Superieur de l'Education. 1978. *La Jungle Administrative du Programme de Formation Professionnel des Adultes.* Quebec: Conseil Superiéur de l'Education.

Development Associates. 1975. *Documentation and Analysis of Development Programs in Canada.* Mimeographed. Edmonton: Divison of Community Development, University of Alberta.

Directeur Générale d'Education des Adultes (D.G.E.A.). 1978. *Présentation Générale.* Quebec: Ministère de l'Education.

Fédération des C.L.S.C. du Québec. 1976. *Définition du Centre Local de Services Communautaires.* Quebec: Fédération des C.L.S.C. du Québec.

Lassonde, G. 1978. *Politique du Post-obligatoire: Dossier 1.* Quebec: Editeur Officiel.

Mansfield, E.A. 1977. "Education Through the Manpower Looking Glass: Some Personal Views." *Journal of the Alberta Association for Continuing Education.* Vol. 5, no. 1.

Ministère des Affaires Culturelles. 1976-77. *Rapport Annuel.* Quebec: Editeur Officiel.

Ministère des Affaires Municipales. 1975-76. *Rapport Annuel.* Quebec: Editeur Officiel.

Ministère des Affaires Sociales. 1975-76. *Rapport Annuel.* Quebec: Editeur Officiel.

Ministère de l'Agriculture. 1974-75. *Annuel Rapport.* Quebec: Editeur Officiel.

Ministère de l'Education. 1978. *L'Education au Quebec, 1976.* Quebec: Editeur Officiel.

———. 1979. *L'Education au Quebec.* Quebec: Editeur Officiel.

Ministère de l'Immigration. 1977-78. *Rapport Annuel.* Quebec: Editeur Officiel.

Ministère de la Terre et des Forêts. 1976. *Rapport Annuel.* Quebec: Editeur Officiel.

Ministère du Tourisme, de la Chasse, et de la Pêche. 1973–74. *Rapport Annuel.* Quebec: Editeur Officiel.

Ministère du Travail et de la Main-d'Oeuvre. 1977-78. *Rapport Annuel.* Quebec: Editeur Officiel.

Organizations for Economic Co-operation and Development. 1976. *Reviews of National Policies for Education: Canada.* Paris: O.E.C.D.

Parti Libéral du Quebec. 1977. *Le Quebec C'est Ton Affaire!* Montreal: Editions du Jour.

Royal Commission of Enquiry on Education in Quebec. 1963-66. *Report.* Quebec: Government Printer.

Superior Council of Education. *Annual Reports.* Quebec: Government Printer.

Willet, G. 1975. *Les Nouvelles Situations de Communications au Quebec.* Quebec: Ministère de l'Industrie et du Commerce.

Part III
Non-Government Institutions

Introduction

Though it is the government structures, including the linkages or lack of them between ministries and departments, that dominate adult education, there are other institutions important in themselves, which illustrate certain provincial characteristics. In Part III, we will look at four groups of such institutions: native organizations, agricultural organizations, labor organizations, and provincial adult education associations. There is a varying order of autonomy among these organizations, both in terms of policy-making and funding, and some are connected in one way or another to the government structures discussed in Chapters 5 and 6. We will take note of those linkages, but the main purpose of the chapters in Part III is to look at the picture from the point of view of the organizations themselves, and to see their involvement in adult education.

These organizations have their own particular approaches to adult education, representing, as they do, people with particular interests. They create their own internal programs, but in view of their importance in society they also make certain demands on and receive special consideration from public authorities. Their development reveals some interesting comparisons between political and educational approaches in the two provinces.

These chapters will study the objectives, structures, and activities of these organizations and their relationships to government. Continuing an analysis of organizational and institutional structures that affect the provision of adult education from Chapters 5 and 6, we will also take note of the kinds of adult education the following organizations provide. This will lead into a study of the broader pattern of adult education in the two provinces in subsequent chapters.

7

Organizations of Native People

General Introduction

The relationships between native organizations and governments have common elements in all the provinces because of the B.N.A. Act, the Constitution Act, and the Indian Act, which are federal laws. The former gives to the federal government exclusive jurisdiction over Indians and land reserved for Indians, and the latter sets out in more detail the governance of Indian affairs. It determines the status of Indians as being those who retain their rights—in Alberta under various treaties—and it sets out the conditions under which an Indian forfeits that status. It therefore creates a legal distinction between status and non-status Indians, and limits the federal government's special responsibilities to status Indians. In all provinces the federal government is an active agent in matters relating to status Indians, including matters of education. According to a Supreme Court decision in 1939, the Inuit people are deemed to be Indian for the purposes of the British North America Act, so they are accorded the same aboriginal rights and treatment as Indians (Cumming and Mickenberg, 1972:7).

So, as far as adult education for Indian and Inuit people is concerned, two departments of the federal government are involved. As with non-natives, the Department of Manpower and Immigration (Canada Manpower) and its offshoot, the Canadian Employment and Immigration Commission, has an important role in vocationally oriented adult education. Likewise, the Department of Indian and Northern Affairs has an important role. There appears to be no clear line between the responsibilities and functions of these two departments with respect to training programs. For example, a training program in communications technology for young natives in Alberta is held at a community college under the auspices of Canada Manpower, while a similar program for young Inuit people in Quebec is held (in Ottawa) under the auspices of the Department of Indian and Northern Affairs' vocational education section.

There is yet another fuzzy (and even contested) area of jurisdiction. Under the B.N.A. Act, education was placed under the provincial governments, which, in particular the Quebec government, claim a right to be involved. Moreover, the affairs of Metis and non-status Indians, including their education, are within the provinces' jurisdiction, so organizations of these people look to provincial governments for financial support while aspiring to participate, as people of native ancestry, in federal government support schemes and in land settlement claims. From the government's point of view the matter is expressed thus in a letter dated 26 July 1976 from a senior member of the Alberta Department of Advanced Education and Manpower:

Historically, the province has viewed matters concerning Indians as being governed by constitutional provisions and by the Indian Act. In order to avoid jeopardizing the rights of Indians and to avoid intervening in what has been viewed as an area of federal jurisdiction, our Department has participated primarily in those programs supported by the federal government. However, we have not adhered rigorously to requiring federal financial participation and have responded, where possible, to needs as identified.

It is important, as well, to distinguish between services provided to treaty and non-treaty Indians. Our Department is extensively involved in providing educational programs and services designed to meet the needs of non-treaty Indians in the province. This is particularly evident in Northern Alberta where AVC Grouard, AVC Lac La Biche, and Keyano College currently provide programs designed almost exclusively for native people in the area. (Harrison, 1977:appendix)

In each of the two provinces there is an association of Metis and non-status Indian people, and one or more associations of status Indians, and at the national level there is the National Council of Canada for Metis and Non-Status Indians, and the National Indian Brotherhood for status Indians.

In 1972 the latter organization presented to the federal government a policy paper urging Indian control of Indian education. One of the reasons for this was that the federal government had begun to negotiate for provincial governments to assume responsibility for some eductional services to Indians, and the Indians saw this as an erosion of their aboriginal rights. They countered with an insistence that such responsibilities be handed directly to the Indian people. Their demands covered adult education, including vocational training (and the training of teachers for Indian schools), and cultural education. The paper demanded the right of band education authorities to control and direct programs in basic literacy and academic upgrading, and such other subjects as business management, consumer education, leadership training, family education, health, crafts, and Indian art and culture. It also stressed the importance of alcohol and drug education. Cultural education, the study of Indian history, culture, language, and values, should be made available through cultural educational centres, according to their demands (Weitz, 1972:12–17).

In August 1973, the Minister for Indian and Northern Affairs confirmed the federal government's acceptance of the proposed policy, and the Native Indian Brotherhood and provincial Indian associations were assisted to employ education consultants to work with bands in planning and implementing local control. By 1978, 82 bands had assumed total control, and 403 had assumed partial control of their education programs.

This insistence on control of their own education, and the list of subjects to be included in adult and cultural education, reveals a duality and an ambivalence in the Indian people's approach to education and training and to their place in contemporary society. On the one hand there is the realization that they need the skills and knowledge to become productive and economically secure in the dominant culture, and on the other hand there is the realization that they have roots in a noble heritage from which they draw personal and collective strength. Expressed in terms of the model set out in Figure 2 in Chapter 2, the purposes of the native people in adult education include a strong counter-cultural element yet acknowledge the importance of the remedial and coping types of education. This creates a disturbing tension.

There is a second source of tension, between local band and tribal loyalties, and the broader identity with native people confronting the dominant white culture, and hence with the political organizations that represent those people. The principle in the policy statement on Indian control of Indian education, that such control should be exercised at the band level, pushes the balance as far as education is concerned down on that side, and since the federal government has accepted that principle, its funding reinforces that push. Furthermore, the increased interest—almost preoccupation—of the larger political associations with land claims, directs much of their energy into that effort, though the preparation of land claims and the process of putting them before the native people is in itself an important educational process.

Alberta

The two principal native groups in Alberta are the Indians and the Metis. In 1976 there were 34,277 registered Indians and approximately 80,000 Metis (University of Alberta Senate, 1978), of whom just over 3,000 live on eight Metis settlements in the northern part of the province. There are no Inuit or Eskimos in the province (the name of the Edmonton football team, the Eskimos, is an example of the licence with which such organizations treat reality). Each of the two Alberta groups has one major provincial organization with mainly political objectives. They represent their members in negotiations with governments and other authorities in matters that affect their lives. While the Indian Association of Alberta represents the interests of the status Indian, the Metis Association represents those of the Metis and non-status Indians.

Status Indians in Alberta

Among the Indians the basic organization is the band, represented by its chief and the band council, who are elected by the people of the band. The bands belong to two major tribal groupings, the Cree in the north and the Blackfoot Confederacy (including the Bloods and Peigan) in the south. While the tribes have a cultural and emotional significance, the bands are the focus of the day-to-day life of the Indian people. This focus is underlined in the policy paper on Indian control of Indian education.

The part of the Indian Association of Alberta in adult educational matters appears to be marginal, and there are some indications that this is perceived by Indians to be properly so. A survey of Indian education in five provincial community colleges in 1976–77 showed that among a sample of Indian leaders—chiefs, band managers, and chairmen of education committees—the perception was that the efforts of the Indian Association to help Indians in regard to college education were poor, secondary to those of tribal government, the Department of Indian and Northern Affairs, and the colleges themselves. None of the respondents felt that the Indian Association of Alberta had a responsibility for initiating improved college education for Indian people (Harrison, 1977:69, 81). The survey emphasized the role of the band authorities who were seen as important in this matter. The Indian Association does, however, have an education research officer responsible for monitoring adult education for native people. The association also has a role in the large oil sands operation in north-east Alberta; it is provided with funds by the Department of Indian and Northern Affairs to hold workshops with bands in different areas to acquaint them with the employment opportunities and skill requirements. Another program for conducting other workshops on matters such as the Indian Act, land claims, and Indian government lacks field staff for extensive implementation. Some of the leaders in the association have been active in organizing seminars for native and non-native groups, involving elders in explorations of Indian culture.

With regard to education, or at any rate the payment for educational services, the Indian people look primarily to the federal government. The letter from the Alberta Department of Advanced Education and Manpower quoted above indicates that the provincial government for the most part recognizes and abides by that division of responsibilities, but that it does not rule out direct involvement when requested. There are, in recent years, instances of Indian children attending schools outside the reserves, and growing attendance by by young Indians at provincial vocational centres, colleges, and universities, whose tuition fees are paid by the federal government. Provincial government authorities have expressed concern (in another part of the letter quoted above) at the possibility of a system of Indian-controlled colleges parallel to the one under provincial jurisdiction. The tendency will be for the higher and adult education needs of Indians to be met in the existing provincial institutions, either under federal funding arrangments or by direct arrangement with native people themselves. On the other hand, Indians are increasingly aware that they are citizens of the province as well as of the country, and should be able to benefit from resources made available through the provincial government in the form, if appropriate, of colleges geared especially to Indian needs. This feeling is reinforced as signs appear of federal funding limitations, and in the light of the great wealth of Alberta as a province.

So the main connection in matters of adult education is between bands and the Department of Indian and Northern Affairs, through the department's six district officers in the Alberta region. Bands are encouraged to approach these district officers directly, since budgetary allocations have been decentralized to these officers. The regional office in Edmonton has a minor role in this respect, restricted to the responsibility for paying tuition fees and transportation costs of Indian students attending non-native institutions. Bands initiate proposals for adult education, and submit budgets to district officers of the department. The first priority in government funding is for what is called non-discretionary funding, that is, funding related to the statutory responsibility of the government under provisions of the Indian Act, such as school education for Indian children. Adult education, education and training for adults beyond formal schooling, does not come under such provisions and is deemed, therefore, to be discretionary.

Within the category of post-school education, the emphasis on funding is heavily on academic, professional, and vocationally oriented education. The following table shows the allocations in the Alberta region of the Department of Indian and Northern Affairs in recent years.

Table 3

Post-School Education, Department of Indian and Northern Affairs Alberta Region

Type of Education	Expenditure 1977–78	Estimated Expenditure 1978-79	Allocation for 1979-80
University & Professional	$993,880	$1,200,000	$1,415,600
Occupational Skills	948,400	820,000	1,204,000
Band Staff Training	279,500	70,000	146,000
Training on the Job	163,500	200,000	155,400
Adult Education	279,300	150,000	81,500
Cultural Programs	27,700	30,000	10,000

Source: Indian Association Analysis of D.I.N.A. Financial Statements

These figures show the heavy imbalance between full-time academic, professional education, and vocational training on one side, and adult and cultural education on the other. While the Department of Indian and Northern Affairs is decreasing its contribution in the vocational field, some of the responsibility is being assumed by Canada Manpower. Adult education covers socially and personally oriented kinds of learning, such as Cree language and home economics, and adult basic education. It is under the adult education heading that the Indian Association is provided with funds to conduct educational and informational meetings with local bands related to socio-economic development.

Table 3 shows not only that adult education and cultural programs have attracted a minor part of the total funding in recent years, but that they were being squeezed even harder in 1979–80. The trend is clearly toward the acquisition of knowledge and skills appropriate to economic integration. This is augmented by the provision of such educational training through provincially controlled vocational centres and colleges. The Department of Advanced Education and Manpower's letter, quoted above, shows that the northern vocational colleges and Keyano College are providing programs designed almost exclusively for local native people. More recently, Lakeland College in the northeast began investigating, with Canada Manpower, the Department of Indian and Northern Affairs, and local Indian band leaders, the possibilities of training natives for work on the huge Cold Lake heavy oil development. Besides the actual provision of courses through the colleges, the Alberta government augments student funding through Alberta training allowances, which are available only through provincial institutions.

One organization that acts as a link between the native people and industry, and which provides adult counselling in this matter of employment and training, is Native Outreach, based in Edmonton. Started in 1973 as a pilot project under the auspices of the Metis Association and with Canada Manpower funding, Native Outreach is funded by both the federal and provincial governments and has two main functions. Counselling and job placement for native people is federally funded, while advocacy on behalf of the native people as potential workers is provincially funded. The latter consists of identifying training needs among native people, job opportunities, and training resources and facilities. The organization's affiliations are now with the Metis Association, Indian Association, and Alberta Federation of Labor, and it has an advisory committee that includes representatives of government, labor, and such industrial concerns as Syncrude, Bechtel, and ESSO. It has helped to initiate training centres such as the New Sun Automobile Training Centre in Edmonton, and training programs such as a welding course for native people conducted by Bechtel Limited in Edmonton.

Native Outreach's adult education interests extend beyond counselling and skill training to labor education in conjunction with the Alberta Federation of Labor, training courses for its own staff, and working with native groups to raise levels of awareness of the impact and importance of oil and industrial developments in the province.

Not everyone is happy with this trend toward integration, especially where the assumptions of white society are dumped on the native people. Within the education institutions, native students sometimes rebel against the process in two ways: by withdrawing in a passive way and dropping out; or by organizing themselves in protest. As native students in the universities and colleges experience the courses of study that have been structured for white high school graduates by white educators, and which fail to take into account the native background and culture, they form student associations to give themselves support and ease their agony. Even when Indian education centres are established, as at Blue Quills in northeastern Alberta, the educational programs are still generated, for the most part, by universities and colleges. There appears to be a concern more for exerting a sort of academic imperialism and being seen to have a presence in native life than with recognizing the special needs and qualities of that life and accommodating the learning process to them. Courses for Indian teachers are not geared to native consciousness or awareness of native needs. The result is a high dropout rate and even—as at Blue Quills in the spring of 1979—student revolt.

This outcome shows a flaw in the admirable principle of Indian control of Indian education as it is implemented. It points to one of the problems being experienced by a people many of whose middle-aged members and leaders tend to have been acculturated into a sense of dependency on white people and authorities, and do not have the experience or competence to set up education programs on their own, nor the inclination to resist the assumptions and importunities of outside experts. The students, on the other hand, represent an increasingly independent and even militant trend among younger native people, demanding more recognition of their culture and former values. There is a certain coincidence of this feeling with those of younger leaders in the Indian Association, which causes some tension between some of the local band leaders and the provincial association.

With regard to adult education, there is likewise a feeling among some native people, including the leadership of Native Outreach, that while vocational counselling, training, and employment are necessary to the future development of native people, an exclusive or over-emphasized concern for that aspect of adult education leaves a wide area of need unfulfilled. Among the elders there is a wealth of untapped wisdom that needs to be brought forth, not only to validate the rising consciousness of the younger native people but also to strengthen the tentative gropings of some Canadians toward an understanding of the elements of Canadian culture.

In relation to this broader movement, initiatives began in respect of cultural education. Under its multi-culturalism policy in the late 1960s the federal government set up funding for activities of this sort, and the Indian people submitted claims on the fund. The intention was that the money should go to any band or Indian agency prepared to develop a cultural component in existing education programs at all levels—from pre-school to adult education. In Alberta, one response to this initiative was made by the Indian Association. They proposed to establish an Indian Education Centre to serve as a kind of provincial college where the curriculum would rest on research in, and the practice of, Indian traditions and history. The amount of money claimed was in excess of the funds for all the other claims, and a contestation resulted within the Indian community. Although federal cabinet approval had been given for funding such a centre in 1971, and work had begun, disagreements among the native leaders frustrated its full development. Individual bands proceeded to apply for separate funding. For instance, the Blackfoot people initiated what has become the Old Sun College at Gleichen, and alongside Blue Quills the Saddle Lake Centre was set up at St. Paul. From 1975 the federal government suspended funding for the provincial centre in favor of funding for local centres on various reserves based on the band organization. This, again, was in conformity with the requests made in the policy paper on Indian control of Indian education.

The early work on the provincial centre was not without results. Between 1972 and 1974 a number of think tanks with elders were organized around the province; these were low-key meetings attended by elders and young people, and had considerable impact on both groups. These experiences and other preparatory work demonstrated the practical possibility of conducting cultural programs based on the teaching resources of the native people themselves. This work also started the momentum by which the other local centres were established.

These local centres, of which there are nine in Alberta, are mostly based at existing Indian school facilities. Formal education programs are financed through the Department of Indian and Northern Affairs district offices as explained above, while the cultural education activities at the centres are financed under a program administered directly from Ottawa. These latter funds are supplemented by others through the Alberta Regional Office. These supplementary funds are shown under the heading of Cultural Programs in Table 3.

These cultural/educational centres are at different stages with regard to their engagement in formal education and cultural education respectively. Blue Quills, for instance, has: a high school program plus three full-time post-secondary programs: a teacher education program from the University of Alberta called Morningstar; a public administration program from Athabasca University; and a social work program from the University of Calgary. The Saddle Lake Cultural Centre, not linked to Blue Quills, runs such cultural programs as a museum, the use of elders as instructors in the schools, and a troupe of singers and dancers.

Old Sun College at Gleichen is another example of an attempt to combine formal education and training programs with a cultural program. The college was started in 1971 in the former Indian residential school on the Blackfoot reserve as a campus of Mount Royal College in Calgary, but in 1972 it became an independent college with its own board of eight Indians and four white members, with the principal as Chief Executive Officer. It conducts three kinds of programs: daytime programs comprising academic upgrading and vocational training taught by the college staff, and a selection of post-secondary courses taught by other institutions such as the Universities of Calgary and Lethbridge and the Southern Alberta Institute of Technology; evening programs comprising adult enrichment and recreation courses, life skills, work-oriented courses such as upholstery, and some Lethbridge University B.Ed. courses; and cultural programs centred on an Indian museum in the building. The evening work-oriented programs aim to promote local business ventures, and in 1979 the college initiated Old Sun Industries to operate an upholstery firm. The college promotes a higher rate of useful employment and economic viability on the reserve. The cultural program aims at complementing this with the renewal of interest and pride in the Blackfoot heritage. This program includes: the operation of the museum as a resource for visitors, both native and non-native; recording native myths and legends and filming dances and pow-wows; providing a meeting place for elders and younger people; and conducting continuing research. It provides a learning resource for student groups from other institutions and other tribes, and for children in the reserve schools. The museum is a separate entity from the college, and the museum program, which has been built up by the first curator, Russell Wright, is financed from Ottawa.

The nine Alberta centres attracted a total of $516,345 in 1979 according to the Department of Indian and Northern Affairs. The largest centres were the Old Sun Community College, Ninastaco Centre at Cardston, the Maskwachees Cultural College at Hobbema, and the Saddle Lake Cultural Centre.

The Metis in Alberta

The Metis are of native and white ancestry, but have become recognized as a distinctive group, emphasized by the exclusion from the status and rights of Indians under the Indian Act. A further distinction is made between the Metis in Alberta and Quebec. From their activity in the nineteenth century, centring around Louis Riel, the prairie Metis have developed a degree of cultural synthesis, a way of life, and a socio-cultural identity. There has been a Metis Association of Alberta since the 1930s. The Metis of Quebec, on the other hand, have tended to be identified with one or other of the ethnic groups in which they originate, and in fact the majority identify themselves with the Indian people and wish for this identity to be recognized in land claims (Laplante, 1979:29; Boudrias, 1979:32).

However, it is only since the mid-1960s that Metis people have begun to assert their claims to recognition as a significant and identifiable element in Alberta society. Since they do not meet the definition of "Indian" under the Indian Act, their affairs fall within the jurisdiction of the provincial government, and they are thus not distinguished for most purposes, including education, from other Albertans. They are, however, distinguished insofar as the Metis Betterment Act of 1938 makes a number of provisions related specifically to what are called Metis colonies in the province. (This term itself says something about attitudes in white society toward the Metis people.) There are eight such colonies, or Metis settlements, in the province. In terms of the Acts, each has an elected council of five, including the chairman.

As in the case of the Indian Association, the Metis Association itself tends not to take the lead in matters of adult education, being rather the political arm of the Metis people. Rather, it supports other organizations that take a more direct role in adult education matters. One of these organizations is related to the settlements, and is a direct offshoot of activities initiated by the Metis Association.

Attention became centred on the settlements and on the Metis people in 1967, when the then president of the Metis Association of Alberta, Stan Daniels, initiated a court action against the Alberta government, charging that the government had wrongfully retained millions of dollars of revenues that were due to the Metis settlements in respect of mineral and other rights on settlement territory. The case failed, on a ruling by the judge that the complainant was not a person properly qualified to bring the action, but the judge gave certain directions as to how a proper action could be initiated by the Metis settlements themselves. As a consequence, the Federation of Metis Settlements was formed, initially as an offshoot of the Metis Association. It is now a quite separate organization.

It was not until 1975 that the federation established a central office, and was organized as a provincial body (in fact, all the settlements are in the northern part of the province). As a federation, its priorities are not directly concerned with adult education, but activity in this field arises out of one of its other needs. The two primary concerns of the federation are the pursuit of the legal case originally brought by Daniels, and housing on the settlements. A third priority is the need for improved local government in the settlements, and this has led to a program of adult education. The low level of experience and competence on the part of local officials and councillors and the need for the settlements to be properly administered called for a training program in such subjects as election law and procedures, parliamentary procedure, writing briefs, and administration. The federation employed a co-ordinator and two facilitators to provide instruction in these subjects.

The federation also worked with the Alberta government Land Tenure Secretariat and the Department of Advanced Education and Manpower to prepare and offer a course in civics through the community vocational centres in the Lesser Slave Lake area, where a number of the settlements are located. Students in the community voctional centres are adults who require academic upgrading before going on to further training or education, and the civics program was introduced as part of the formal social studies curriculum. It incorporates material designed more for native needs than is the case in the Alberta Schools Social Studies Curriculum. But it is also used as a tool for community education, imparting information to settlement residents about Metis history, the identity of Metis settlements as distinct from other native communities, and the Metis Betterment Act (Davis, 1979). Another organization initially sponsored by the Metis Association, and which remains affiliated to it, is Native Outreach.

A third and important organization to be linked to both the Metis and Indian associations is the Alberta Native Communications Society. This society began in 1968, when one man, Eugene Steinhauer, later President of the Indian Association, started it as a producer of Cree radio programs for broadcasting on Station C.K.U.A., which was then a government-owned station and has since become part of the ACCESS network (*see* Chapter 5). The society has since expanded to employ a full-time executive director and a staff of producers, writers, and reporters. It is governed by a board of twelve persons, six Metis and six status Indians. The society started with funding from provincial and federal governments and in 1979–80 it received $335,000 from the Alberta Department of Culture, and $357,000 from the federal Secretary of State. It was the first such service to be funded by the Secretary of State, and became a model for other similar societies in other provinces.

The services of the society now include a weekly newspaper, *The Native People*, with a circulation of about ten thousand, a radio department producing Alberta Schools broadcasts and other programs aimed primarily at native communities, a film-making department and a television department. Radio programs are broadcast on four stations, some in Cree and some in English, and native speakers, musicians, and singers, contemporary and traditional, are featured. The society broke new ground in educational programming and transmission via radio and then via the satellite Hermes in a project called Ironstar. Project Ironstar had two phases, the first being a radio link-up of a studio in Edmonton with communities in northern Alberta in 1976, and the second phase being video link-up via the Hermes satellite. In this phase, between August and December 1977, after consultation with local people, and using field worker/facilitators, the Edmonton production centre could communicate with three northern communities—Assumption, Fort Chipweyan, and Wabasca/Demarais—by satellite transmissions. Intercommunity discussions were organized, and many native organizations, notably the Indian Association and the Metis Association, and government departments, provided material for the transmissions. Apart from programs designed for the schools in the three communities, adult programming covered such topics as land tenure, land rights, Indian rights for Indian women, alcohol problems, preventive medicine, and fishing and trapping.

Following the success of the Ironstar project, the Alberta Native Communications Society began in 1979 to plan and prepare for a second project, Native T.V. Programming Services, this time using the Anik B satellite. The aim was to develop and broadcast a series of programs addressed to sixteen native communities, mainly in isolated northern areas. Six of the communities would have the capability of "talking back" via the satellite, and the ten others would simply receive the broadcasts. The signal would go to color T.V. monitors set up in central locations in the community, and in three comunities the proposal was to have low-power T.V. re-broadcast transmitters for broadcasting directly into homes in the community. Each community would have a Community Advisory Committee comprising local residents to advise on and react to programs. Part-time animators would be hired in each community to operate the equipment, publicize the programs, and encourage participation.

The matters identified, partly through Project Ironstar, as being high priority subjects for programming and discussion are: physical and mental health services and information; employment and career counselling and information; educational services especially for preschool children, young adults, and adults; native-oriented cultural, information, and entertainment programs; programming for women; programming addressing teenagers' concerns such as alcohol and drug abuse, stages of adolescence, anti-social and criminal behavior, and entertainment; "specials" dealing with problem or topical issues such as housing, welfare, income tax, gun control, and politics; and information and cultural exchanges among communities.

Alongside this broader approach to adult education through the media, the Alberta Native Communications Society (A.N.C.S.) initiated a training program for native workers in communications—journalism, photography, radio and video production, Cree language, and native culture. This program, whose students are funded by Canada Manpower, is now run by Grant McEwan Community College in Edmonton.

The Communications Society originated as an effort on the part of a few individuals to improve communication among native people in the province, as a means of consciousness-raising and cultural development. The late 1960s and early 1970s were a period of active growth in the native organizations and of a growing sense of ethnic identity. It is possible that in Alberta this had some connection with the provincial government's Community Development Branch, whose field officers, both native and white, were active in native areas and communities to the point of being an embarrassment to the government in the 1960s. For whatever reasons, the first efforts of the communications society grew to the present high and sophisticated level because they found a good response among native people as the latter became more aware of their problems and energies, and more confident in articulating them. Among northern people there were misgivings about the ways that southern white culture was exacerbating the problems of native and mixed communities and enthusiasm for attempts to promote native culture and language.

In the southern part of the province a similar and complementary development took place through the Indian News Media organization, based at Standoff on the Blood Reserve. This organization produces what is claimed as Canada's leading Indian newspaper, *Kainai News*, and it runs the Blackfoot Radio, a service dedicated to the promotion of Indian culture. The radio program, produced by native people, features community news and cultural items, making use of elders in the five southern tribes. The programs are transmitted through four local radio stations.

There are a number of other native organizations involved in some form of adult education, connected with or sponsored by both Indians and Metis. There are Native Friendship Centres in a number of towns, which employ program co-ordinators and offer programs of both a recreational and cultural nature. The Voice of Alberta Native Women has been active for some years in a program of consciousness-raising and organization among native women, and runs workshops on various aspects of leadership and administration. Native Counselling Services offers counselling to native people coming before the courts, and has a training program for such counsellors and court workers. Altogether, the Native Secretariat of the Alberta government has listed twenty-one such organizations. Much of their funding comes through the Native Secretariat. Prior to 1979–80, grants to the major organizations were identified in government estimates of expenditure—in 1978–79, for instance, the Native Friendship Centres received $200,100, and the Voice of Alberta Native Women received $55,000. Since 1979–80, however, the estimates show only one item for $1,028,000 under "assistance to native organizations." Funding was thenceforth provided on a project basis.

The impression is that Alberta government funding in this field is tied relatively less to vocational training and manpower development, and more to cultural affairs, than is federal government funding. The federal government's funding for cultural education, either direct from Ottawa or through the district officers, is small compared with funds for vocationally oriented training.

Quebec

The White Paper published by the Minister of State for Cultural Affairs in 1978 estimates that including non-status Indians and Metis, there are an estimated 60,000 people of Indian blood in Quebec, and 4,500 Inuit, in respect of whom the term *autochtones* (indigenous people) is used as a general classification, possibly because the term sometime used, Amerindian, would seem to exclude the Inuit. Though the Department of Indian and Northern Affairs is concerned with both Indians and Inuit, the two peoples see themselves clearly separate, with their own cultures and needs. This separateness is reinforced geographically, in that the Inuit all live in fourteen communities along the coast of northern Quebec, and the majority of Indians live in the central and southern parts.

Whereas in Alberta the one important division in terms of native organizations is between the Indians and Metis, a division which is reinforced by differing federal and provincial government jurisdictional responsibilities, in Quebec the main division is between the Indians and Inuit, and both stand in the same relationship to the federal government.

The federal government accepts responsibility for education among the two main native peoples of Quebec under section 91(24) of the British North America Act. This extends to adult education. However, in section 93 of the Act, the Quebec government also has an interest in adult education, and in recent years when feelings of Quebec nationalism and autonomy have been growing, the provincial government has shown increasing activity in this field. In the early 1960s, under the Lesage regime, Quebec government activity in northern Quebec began in earnest. In 1963 the Directorate-General of New Quebec was set up to provide schools and other services.

In his 1978 White Paper, the Minister of State for Cultural Affairs makes special reference to the responsibilities of the Quebec government in regard to the autochtones, at the same time taking a dig at the record of the federal government: "We find ourselves faced with a sort of political limbo to which the federal government, which has jurisdiction under the Canadian constitution, has finally condemned the indigenous peoples" (Ministère d'Etat, 1978:86). The White Paper states three principles influencing the Quebec government's stance: the native people should decide on their development through free discussion of their social and cultural status; the native people should not, however, be left to their own resources, but should, as citizens of Quebec, be able to count on the support of the "State of Quebec;" the native people have the responsibility to create institutions and strategies needed for their own development (Ibid.:89–90). In 1978 the Quebec government created a secretariat for government activities among Amerindians and Inuit (S.A.G.M.A.I.) in the executive council office. This appears to be the equivalent of the Native Secretariat in Alberta, which also comes under the office of the executive council.

For some years there was a confusion of roles and responsibilities between the federal and Quebec governments, but more recently a more co-operative mode of operation has emerged. Involvement by the two levels of government in adult education for native people in the province is now co-ordinated by a Liaison Committee for Adult Education and Training for Indigenous People, based in Quebec City and comprising representatives from the Quebec Regional Office of the Department of Indian and Northern Affairs, the Canadian Employment and Immigration Commission, and the Quebec Ministries of Education (through the D.G.E.A.) and Labor. This liaison committee works with the Inuit and Indian Associations. Many of the programs are held in schools coming under the Quebec school-boards and financed by the Quebec government.

One event that has affected the whole picture is the James Bay Agreement, which covers the vast hydro-power project in the northern part of the province. The preparation for and negotiation of the agreement, and its final conclusion, has had important repercussions among the two native peoples. The James Bay and Northern Quebec Agreement was signed in 1976 by the governments of Canada and Quebec, Hydro Quebec, the James Bay Development and Energy Corporation, the Grand Council of the Crees (Quebec), and the Northern Quebec Inuit Association.

Status Indians in Quebec

Unlike in Alberta, where the Indian Association of Alberta represents all the status Indians, the Indians of Quebec have a number of organizations. They belong to two broad linguistic groupings. The Algonquin group includes: the Cree who live in the James Bay Region; the Naskapi, a small tribe living in Labrador and eastern Quebec; and the Montagnais, Attikameks, Abenakis, Algonquin, and Mic Macs, who live in the south (the Mic Macs spread to the Gaspé Peninsula and the Maritimes). The Iroquois grouping, of Mohawks and Hurons, live in the region south of the St. Lawrence and extend into the U.S. In the years before 1974 all these groups came together in the Indians of Quebec Association, and therefore formed a reasonably common front in terms of demands for education and development. The beginning of the planning and negotiations around the

James Bay project revealed the more particular interests of some of these sub-groups. In 1974 the Cree left the Indians of Quebec Association and formed the Grand Council of the Cree, in preparation for negotiating their proper rights as part of the proposed project, which threatened to impinge heavily on their traditional lifestyle and economy. This left the southern group in some disarray, some of which appears to arise from the preoccupation of each group with the question of land claims, and the lack of consensus about what these claims should contain. The process of the James Bay negotiations, and its outcome in terms of the rights established for the northern Cree, Naskapi, and Inuit, gave an impetus to the aspirations of the southern groups, but there is not unanimity about the benefits of that agreement. There are now a number of associations of Indian people: the Grand Council of the Cree; the Council of Attikameks; the Council of Algonquin; and the Conference of Indians of Quebec (Mohawk, Abenaki, Huron, and Mic Mac).

A look at the James Bay Agreement will indicate that the conditions now enjoyed by the Cree are conditions to which other groups can aspire. The agreement set up a Cree school-board, which, subject to the Quebec Education Act, has exclusive responsibility for elementary, secondary, and adult education among the Cree in the region covered by the agreement. The board comprises one commissioner from each of the eight Cree communities in the region and one designated by the Grand Council. Its role is to make agreements for educational purposes with other groups and with the federal government for programs not available through the Quebec government; develop courses, books, and materials in native literature and culture; establish training courses for teachers (native and non-native); and hire community education administrators. Funding for the board and its operations is provided in the proportion of 75 percent from the federal government and 25 percent from Quebec (Department of Indian and Northern Affairs, 1976).

A number of services relating broadly to adult education and development have been set up under the agreement. The James Bay Native Development Corporation has a responsibility for the general economic well-being of the Crees, and among its activities is the sponsoring of training programs in trapping, traditionally the mainstay of their economy, and particularly in fur grading, marketing, and depot management. It also sponsors the Cree Native Arts and Crafts Association. The Joint Economic and Community Development Committee, with nine members (five Cree, two federal government, and two Quebec government), reviews and makes recommendations on programs of vocational upgrading, and other training, and examines and makes recommendations on community development programs. Subject to financial limitations and mutually acceptable priorities, the federal and Quebec governments will fund community centres in each Cree community, an economic development agent to provide expert business consultation, and a community affairs service, including community workers. The two governments undertake to advise the native authorities when proposing field studies as part of research projects affecting cultural and social life of the native people.

The other three Indian associations work more directly with the two governments and regional school-boards in their areas. Requests and proposals for courses are generated locally, at the band level, and are considered by local committees including representatives of the associations and the local Adult Education Counsellor of the Department of Indian and Northern Affairs. In the Attikamek and Algonquin Councils there are regional committees for adult education, which consider the proposals before forwarding them to the liaison committee in Quebec. In the Conference of Indians (Mohawk, Abenaki, Huron, and Mic Mac) there is no such regional committee and proposals go to the liaison committee through officials of the department. The liaison committee then purchases the necessary courses from the school-boards in the region. In 1978–79 the committee purchased 40,000 student days of adult basic education (adult literacy and basic academic courses) and 25,000 student days of vocational education. The education courses requested and offered to native people under these arrangements are of four main types: part-time general education; vocational training and popular education; training for band and other officials; training in fire-fighting. The part-time courses, of which there were 55 with 886 students in 1977–78, are funded in three ways: entirely by regional school-boards, that is the Quebec government; jointly by provincial vocational training commissions, school-boards, and the Department of Indian and Northern Affairs, that is, by the Quebec and federal governments; and entirely by the department, or the federal government alone. Full-time courses, of which there were 56 with 812 students in 1977–78, are all vocationally oriented and funded by Canada Manpower, but are organized jointly by school-boards and by the department. The band training, comprising 29 courses with 436 students in 1977–78, comes under the department and is co-ordinated at the Quebec Regional level; it covers such subjects as local government administration, management, economic development, school affairs, housing, social services, and cultural affairs. The fire-fighting program, comprising eight courses with 82 students in 1977–78, is for volunteers and regular firemen in the native communities, and is an important element in native life, in view of the frequency of large forest fires.

From this it is clear that the education programs requested of and funded by government are mainly utilitarian in nature, designed to help native people cope better with their changing milieu by acquiring knowledge and skills related to economic and administrative affairs. This is particularly so in the full-time programs, though in some districts, such as Pointe-Bleu and Sept-Iles, there are a number of courses in literacy, family affairs, and adult basic education. In the part-time programs there is a higher proportion of general interest and developmental courses, such as French language, English and native languages, yoga, nutrition, cooking, and sewing, than is the case in Alberta.

In the administrative procedures drawn up for school-boards, in respect of education for Indian people, the D.G.E.A. of Quebec declares that "we must take into account their particular characteristics, such as their ways of living, their environment, their mother tongue and their choice of a second language, their collective spirit, the essence of their culture, their rhythm of learning, etc." (D.G.E.A. 1978–78). It is not yet clear to what extent or how the efforts of the Secrétariat des Activités Gouvernementales en Milieu Amérindien et Inuit, (S.A.G.M.A.I.), will make an impression in this area of cultural development but the thrust of such development is not through the educational institutions but through the federal program for cultural centres, referred to in the discussion of the Alberta situation.

The first venture as an Indian cultural/educational centre in Quebec had a short history similar to that of the Indian Education Centre in Alberta, though the Quebec venture did establish a physical centre and accepted students for a few years. In 1972, with the backing of the Indians of Quebec Association and the Northern Quebec Inuit

Association, Manitou Community College was started at La Makaza, a former Canadian Forces base north of Montreal. It was a CEGEP in the Quebec system, but with a particular objective of helping preserve and strengthen Indian culture and identity. Its college-level courses were accredited by two CEGEPs in Montreal—Dawson College and Ahuntsic College— and it ran a training program for teachers of native children accredited by the University of Quebec. It accepted native students from inside and outside Quebec, the mainly social science courses had a strong native emphasis, and the staff encouraged the growth of Indian culture and values. Sponsors and staff saw Manitou Community College as an element in the move toward Indian control of Indian education (Rice, 1975).

The main funding for the college came from the federal government cultural educational program. In 1975 the government notified the college that it should not accept students beyond May 1976, and suggested that the cost of maintaining the college in the existing facilities was prohibitive. It also introduced a provision that native persons must, in most cases, receive their post-secondary education at an institution close to their homes, and since most of the Manitou College students were from outside Quebec, this meant cutting the student body by over a half (C.A.S.N.P. Bulletin, 1975). Despite bitter protests by staff and students, the college was closed in 1976. One of the staff alleged that the federal department was afraid of the growth of Indian culture and values, that it did not really wish to see Indian people gaining strength by working together for themselves. We have seen from the Alberta account that the federal government's reasoning might be that the policy of decentralization implicit in and pursuant to the acceptance of the Indian control of Indian education principle meant an allocation of funding and major control to the bands, rather than to one or a few provincial centres such as Manitiou Community College. These two views again reflect, as in Alberta, the tension between two forces among the Indian people themselves: on the one hand a need for the assertion of a shared, collective native culture and a political voice expressing the rights of people in that culture at the regional and national levels; and on the other hand a narrower identification of people with their local bands, and the influence of older, more traditional, and often more conservative, leaders at that level.

At any rate, since that time, nine Indian cultural centres have been established in Quebec, with direct funding from Ottawa amounting to $525,157 in 1979, according the the Department of Indian and Northern Affairs. The largest centres were the Kan'ien'keha: ka otiokwa serving the Mohawks of Caughnawaga, the Institut Educatif et Culturel serving the Attikamek Montagnais, the Restigouche Institute of Cultural Education serving the Mic Mac, and the Centre Culturel et Educatif serving the Huron. Typically the centres were engaged in research into language and customs, applying that research in teaching children and adults, training for and promoting arts and crafts, organizing teachers' workshops, and operating museums. The Mohawk Centre proposed for 1979–80 the establishment of a community television station to broadcast on the Caughnawaga Reserve.

Metis in Quebec

As indicated in the section on the Metis in Alberta, the Metis of Quebec have not been prominent as a group asserting their particular interests. They do not have any identified or recognized settlements, and have been grouped with the Indian people. The Laurentian Alliance of Metis and Non-Status Indians has been in existence only since 1974, and is still at an early stage of re-grouping the Metis people to safeguard and reconstruct their culture, and to prepare land claims. But the Quebec Metis' main concern is that they should be recognized as an integral part of the native people of Canada and not be defined as otherwise by the Indian Act (Boudrias, 1979).

Inuit of Quebec

Among the Inuit, the formation of co-operatives was the earliest stage of uniting the people of the fourteen settlements strung along the northern coast. The first co-operative began in 1954 at Povungnituk, and by 1974 there were about forty in the region, in such activities as fishing, handicrafts, saw milling, hunting, and house building. These co-operatives received help and advice from the federal government, the Caisse Populaire Movement of Quebec, the Co-operative Union of Canada, and from locally based Oblate priests. In 1967 the Federation of Co-ops of New Quebec was formed. This movement—as in Alberta and southern Quebec—provided in itself a process of adult education, and many of the present Inuit leaders received valuable experience and training in it (Crowe, 1974:190–91). The Federation of Co-ops was in effect the first Inuit political movement. Learning was not confined to administrative skills, but extended to the arts and crafts of printmaking, sculpture, ceramics, and leather work.

Because of the relatively late coming of the Quebec government, after many years of the influence of the federal government, the Hudson's Bay Company, and the Anglican Church missions, the dominant second language of the Inuit has been English. Because of this, many Inuit people did not take well to French language legislation of the Quebec government, nor to the increasing interest on the part of the Quebec government in providing administrative and educational services. There is evidence that some Inuit preferred to relate to and take advantage of facilities offered by the federal authorities in Ottawa. On the other hand, a few Inuit were attracted to Quebec and the French language because they interpreted the nationalist, independent movement in Quebec as promising a sympathetic ear to their own aspirations of regional autonomy. In recent years there have been expressions of support for the natives of Quebec on the part of the Quebec Teachers' Federation (Crowe, 1974:205–6) and in the form of resolutions at the P.Q. Congresses (The Alliance, 1979:2).

The negotiations leading to the James Bay Agreement caused a split among the Quebec Inuit, between those in favor of the settlement and those against it. In the negotiations the Inuit were represented by the Northern Quebec Inuit Association, whose stance was opposed by some of the members of the Federation of Co-operatives, particularly from the settlements of Povungnituk, Ivujivik, and Sugluk. When the agreement was eventually signed the dissentients formed a new organization, Inagtigut Tunngavinga Nunaminni (I.T.N.) (Hill and Valaskakis, 1979:1.13).

Under the terms of the agreement the Inuit, like the Cree, were given the authority to establish their own school-board, the Kativik School-Board, to cover the territory north of the fifty-fifth parallel excepting the Cree settlement of Great Whale River, which comes under the Cree School-Board. Subject to the conditions of the

Quebec School Act, it has responsibility for elementary, secondary, and adult education (Department of Indian and Northern Affairs, 1976). The council of the board comprises one representative of each of the municipalities in the territory and one representative of the regional government responsible for the whole area. In each municipality there is a parents' committee to advise the principal of the school. The board may, for educational purposes, enter into agreements with the federal government, or with any other school-board, education institutions, or individual. It may establish a curriculum development centre to select courses, books, and materials appropriate to the native people. The funding for the school-board is provided in the proportions of 75 percent from the Quebec government and 25 percent from the federal government, which is the opposite of the position in the Cree area, where 75 percent is from the federal government and 25 percent from the Quebec government.

With regard to broader economic and social development, a series of Native Economic Development Programs was established. Such programs would continue to be funded as previously by the federal and Quebec governments, but would be administered wherever possible by the regional government and municipalities. The regional government is responsible for establishing and maintaining hunter, fisherman, and trapper training programs, and for making proposals to the federal and Quebec governments for training programs and facilities for Inuit people, to enable them to qualify for jobs created by existing and planned developments in the territory. To co-ordinate the federal and provincial manpower training efforts, an interim joint committee was formed, which was eventually due to hand over responsibility to the regional government. A particular concern was to promote the training of Inuit people for government work within the territory, including work in federal and provincial government services.

As with the Indian people, the emphasis in formal adult education and training programs for Inuit people is on utilitarian skills and knowledge—predominantly training for improved performance in traditional economic pursuits or new administrative and technical occupations. For instance, ten courses with 134 students were mounted in 1977–78 in Arctic Quebec through the Regional Liaison Committee in Quebec City; they covered crafts, telephone linesmen training, instructions for school-board members and officials, and fire-fighting. Other training in new technical occupations is provided by the Vocational Education Section of the federal Indian affairs department in Ottawa. This service has a group of Inuit education and social counsellors, and an education centre in Ottawa, to which Inuit students come from the Northwest Territories and Northern Quebec (despite the facilities offered by the Quebec government). The centre responds to demands from the native organizations and its field staff, and offers courses that are not available readily elsewhere, such as typing and typewriter repairs. It purchases some courses from other community colleges, such as Algonquin College in Ottawa and Manitou College in Quebec while it existed. At a higher level of expertise this section of the department has negotiated a university-level program in business management to be offered by the University of Regina through the Anik B satellite, and courses in television technology and production.

This introduces the question of education and cultural development by long-distance methods. For many years the CBC has transmitted to the Inuit people programs related to their culture and development; it has a staff of Inuit broadcasters based at Montreal. But there was dissatisfaction with this service among the Inuit and in 1972 the Northern Quebec Inuit Association (N.Q.I.A.) appointed Mr. Josepi Padlayat to enquire into the state of communications in Northern Quebec Inuit settlements. In 1973 Mr. Padlayat intervened in C.R.T.C. hearings into a CBC application to operate Anik-fed T.V. stations in Fort Chimo and Great Whale River. His case was that the CBC radio coverage had been inadequate, the communities had not been consulted, and no local programming was planned. What many Inuit wanted was a community-based communications system. In 1975 the Tagramiut Nipingat Inc. (T.N.I.) was formed as a native communications society, on the lines of the A.N.C.S. in Alberta. It was not affiliated with the N.Q.I.A., in order that it should be seen to be neutral in the political conflict between the N.Q.I.A. and the I.T.N., and to be available to all parties (Hill and Valaskakis, 1979: 1.11–1.13).

Five Inuit communities had access to the telephone through the Anik B satellite, and the Hermes satellite provided further transmissions in socially related subjects such as health care. The Tagramiut

Nipingat Inc. proposed that the system be extended to put eight northern communities in touch with one another through a programming unit at Sugluk. There should be radio telephone lines for intercommunity broadcasting, a radio program production centre in Sugluk, intercommunity programming, and short-wave programming fed in from Montreal. An evaluation of the project, which was called Project Naalakvik, in 1978-79 indicated that these objectives were being met. The project had the support of the native people; it provided news and general reports and information to help people make decisions affecting their local affairs; it had created an interactive communications system between communities; and it was helping the cultural development and political unity of the Inuit (Ibid.: SX.1-18). The latter outcome resulted from the ability of T.N.I. to act as a link between the N.Q.I.A. (now absorbed into the Makivik Corporation) and the I.T.N., in that they were each able to use the system to discuss their differences and enable the community people to be aware of and more sensitive to the complex problems arising from the James Bay Agreement. The frequency of the transmission of intercommunity discussions, under a number of broad headings, gives an idea of the priorities of interest among the contributors and listeners. The headings are as follows, with the percentages of time devoted to them (Ibid., 1979 : 2.23):

Economic Matters	23.7%
Land Claims	9.1%
Legal Matters	6.5%
Cultural Preservation	6.0%
Land Use	5.6%
Health	5.3%
Education	4.3%
Other (including Political)	20.5%

Under Economic Matters are included topics such as the traditional economy, Inuit control of enterprises, new co-operatives, and calls for unity; the people bring considerable cultural concerns to this subject. The increase in activity under this project appears to have a livening effect on community affairs; in the communities linked through the Hermes satellite there are active community councils, co-

operatives, school committees, women's auxiliaries, and radio committees. Some of the organizations that made use of the project were
the Makivik Corporation, the Federation of Co-operatives, I.T.N.,
the Quebec Government, the churches, N.Q.I.A. Cultural Teachers,
the Women's Auxiliary, and the Kativik School-Board. The project
appears, therefore, to have been an important element in the total life
of these communities, and has indicated the usefulness of such a
communications system in the general advancement of a developing
region.

There is one cultural/educational centre among the Quebec
Inuit, under the Ottawa-based program. It is attached to the Kativik
School-Board and attracted, in 1979–80, federal funding of $122,175.
Besides preparing and publishing the history of the Inuit communi-
ties and a geography book, it is involved in using the satellite com-
munications program to disseminate cultural material.

Conclusions

The ambiguities of life for the native peoples of Canada in a society
dominated by forms and values different from their own are reflected
in the patterns of adult education in Alberta and Quebec.

Extensive resource development shapes the content, structure, and
motivation of community development in Alberta, and the main
thrust of government-supported activities is to adapt native people
directly or indirectly to the demands of the resource development
economy. The account of adult education activities among native
people in Alberta supports this observation; insofar as these activities
depend on government funding and are carried out in government institutions they are overwhelmingly work-oriented, and much of the
training, at any rate in the north, is in the resource industries of
timber and oil. The observation is true in the broader sense that the
whole society of Alberta is shaped by the economy of resource exploitation, and the main thrust of adult education among native people is to help them adapt to that society, either as workers in the main
economic enterprises or as administrators, leaders, and members of

communities that are having to come to terms with the dominant culture. Conformity with norms of white society is an underlying purpose. For instance, the training program under the government's Opportunity Corps in the Lesser Slave Lake area, which is referred to in Chapter 5, has been characterized by a field worker in the area as a kind of behavior modification process whereby punctuality, good grooming, and "positive attitude" are rewarded (Davis, 1979).

The situation in Quebec can be said to be similar, insofar as the huge resource development project of the James Bay region in the 1970s has dominated the thinking of governments and of native people directly involved and has influenced the thoughts of the other native groups. The provisions of the James Bay Agreement affect the Cree and Inuit in two ways related to education. First, it provides, through the Development Corporation and Joint Economic and Community Development Committees in Cree Territory, and through the Regional Government in Inuit Territory, for the "full range of training programs or facilities they require in order to qualify for jobs created by existing or planned developments." It sets up procedures for the building and maintenance of skills in the more traditional occupations of hunting, trapping, and fishing. Secondly, it gives the Cree and Inuit a good deal of autonomy in education at all levels including adult education. This agreement sets a standard for the other Indian groups in their preparation of claims based on aboriginal rights and their desire to share in modern development. The native people, in other words, have shown that they wish to share in the development of their lands by learning the skills related to that development.

But in counterpoint to this theme, and partly as a reaction to it, there has grown, in both provinces, a greater self-consciousness, and a concern for their own native culture. Among the Inuit this has manifested itself in a political split between those in favor of the James Bay Agreement and those against. In both provinces there are groups pulling in different ways, debating the matter among themselves—as, for instance, in the case of a group of native students at a University of Alberta symposium in 1978. One comment made to a Senate Task Force on Native Students at that university in 1978 was that some native students do not wish to be identified as native (University of Alberta Senate, 1978:34). In terms of adult education this counter-trend shows itself in the activities of cultural education centres: research into native history, recording that research in writing, videotapes, audiotapes, and film, and the articulation of that history among native and non-native groups. While public expenditures and the proportion of culture-oriented programs to work-oriented programs, weighs heavily in favor of the latter, an evaluation of the cultural/educational centres program in 1979 found that it had made a great deal of impact on the Indian and Inuit communities served by it. Indian and Inuit leaders viewed it as being important to their people. There had also been some impact on non-native groups in the form of curriculum materials, teacher training, and the provision of resources for teaching. The evaluators recommended that native people should have more input into the overall program, which should receive higher priority within the federal department – and ideally even placed outside the department, under a National Association of Cultural/Educational Centres.

One of the interesting things about the developments outlined above is the way that the most modern communications technology has been taken farther in the service of cultural education among native peoples, on their initiative, than it has by any other Canadian group. This stems from the geographical situation and needs of a large part of the native population, but it is, nevertheless, an interesting commentary on the integration of one culture with another, of the use of the technology of one culture in the interest of the values of another, in a deliberate and compensatory way to counteract the same technology's adverse effects. The A.N.C.S. in Alberta and the T.N.I. in Quebec are gaining and providing valuable experience in the use of such technology in popular education.

References

The Alliance Journal. 1979. "Péquistes Recognize Strong Native Rights Within Sovereignty Association." Val D'Or: Laurentian Alliance of Metis and Non-Status Indians Inc.

Boudrias, R. 1979. "Speaking For His People." *Monchanin Journal*, vol. XII, no. 2, issue 63.

Canadian Association in Support of Native Peoples (C.A.S.N.P.). 1975. "Manitou College." *C.A.S.N.P. Bulletin*, vol. 16, no. 4 (December 1975).

Crowe, K.J. 1974. *A History of the Original Peoples of Northern Canada*. Montreal: McGill-Queeen's University Press.

Cumming, P.A. and Michenberg, N.H., eds. 1972. *Native Rights in Canada*. Toronto: Indian-Eskimo Association of Canada.

Davis, M. 1979. "Education for Local Control: A Curriculum Development Project in Community Development." M.A. thesis, University of Alberta.

Department of Indian and Northern Affairs. 1976. *The James Bay and Northern Quebec Agreement*. Ottawa: Department of Indian and Northern Affairs.

Directeur Générale d'Education des Adultes. 1977–78. *Procédures Administratives et Renseignements Pédagogiques a l'Usage des Commissions Scolaires et Régionales*. Quebec: Ministère de l'Education.

Harrison, W.G. 1977. *A Survey of Indian Education in Five Alberta Community Colleges*. Edmonton: Department of Indian and Northern Affairs.

Hill, C.W. and Valaskakis, C.G. 1979. *An Assessment of Project Naalakvik I*. Ottawa: Tagramuit Nipingat Inc.

Laplante, R. 1979. "Introduction." *Monchanin Journal*, vol. XII, no. 2, issue 63.

Ministre d'Etat au Développement Culturel. 1978. *La Politique Québecoise du Développement Culturel*. Quebec: Editeur Officiel.

Rice, K. 1975. "First Graduates of Manitou's Amerindian Program." *Native Perspectives*, vol. 1, no. 11 (August 1975).

University of Alberta Senate. 1978. *Report of the Task Force on Native Students*. Edmonton: University of Alberta.

Weitz, J., ed. 1972. *Indian Control of Indian Education*. Ottawa: National Indian Brotherhood.

8

Agricultural
Organizations

Alberta

Agricultural organizations have been active in adult education in Alberta since before World War I. Both the United Farmers of Alberta (U.F.A.), which formed the government of the province from 1922 to 1935, and its counterpart, the United Farm Women of Alberta (U.F.W.A.), were leaders in rural development, by nature of their very being. By 1915 they had about 30,000 members, and they were involving people in almost every locality in the process of organization and political discussion, which in itself was an educational process. They also ran more formal education programs in such matters as bank credit, interest rates, health, and legislation—especially legislation affecting the rights of women (Cameron, 1977:18). Cameron (later to become Senator Cameron) writes of his own experience in the early 1920s as president of the Junior Branch of the U.F.A.—which accepted persons up to the age of 26 as members—and which also had its own active educational program (Ibid.:19). So in these relatively early years of the province's history there began a tradition of rural education at the grass roots level in matters social and political, as well as agricultural.

An important feature of agricultural education in the province has been, and is, the co-operation of the farm organizations with the Extension Branch of the Department of Agriculture, and with the University of Alberta, particularly its Department (now Faculty) of Extension. The Department of Agriculture has been active in agricultural extension since the early days of the century, and a Department of Extension was established by the University in 1912, and in its early years, up to World War II, it worked almost exclusively in rural areas.

This is primarily an account of the work of the agricultural organizations, but since they co-operate so much with these two institutions, it illumines the account a little to explain the relationships between the latter. These relationships revolve around two activities: agricultural extension in the field, and in the publication of reports and bulletins for the agricultural industry. Regarding the first of these, in 1915 the Department of Agriculture suggested that the university set up a provincial agricultural extension service, on the lines of the Co-operative Extension Service in the United States. The university declined to do so, so the Department of Agriculture began to appoint its own district agriculturalists, and later its own district home economists. Ever since then, there have been periods and episodes of confusion about the respective roles of the two institutions in the minds of the farmers, the members of the university faculty, and Department of Agriculture personnel. While the latter have been the first and major points of contact in the field, working with farmers on basic production problems, they are not able to provide the latest and more specialized information that results from university research, so the Faculty of Agriculture staff are sought out for this purpose. (The University of Alberta is the only one in the province with a Faculty of Agriculture.) These staff, in turn, are not sure where agricultural extension work fits into the university's priorities with regard to academic rewards and advancement, but the evidence indicates that it is fairly low in priority. Meanwhile, the Department of Extension played a third, at times almost independent, role in arranging lectures, short courses, and other learning occasions. For instance, since 1950, it has conducted Leadership Techniques and Rural Leadership courses at the Banff Centre in conjunction with the wheat pools, agricultural co-operatives, and farm unions. At times it appears to have shown an aggressiveness and a desire to control that has aggravated relationships between all parties.

The second of the two activities around which revolve relationships between the university and the Department of Agriculture has been with the publication of agriculture bulletins and reports. An Agriculture Publications Committee has been in existence at the university since 1922, combining the academic input of the Faculty of Agriculture and the administrative and distributive work of the Department of Extension (the secretary has always been a member of the Department of Extension). Again, over the years there have been conflicts between the university and the Alberta Department of Agriculture about these publications, each side accusing the other of a lack of understanding of their concerns. One dilemma has been the need, as seen by the academics, to produce properly respectable academic papers and the need, as seen by the Department of Agriculture, to produce information in a form readable by and interesting to lay farmers. There have been accusations of plagiarism against government officials.

In the last decade or so, all these relationships appear to have improved and become clearer and more stabilized. Modes of co-operation and complementary activity have superseded attitudes of competition and acrimony. An Extension Committee of the Faculty of Agriculture and Forestry now exists within the university, and two members of the Faculty of Extension—one of whom serves as secretary—are on that committee. It has absorbed the functions of the former publications committee. In the broader sphere there has, since 1965, been an Alberta Agriculture Co-ordinating Committee, with a number of subcommittees, one of which is the Agricultural Extension and Rural Extension Advisory Committee, which advises the provincial Departments of Agriculture and Advanced Education and Manpower, and which includes in its membership the University of Alberta and the public colleges that offer agricultural programs, for example, Lethbridge, Lakeland, Olds, and Fairview colleges (the last three of these being former agriculture colleges.

The present *modus operandi* is that the district agriculturalists and home economists have a role in education having to do with day-to-day production and farm and home management. Members of the university's Faculty of Agriculture and Forestry have a role in education at a higher level of professional and technical concern, serving professionals in the field, top level and large farm innovators, and leaders in rural communities and farm organizations. The Faculty of

Extension has a role in planning and providing learning experiences of various sorts, from a professional adult education and extension point of view and in conjunction with other faculty and other agencies, and in distributing the quarterly *Agriculture and Forestry Bulletin* and other reports.

This is an important part of the framework in which the adult education activities of agricultural organizations take place. To a greater or lesser extent they use the services of the Department of Agriculture, both district and head office staff, and of the University of Alberta, both the Faculty of Extension and the Faculty of Agriculture and Forestry.

There are, in general terms, two types of agricultural education: the first addresses problems of production and farm and home management, and the second addresses problems of rural development and social change that affect agricultural life. The first has been carried out under the auspices of producer organizations that emerged in the early years, such as the Alberta Livestock Co-operative, the Alberta Wheat Pool, and United Grain Growers, and their successors. For example, the Western Stock Growers Association sponsored an annual cattlemen's short course at the Banff Centre for some years, and the Holstein-Friesian Association of Canada holds field trips and short courses and issues publications giving practical information (Farm and Ranch Management Consultants Limited, 1970:7.4). The Alberta Wheat Pool, as another example, has an internal program for its own members in technicalities of marketing, accounting, and so forth.

Most of the actual courses, as distinct from the preparation of internal information bulletins, in-service courses for association members, and individual services to members, are arranged in conjunction with other agencies. For example, the annual cattlemen's short course referred to above was administered by the University of Alberta Faculty of Extension, which also continues to administer an annual Feed Industry Conference for the Alberta Division of the Canadian Feed Manufacturers' Association, and a number of other such conferences and seminars.

A consultants' survey of this whole field in 1970 points out that some of these activities, particularly those carried out by agri-businesses, tend to look primarily at short-term problems as they affect profits of the businesses, while relatively few address long-term growth and the general improvement of society (Farm and Ranch Management Consultants, 1970: chap. 8). Furthermore, some of the grass roots needs expressed by farmers and farm service businesses are sometimes at variance with the way agriculture is or should be developing—that is, a conflict between immediate individual perceptions of need and wider perceptions of economic and social need (Ibid.: chap. 5). This all leads to the need for the second type of education, a broader social kind, and requires the introduction of other resources and their co-ordination. And it is here that representative farm organizations such as Unifarm come into the picture.

Unifarm is the present form and title of a succession of farm organizations stretching from the 1920s, which at times amalgamated, and broke away, stirring discontent, and then amalgamated again, and so on. This very process is an illustration of the pulls and tensions between those forces in rural Alberta referred to in Chapter 4—a sense of individualism and intolerance of organization on the one hand, and a sense of co-operativism and social activism on the other. In 1948 the U.F.A. joined with the Alberta Farmers' Union (A.F.U.) to form the Farmers' Union of Alberta (F.U.A.). In 1970 the F.U.A. and the Alberta Federation of Agriculture formed Unifarm. Now the National Farmers' Union (N.F.U.) stands out in opposition. Alongside these have been the United Farm Women of Alberta, which is now called Women of Unifarm, and the Women's Institute, both of which have been active for decades in the education of women in particular matters related to the home, such as nutrition and household hygiene, and in education for wider social roles, such as women's rights, group organization, and committee work. While the Women's Institute reached the peak of its influence and activity many years ago, Women of Unifarm is still very active as a constituent body of Unifarm.

Unifarm has two types of member, individual and organizational. There are about 10,000 individual farmer members of Unifarm, but most Alberta farmers belong indirectly through their membership in a particular commodity association—cattle, poultry, and so on. While Unifarm has an advisory service for its members, for example, on income tax and surface rights, it leaves educational programs to the commodity associations, to the Rural Education and Development Association, which is referred to below, and to the University of Alberta and the Alberta Department of Agriculture.

As indicated in Chapter 4, agricultrual co-operatives have been active and important in rural Alberta since the early years of the century, and through the nation-wide Federated Co-ops Limited, which is based in Saskatoon, they have also come to constitute an important commercial enterprise in the form of consumer co-operatives in the towns, in competition with conventional commercial enterprises. They have been linked with the Credit Union movement and have branched out into a wide range of insurance businesses. While co-operatives provide their own instruction to members in various technical farm matters, the general view held by proponents of the co-operative movement is that the participation of the members in itself can be an important educational process. Some of the larger co-operatives in Alberta are the Alberta Wheat Pool, the United Farmers Co-operative, the Central Alberta Dairy Pool, and the Northern Alberta Dairy Pool.

In 1968 the Federation of Southern Alberta Indian Co-operatives was formed, aided in terms of funding and staffing by the other large co-operatives and supported by the Human Resources Development Authority. Eight co-operatives were formed within the federation, and from 1968 to 1972 the Farmers' Union and Co-operative Development Association provided an officer to help these co-operatives, an exercise which was funded by the government.

All these co-operative ventures are linked to the national co-operative movement through the Co-operative Union of Canada, and to the Co-operation College of Canada at Saskatoon, which is an important element in the co-operative education system, and of the adult education system as a whole. In 1959 representatives of the F.U.A. and the co-operatives formed a new organization to be aimed specifically at rural education and development—the Farmers' Union and Co-operative Development Association (F.U.C.D.A.). The Farm and Ranch Management Consultants' report of 1970 points out (pp. 7–13) that most farm organizations concerned themselves much more with the quantity of living than with the quality of living, and the F.U.C.D.A. (as well as the Women's Institute and the Women of Unifarm) was established in large part to create a balance. Here was a re-emergence of the spirit of the 1920s and 1930s, which had brought forward the U.F.A., the co-operatives, and the thrust of agrarian populism. The F.U.C.D.A., or as it is now called, the Rural Education and Development Association (R.E.D.A.), comprises Unifarm and all its constituent associations including Women of Unifarm and many of the co-operatives, the Federated Co-operatives Limited, the Co-operators (insurance) and the Credit Union Central. It has an executive director and a small staff of organizers and educational administrators, and pulls together the energies and resources of government departments, the universities, co-operatives, and farm organizations, in continuing education programs designed to improve the social and communal aspects of rural life. The objects of R.E.D.A. are: through continuing education programs to develop in rural people commitment to and responsibility for agriculture, co-operatives, and the quality of rural life; and to develop leadership and organizational expertise in and for farm, co-operative, and rural organizations in the agricultural community. It therefore offers a wide range of instruction and consultative services for individuals and for groups. For individuals the programs include workshops for presidents and secretaries, courses and seminars in leadership skills, agricultural policy workshops (both of these jointly with the University of Alberta Faculty of Extension), and a Rural Humanities and Issues Program. This last program is held at a residential centre in the foothills of the Rockies owned and operated by R.E.D.A.–Gold Eye Centre. This centre is used by R.E.D.A. for its own programs, and is available to other organizations for their own educational programs.

Examples of R.E.D.A.'s programs for groups are: lobbying skills, negotiation skills, parliamentary procedure, skills for rural living, and board of director workshops. It also conducts summer programs at Gold Eye Centre for young people covering aspects of co-operative and community life.

This short account indicates that though an important component of agricultural education and training in Alberta relates to skills and knowledge that help rural people in their capacities as producers and marketers, there remains in this sector of Alberta life a strong concern for social and community development, which stems from the early agrarian years of the province.

Quebec

Agricultural organizations in Quebec date from earlier times than in Alberta. Since the mid-nineteenth century there have been producer associations for horticulture, dairy products, and fruit (U.P.A., 1974: 15). And as in Alberta, there has been a parallel movement among farmers for the formation of organizations with a more social and broadly political aim. Unlike the emergence of the U.F.A. as a political party and a government in Alberta, the movement has never in Quebec found expression in an official political party. But the two streams of development – production and marketing-oriented, or economic, and social and human-oriented or political – have been a feature of the agricultural scene as in Alberta.

One major difference between the two provinces is the line between the numerically dominant francophone farmers and their associations, and the smaller number of anglophone farmers, who are found in clusters in different areas of the province. All Quebec farmers, including anglophones, have to belong to the Union des Producteurs Agricoles (U.P.A.), which is discussed below, but the anglophone farmers also have their own association, and they lean heavily on Macdonald College of McGill University for technical and socio-cultural support in English.

The main elements in the educational support system for Quebec farmers and their associations are: (i) the corps of government agronomists who come under the Quebec Ministry of Agriculture and provide at the local level the same kinds of technical farming advice as do the District Agriculturalists in Alberta; (ii) the Ministry of Agriculture and its information service, which publishes regular newsletters in French and English, and provides co-operation and funding to institutions providing educational programs; (iii) the CEGEPs, some of which offer courses related to farming, and among which can be included the two agricultural institutes at Ste-Hyacinthe and La Pocatière, which were referred to in Chapter 6 in the discussion of the role of the Quebec Department of Agriculture; and (iv) the Faculty of Agriculture and Food Sciences at Laval University, and Macdonald College (which is in effect the Faculty of Agriculture) at McGill University.

These elements serve the industry's needs for technical production and marketing knowledge and skills. As in Alberta, such needs at the local level are met mainly by the District Agriculturalists, while the two universities generally operate at the more professional level, offering courses both to farmers and to agronomists. Laval University's courses for farmers are advertised through the medium of the publications of the U.P.A., but registration and attendance are individual matters. Macdonald College has its own monthly English language journal as a means of communication with farmers and others, and it puts out a bilingual agricultural bulletin. It is also the centre for the Quebec Farmers' Association and Quebec Young Farmers, the two main rallying points for anglophone farmers in the province. The former has as its objectives the provision of information, educational and socio-cultural opportunities, and leadership to English-speaking people in rural areas, and it works in close co-operation with the U.P.A. and the Department of Agriculture in providing English information to rural people. The Quebec Young Farmers, like its francophone counterpart, Jeunes Cultivateurs du Québec, is the equivalent of the 4H clubs in western Canada, providing leadership to young rural people.

In fact, Macdonald College has a long record of service in agriculture in Quebec, mainly through its Extension Department, and not just in technical agricultural education. Nor is it purely English-speaking; its staff are bilingual, and it makes its services available to all farmers. In 1940–41 the first talks under the "Canadian Farm Problems" radio series were organized for Ontario and Quebec farmers by a group at Macdonald College, under W.H. Brittain, and this developed into the famous "National Farm Radio Forum," which dealt with major economic and social issues of the day (Faris, 1975: 98). Through the following years, up to 1954, these radio broadcasts, with 1,600 listening and discussion groups and about 30,000 participants across the country, focused on problems of distribution and marketing, leaving the more technical questions of production to the government services and colleges of agriculture. The series also raised matters of broader economic and social policy, which brought it and the CBC under pressure from the federal government during the 1940s (Sim, 1954).

Macdonald College also works with producer organizations such as the Holstein Association, and with farm implement businesses, in extending new technical knowledge to farmers. One of its largest and most important extension efforts is the Dairy Herd Analysis Program, under which 85 supervisors work in local areas—English-speaking and French-speaking— with 5,000 farmers in the upgrading of their production. Finally, the college offers a range of evening courses to the public in subjects related to agriculture or rural pursuits, such as hobby greenhouses, horse management, and bees and beekeeping (Macdonald College, 1976–77).

While the Quebec Farmers' Association has 500 active members, the Union des Producteurs Agricoles has over 40,000 members. All farmers in the province are obliged, under Law 64 of Quebec, to be members of U.P.A. This law permits the accreditation of only one professional association of agriculture producers in the province, and in 1972 70 percent of Quebec's registered producers voted in a referendum; 74 percent of the voters favored the U.P.A. as the accredited body, assuring it of an obligatory subscription from every farmer and contributions from specialized federations. The U.P.A. sees itself, and is seen, as a labor union rather than an agricultural association like Unifarm in Alberta. It sees its educational role as being related to the social and political needs of the farmers of Quebec, as a class.

The U.P.A. emerged in 1972 from a century or so of effort on the part of Quebec farmers to better their condition against the effects of changing markets, poor communications, lack of capital, and a provincial government intent on resisting the organization of rural people, even though this was not a party political movement. The aims of the first and abortive National Agricultural Union, formed in 1875, expressed what continues to be the thrust of the existing union: "to better the intellectual and material condition of the agricultural class, to lead farmers to act together in their own interests, to advance their cause and protect it by all possible means ... to work to bring about respect for, and to enforce, all laws and regulations for the benefit of agriculture" (U.P.A., 1974:6). Like those of the U.F.A. in Alberta, the leaders of this movement saw it as important to distinguish members of the agricultural class, independently of all considerations other than those relating to the profession (Ibid.: 8). They saw it as necessary to overcome the individualism of farmers, which they saw as being detrimental to their collective interests as a class.

In its early years the movement had strong support from the Roman Catholic church in Quebec, at all levels of the hierarchy, because the clergy were anxious to preserve the nature of rural Quebec life. One of the aims of the movement was "to work toward maintaining in the hearts of the rural population the traditions of Catholic French

Canada" (Ibid.: 8) and the name of the first successful association was the Union of Catholic Farmers. This went along with a concern, in those earlier years, for farmers as people: "In one sense, we can say that professional and union concerns gave way to the promotion of the family and of man as a rural person. There was the direct influence of the social doctrine of the Catholic church, in which the farmer is a person before being a producer. And even today this characteristic distinguishes the U.P.A. from other agricultural associations in Canada and elsewhere" (Ibid.: 10). Later, however, the emphasis on the syndicalism and professional interests increased, and in 1972 the name was changed from the Union des Cultivateurs Catholiques (U.C.C.) to the Union des Producteurs Agricoles (U.P.A.): "The professional association can at the same time be an educational and an economic instrument, to the general benefit of the health of society" (Ibid.: 11). During the time of the struggle of the U.C.C. and the U.P.A. for outside recognition and membership support, there was also the rise of the specialist agricultural organizations referred to earlier—related to such production as horticulture, forestry, dairy, and fruit products: "In fact, we can say that the association of farmers according to their special interests came about more spontaneously than that of farmers as a social class" (Ibid.: 15). The U.C.C. adapted program includes: the operation of the museum which became even more marked as agriculture became more diversified and specialized. The union started to take more interest in marketing and the rational organization of production and to the negotiation, on behalf of farmers, of better marketing arrangements. It became evident that the U.C.C. must work toward a syndicalist structure adapted to solving the particular problems of specialist groups, as well as, and parallel to, a structure related to general class needs, that is, an integration of specialist unions with a general professional union.

As in Alberta, the farm organizations received much of their impetus from the farmers, who felt that they were being exploited by the manipulators of the eastern Canadian markets, the big purchasers of agricultural produce. In Quebec the fight of the farmers was for a more equitable bargaining position *vis-à-vis* the large industrial users of produce, such as the Carnation milk enterprise. In forestry there were many small woodsmen and many employees who were dependent on the larger sawmill operations. In such circumstances the specialized federations had an important bargaining role on behalf of their members. In Quebec there was the added element of nationalism; the large entrepreneurs were also exclusively English-speaking, and the large enterprises were controlled by English-speaking persons, while the farmers, woodsmen, and woodworkers were predominantly French-speaking. These circumstances helped to explain both the syndicalist emphasis in the Quebec scene, and the evidence of some support in the present-day U.P.A. organization for nationalist and even separatist ideas.

In the 1960s, during the new wave of the quiet revolution, Premier Lasage was a supporter of the farmers and their efforts to confront the large companies who provided the outlets for agricultural products. This gave encouragement to the whole movement and strengthened the U.C.C. and the producer federations. The U.C.C. in particular led a campaign in which mass marches, demonstrations, and press conferences became important strategies. In other words, there was a move away from the earlier subordination of the economic to the traditional standpoint, an assertion of the general interest of Quebec farmers in the wide political area.

Today the U.P.A. comprises sixteen regional federations of farmers and twelve producer federations, for example, dairy products, poultry, pork, beef, and forestry products. The membership stands at over 40,000. With regard to educational activities, both the union and its affiliated federations have their own education and information services. Each local or grass root union is, in a sense, a study group as well as a union (U.P.A., 1974(b):9). Each regional federation has at least one education officer, who works with farmers; some of these come to the job with an agricultural background, and others from the social sciences. The emphasis of their work is on social and union education (éducation syndicale), some of it along the lines of the work of R.E.D.A. in Alberta. The Education and Information Service of the U.P.A. acts in a supplementary and support role to those field workers from the federations.

With regard to more formal types of instruction in socio-economic and leadership matters, the U.P.A. negotiates with the universities for workshops and seminars as required, in addition to acting as a channel for advertising to its members the more technically oriented courses offered by the universities. In common with the other

Quebec union organizations, the U.P.A. sees the universities as explicitly responsible for providing services to the community (Service à la Collectivité), that is, a third mission, alongside teaching and research. In light of this expectation, the U.P.A. has negotiated an agreement with the University of Sherbrooke to provide a program of instruction to members and officials according to needs and purposes defined and elaborated by the U.P.A. This is similar to agreements negotiated by the University of Quebec in Montreal and the University of Montreal with other union organizations (refer to Chapter 9) except that under the latter agreements the co-ordinators of the projects are employees of the universities, whereas under the U.P.A./Sherbrooke agreement the co-ordinator is an employee of the U.P.A. The agreement is financed through the University of Sherbrooke. The kinds of subjects covered in the project are: job evaluation, business organization, the Canadian Labor Code, and the economic situation as it affects agriculture.

As in Alberta, there has in Quebec been a longstanding relationship between the agricultural union – the U.C.C. and then the U.P.A. – and the co-operative and credit union movements, support for which has always been a feature of the activity of the Quebec church over the years. Just as the U.C.C. movement had a strong parish base in the earlier years, so did the co-operatives. The U.C.C. played an important role in the creation of caisses populaires – local savings banks or credit co-operatives – throughout the province, as well as producer co-operatives. One of the earliest of these was a cheese co-operative formed in 1910; a seed co-operative was formed in 1914, followed by others. In 1922 the Federated Co-operative of Quebec was formed, and in 1939 a Superior Council of Co-operation was formed and a chair in co-operation was established at Laval University. In the 1930s and 1940s the U.P.A. formed its own mutual life, fire, and automobile insurance societies. One of the interests people had in co-operatives stemmed from the view that co-operative education, as a participative process, was a good means of establishing economic and social democracy.

The caisse populaire movement has been one of the important features of rural (and now urban) life in Quebec. The fiirst caisse was formed by Alphonse Desjardins in 1900. His motives were not simply to help people save and generate financial capital, but also to raise their social aspirations. Desjardins and his colleagues were influenced by the Rochdale Co-operative movement in Britain, in its concern both for effective use of people's savings and for their broader social and mental development (Coté, 1963:105). Again, he was supported by the church, with its interest in keeping a viable rural society in Quebec.

Today the Quebec Federation of Caisses Populaires comprises ten regional unions, with 1,250 local caisses, and a total of 3.5 million members. It also includes five major insurance and trust companies. It has a permanent Commission on Education with a mandate to: set up training programs for employees and leaders in the movement; support any activity which promotes knowledge of the co-operative movement, and greater participation of members; and spread knowledge of co-operative thought for the promotion of co-operative democracy.

The federation also has a Human Resources Division, concerned with leadership, management, and employee training in such subjects as planning, decision-making, and interpersonal relations (La Fédération du Québec des Caisses Populaires Desjardins, 1978).

There are, then, some strong similarities in Alberta and Quebec with regard to adult education among rural people. In both provinces there is an awareness of the need for learning related both to the processes of production and marketing, that is, economic education, and to the quality of rural life in general, that is social education. In both, there is an infrastructure of government, college, and university services and facilities designed particularly for meeting the economic needs, and there is a system of producer organizations through which demands in this field can be articulated to those agencies. There is one interesting trend which appears to distinguish developments in the two provinces. In Alberta the early activities of farmers to organize themselves to improve the general conditions of rural life and to take a bigger part in political life in the broad sense, were in tune with, and supported by, government. In fact, the U.F.A. government in the 1920s and early 1930s arose out of that very movement. So the institutions, such as co-operatives, which are both socially oriented and production oriented, remain and are active in the province. They bring into the second half of the twentieth century a spirit of the first half, that is, a concern for social issues and the quality of life, which it is the role of R.E.D.A. to explore. But they become less congruent with the changing economic interests of the majority of the people in the province, with the managerial, technological, non-renewable resource development philosophy of the government, and therefore with the culture of the province. And as agriculture becomes increasingly business oriented, in larger non-family units, the thrust becomes weaker in the rural areas. In Quebec, on the other hand, the early efforts of rural people to organize met with continuous antagonism from the governments of the day, even up to the 1960s. This opposition thwarted a number of early attempts to form agricultural unions. Since the quiet revolution, however, there has been more sympathetic government reaction to such efforts. And there has been a growing coincidence between the nationalist, culture-sovereignty tendencies of the governments, and the strong French-Canadian nature of the farm organizations. Though individual farmers tend to remain traditionalist and individualist, a major aim of the U.C.C. and the U.P.A. has been to break down that individualism and engender a corporate, co-operative spirit. The strong francophone roots of the U.P.A., and its syndicalist nature, place it in the favor of strongly nationalist provincial governments. One result is that though English-speaking farmers belong to the U.P.A., and though the U.P.A. provide services to them in English, these farmers appear to seek their cultural and educational support increasingly from their own associations.

The emphasis in the specialist federations in Quebec is far more syndicalist than in Alberta; in fact, there is in Alberta no exact equivalent of these federations. This philosophy and practice in Quebec appears to be related to the nature of the industry, in that agriculture in Quebec is more mixed and relies more on provincial and local markets than is the general case in Alberta, where grain markets particularly are international. The Quebec producers, therefore, tend to be much more in direct relationship with the buyers of their produce—industrial milk and poultry enterprises, sawmill companies, and so on. So the area of confrontation is more immediate and discernible, lending itself to union organization on the part of the primary producers. The whole Quebec context therefore engenders a different perception of the need for education and action than does that of Alberta.

References

Cameron, D. 1977. *The Impossible Dream.* Banff: By the Author.

Coté, M. 1963. *Le Mouvement Coopératif Dans La Province du Québec.* Quebec: Faculté des Sciences Sociales, Université Laval.

Faris, R. 1975. *The Passionate Educators.* Toronto: Peter Martin.

Farm and Ranch Management Consultants Ltd. 1970. *Tradition and Transition.* Edmonton: Government of Alberta, Agriculture Department.

La Fédération du Québec des Caisses Populaires Desjardins. 1978. *Rapport Annuel.* Levis, Quebec: La Fédération du Québec des Caisses Populaires Desjardins.

Macdonald College. 1976–77. *Annual Report, Extension Department.* Ste. Anne de Bellevue: Macdonald College.

Sim, R.A. 1954. "Canada's Farm Radio Forum." In *Learning and Society,* ed. Kidd. Toronto: C.A.A.E., 1963.

Union des Producteurs Agricoles (U.P.A.). 1974(a). *Evolution Historique.* Montreal: U.P.A.

———. 1974(b). *Organization et Fonctionnement.* Montreal: U.P.A.

9

Trade Union Organizations

The term "union education" means education for union members about union matters: organization, negotiation, roles of shop stewards, and so on. "Workers' education" is more general in scope and is designed to enable workers to learn about the conduct and conditions of society (Dickinson and Verner, 1973). The study by Dickinson and Verner indicates that in Canada as a whole there was at that time relatively little activity in both these areas. Only 18 out of 112 national and international unions affiliated to the Canadian Labor Congress (C.L.C.) had education departments; these unions represented half of all the members of affiliated unions, since they were some of the larger unions in the country. A similar condition existed in local unions directly chartered to the C.L.C. And of what education there was, the great bulk was in union education, "tool" courses such as the study of collective agreements and shop steward training.

There was, according to the survey, more interest and activity at the level of provincial federations and local labor councils. The study found that the Alberta Federation of Labor (A.F.L.) had sponsored more programs than any other provincial federation in 1971, some conducted by the A.F.L. itself and others in co-operation with other labor bodies. Among the labor councils in each municipality, the Edmonton council was one of four with education budgets over one thousand dollars.

Significantly, the returns of survey instruments received by the researchers from Quebec unions were generally much lower than from other provinces, while no response to the survey was provided by the Quebec provincial federation—the only federation to fail to participate. And this begins to point to differences between the situation in Quebec and other provinces.

Before going on to look in more detail at the situations in Alberta and Quebec, we should outline the roles of the Canadian Labor Congress and the federal Department of Labor (Labor Canada) in this field. The C.L.C. has taken an active interest in union education since 1956. It has an Education Department with the second largest departmental budget in the congress, and a director of education. The Congress operated a National Labor College for many years, situated in Montreal and run in co-operation with McGill and Montreal universities. In 1975, as a result of the feasibility study instituted by the congress, it was decided to centralize the education function, including the college, in Ottawa, within a Labor Education and Studies Centre. One other contributing factor to this move appears to have been the lack of enthusiasm for what was seen as an almost "foreign" institution on the part of the Quebec Federation of Labor and the other central labor organizations in Quebec. Except with the Quebec region, the C.L.C.'s Education Department works with the provincial labor federations, through its five regional offices, one being the prairie region office in Regina.

The Dickinson and Verner report referred to above arose out of the work of an advisory committee convened in 1970 by the Education Director of the Congress, with members from the unions and universities, to advise the Congress about its role in education, both centrally and regionally. One of the report's recommendations was that the C.L.C. should sponsor a national conference on union education. This was done in co-operation with Labor Canada. The conference report concluded with a policy statement containing among others, the following points: labor education is essential not only for workers, but for the full development of a just and democratic society; the primary responsibility for worker's education and training lies with labor organizations; labor education is oriented toward collective action; the need for collaboration between trade unions and post-secondary institutions in the field of workers' education must be recognized. Universities and colleges, in collaboration with the labor movement, should devote substantially greater attention and effort to labor education; the co-operation between post-secondary institutions and trade unions requires specific organizational forms which reflect the distinctive characteristics of both parties; provisions for paid educational leave should be set up; the follow-up to the conference will take fully into account the two main linguistic communities in Canada (Pearl, 1975).

Two important points come out of this, in terms of procedures. First, the initiative and responsibility in this field lies with the labor organizations, and it is in accordance with their needs and purposes that any programs should be worked out with educational institutions. Second, in effect the special nature of conditions in Quebec was recognized.

Following that conference, the federal government, through Labor Canada, co-operated with the C.L.C. in formulating a new Financial Assistance Program for Labor Education. This program came into effect in 1977. Its objectives were "to encourage a better informed union membership and smoother collective bargaining, to help labor to participate more fully and knowledgeably in social and economic matters" (Labor Canada, 1977–78). A total amount of $10 million spread over five years, that is, $2 million per year, was to be distributed to three main categories of organizations: central labor organizations, post-secondary educational institutions, and independent unions and individual union members (as bursaries). The last of these three categories indicates an acknowledgment that there are many unions not affiliated to the C.L.C., representing some 25 percent of the total union membership in Canada (Dickinson, 1973). Some are affiliated to other central organizations such as the Confederation of National Trade Unions (Confédération des Syndicats Nationaux) in Quebec. The funds available through this program were to be allocated thus: one-half to the central organization (C.L.C.) in Ottawa, and the other half to be divided equally between the five regions, and administered by regional boards of the Labor Education and Studies Centre—with the exception that the Quebec region's funds would go direct to and be administered by the labor federations in that province. So each region had a total of $200,000 for the period of five years, and it could be used for specific projects submitted from the three categories of organizations referred to above. One example of the work of the Labor Education and Studies Centre in the provinces is a series of three courses offered in Alberta in September 1979 in instructor training, economics, and labor and politics.

Alberta

Out of a total population of 1,838,000 in 1976, the number of people in the labor force in Alberta in that year was 871,000 (Alberta Statistics, 1979). The total number of members of trade unions in 1976 was 180,172. So when we are considering the possible scope of education for workers, as a part of the total population, we have in mind almost half of the population (46 percent). But when we are considering the possible scope of union education as defined at the beginning of this section and as discussed above, we have in mind only 21 percent of that work-force. This is still a substantial number of adults, and programs that reached those people would be a considerable part of total adult education activities in the province.

Since we are looking at this from the point of view of the unions and union organizations, we should first see the ways in which unions are affiliated to central organizations. First, the main breakdown is into international unions, those with central offices and chief officers outside Canada (in effect, the U.S.), and national unions or autonomous and indigenous Canadian unions. Table 4 shows this breakdown and then the more detailed affiliations of the unions to larger organizations. We see that the membership is split roughly equally between international and national unions, while the number of branches of national unions is considerably larger than those of international unions. The indication, therefore, is that the average membership of the national union branches is lower than for the international unions. The largest affiliation is with the Canadian Labor

Table 4

Trade Union Membership and Affiliations in Alberta, 1976

| | International Unions | | National Unions | |
Affiliation	*Branches*	*Members*	*Branches*	*Members*
A.F.L./C.I.O./C.L.C.	235	78,495		
A.F.L./C.I.O. only	2	5,024		
C.L.C. only	8	2,155	173	61,008
P.S.A.C.			96	8,951
Unaffiliated	10	6,455	124	18,084
	255	92,129	393	88,043
	average: 361		average: 224	

Source: Statistics Canada. 1978. Cat. 71-202. *Labour Unions*. Ottawa: Ministry of Trade and Commerce.

Congress, either uniquely or with a secondary affiliation to the U.S.-based American Federation of Labor/Congress of Industrial Organizations. Ninety-six of the Canadian union branches are in the Public Service Alliance of Canada.

In Alberta the provincial affiliate of the C.L.C. is the Alberta Federation of Labor. Unions affiliated to the C.L.C. at the national level are affiliated at the provincial level to the A.F.L. which, like the C.L.C., has an Education Committee. At the next level downward, the Labor Councils in the bigger centres have education officers who provide courses on demand, and at the branch, or local, level some of the larger unions, such as the Alberta Union of Provincial Employees, the Canadian Union of Public Employees, and the Railway, Transport, and General Workers, have education or training officers. Some of the craft unions, such as the plumbers and pipe fitters, have training co-ordinators, but their responsibility is rather for trades training than union education.

The main efforts of the A.F.L. Education Committee have been the organization of an annual union education school at the Banff Centre, while the labor councils run week-end institutes. In all of these, as well as courses within the unions, the emphasis is on "tool" courses, those dealing with union management and matters of organization. There is little workers' education, or courses of a more general interest such as aspects of political economy.

Two developments have occurred as a result of the Financial Assistance Program initiated by Labor Canada and the C.L.C. In co-operation with the A.F.L. Education Committee, and with finances from the assistance program, Athabasca University commissioned an assessment of labor education in the province in 1978, including existing provisions and future needs and interests. Some of the information provided by the survey can be summarized as follows: only 23 percent of those surveyed were taking work-related courses at the time, and 32.6 percent were taking union-related courses; less than half of the respondents perceived the offerings of work-related and union-related courses to be adequate; there was a tendency for preferences for personal interest and work-related courses to rise with the level of education of respondents and vice versa for union-related courses; the most common barriers to attendance were, inconvenient course times, job responsibilities, not enough time, wrong location, and home responsibilities, and 22 percent said that they had too little information about courses; the subjects in which greatest interest was declared included public speaking, money management, collective bargaining, labor-management relations, unions and the law, learning a second language; the subjects in which least interest was declared included basic education, the appreciation of art, music and drama, report writing, retirement planning, and the history of labor; preferred modes of learning were weekly classes in a centre, week-end seminars or workshops, short courses at a university or college, and on-the-job training; and a management perspective pervaded most courses offered in labor matters by business and industry, government and educational institutions (Centre for the Study of Post-Secondary Education, 1979).

One of the indications given in the survey was that many union members would be interested in some type of credit or recognition for course completion. Subsequently, Athabasca University has negotiated with the A.F.L. Education Committee for a one-year university-level program leading to a Certificate in Labor Studies. The themes proposed for the course are: labor and industrial relations (collective bargaining, labor law, arbitration); administrative principles and union practices (administration theory, interpersonal communications, written communication, worker motivation); work, labor, and contemporary society (sociology of work, labor history in Canada, political ideologies, theories of conflict); the Canadian mosaic (native populations, theories of ethnicity, immigration patterns); and science and technology (technology and work, industrial health, safety standards in training, politics of technology). Instruction was to be given by people identified and hired by the Athabasca University/A.F.L. Program Advisory Committee and it would be available in course modules to be taught at union halls, work-places, and/or community centres.

The second potentially important development following the introduction of the financial assistance program was a labor education conference held at the Faculty of Extension of the University of Alberta in March 1978. A joint program for the conference was prepared by representatives of the A.F.L. and the Faculty of Extension. The objectives were to provide a face-to-face meeting between union leaders and the staff of post-secondary institutions in the province to review the existing offerings, the general needs of the labor movement, and possible models of co-operation. The conference was attended by representatives of the A.F.L., the provincial universities and colleges, and the Department of Advanced Education and Manpower. The attitudes the labor representatives brought to the conference were generally ones of caution, and even suspicion. Their perception was that the programming of the post-secondary institutions was heavily management-oriented. This perception was confirmed in a more general sense by the Athabasca University survey mentioned above. After comparing resources and needs, no firm conclusions were reached with regard to future programs, excepting that Athabasca University and the A.F.L. went on to plan the certificate program. A committee of three A.F.L. members and three representatives of post-secondary institutions was set up to monitor and report on any developments in labor education in Alberta in the following year, and to initiate other conferences and meetings as deemed desirable.

Each institution was asked to nominate a staff member to keep this committee in touch with activities in this field, and to be primarily interested in working with the labor movement. Since then, Grant McEwan Community College in Edmonton, has reported that it has extended the use of its facilities for labor institutes and meetings organized by the C.L.C. and the Edmonton Labor Council, and is working with the A.F.L. on a possible program of labor education for native peoples in the Cold Lake area.

One of the matters of increasing interest to trade unionists and adult educationists in recent years is paid educational leave. A convention on this matter was adopted by the International Labor Organization in 1974, providing that paid educational leave should be implemented by collective agreements or be given effect by national laws or regulations. In 1976 the C.L.C. adopted a policy statement endorsing this convention, and urging that the right to paid educational leave be recognized, so that it became a goal of collective bargaining in Canada and a legislative right for all employees. In 1978 the federal government set up a national task force to study, report, and make recommendations on the matter. In the meantime it has been increasingly publicized as a desirable component in collective bargaining between unions and employers. In reality, however, it appears in Alberta to be still a low priority in the minds of union negotiators. Though in the Athabasca University survey there was some evidence that paid educational leave would increase participation in labor education programs, the statistical evidence indicates that it is not a big issue in bargaining. In 1978 in Alberta only 49 out of the total 394 collective agreements analyzed by the Department of Labor Research, or 28.9 percent, contained provisions for leave of absence for educational purposes. This covered 24,154 employees out of a total of 180,172 union members in the province. Moreover, all the provisions did not extend to full payment of wages during the period of study, as proposed in the I.L.O. convention. However, this was an advance on the situation in 1971, when 16 percent of agreements contained such provisions. In the political and ideological climate described in Chapters 4 and 5, it is not unexpected that trade unionism has been grudgingly tolerated by the government and business leaders in Alberta. For instance, in contrast to what we shall see in Quebec, Alberta law does not allow for the recognition of unions of agricultural producers. This set of attitudes is complemented, particularly in recent boom years, by economic conditions in which wages and employment levels have been relatively high, thus diminishing the reasons for union militancy and enthusiasm directly, and diminishing the demands for union education indirectly. Apart from the historical tendencies among some rural people toward mild forms of co-operation and collectivism, and some early support for communism among southern Alberta coal-miners, workers' organizations have not attracted strong support in the province.

Quebec

The same cannot be said of Quebec. The story of the U.P.A. in the preceding chapter has intimated that there is a strong syndicalist tendency in the province, an awareness that economic gain for producers and workers comes not just as a natural component of general economic profitability, but that it needs the assertion of a collective power. As the account of the U.P.A. indicates, this to some extent went along with and even arose out of circumstances where the control of marketing and, as in forestry, much of the production, was in the hands of English-speaking Canadians and foreigners. These elements of syndicalism and nationalism are features of the broader labor field in Quebec. Moreover, in recent decades, since the late '50s there has been some identification with the interests of workers on the part of some political figures such as Trudeau, Marchand, and Lévesque.

In terms of the proportion of the work-force that is unionized, Quebec is only slightly in advance of Alberta—26 percent compared to Alberta's 21 percent. The Quebec labor force as a proportion of the total population is slightly lower than in Alberta—43 percent compared with 46 percent. But the absolute number of trade union members in Quebec, 788,668, constitutes a very large potential field of adult education.

Table 5 gives an indication of some features of the labor scene in Quebec in comparison to Alberta, as outlined in Table 4. In Quebec there are far more members in the national unions than in the international unions, whereas in Alberta there is a fairly even split. And the average membership of national union branches in Quebec is lower than both the average for international unions in Quebec and

Table 5

Trade Union Membership and Affiliations in Quebec, 1976

Affiliation	International Unions		National Unions	
	Branches	Members	Branches	Members
A.F.L./C.I.O./C.L.C. (F.T.Q.)	796	288,026		
A.F.L./C.I.O. only	1	7,124		
C.L.C. only (F.T.Q.)	23	9,475	450	80,084
C.S.D.			146	24,987
C.N.T.U. (C.S.N.)			1,075	149,969
P.S.A.C.			261	24,570
Unaffiliated	20	20,724	581	182,709
	840	325,349	2,513	462,319
	average: 387		average: 183	

Source: Statistics Canada. 1978. Cat. 71-202. *Labour Unions.* Ottawa: Ministry of Trade and Commerce.

national unions in Alberta. The lower average in Quebec appears to be a reflection of smaller branches in all the groups—those unions affiliated to the C.L.C. as well as those affiliated to the other central organizations in the province. This is not an unimportant point, because it is found that union education within unions themselves is restricted almost entirely to the large unions with large branches.

The presence of these other organizations in Quebec makes for one of the most important differences between the two provinces. Whereas in Alberta there is one major provincial federation, the A.F.L., affiliated to the C.L.C. in Ottawa, in Quebec there are four important provincial federations, and apart from the U.P.A., only one is affiliated to the C.L.C. This is the Quebec Federation of Labor, known better in the province as the Fédération des Travailleurs du Québec (F.T.Q.). The others are: the Confederation of National Trade Unions, better known locally as the Confédération des Syndicaux Nationaux (C.S.N.), the Confederation of Democratic Trade Unions, or the Centrale des Syndicaux Démocratiques (C.S.D.), and the Quebec Teachers' Federation or the Centrale de l'Enseignement du Québec (C.E.Q.). The last of these is treated as one unaffiliated union, and with 97,405 members in 1976, it was the third-largest national union in Canada. This, again, represents a difference from Alberta, where the Alberta Teachers' Association is not legally a trade union; it is a professional body under the Teaching Profession Act, though it does bargain collectively on behalf of Alberta teachers. In the late 1970s there was discussion about the possibility of the A.T.A. being split into two organizations—one professional association and the other a trade union in terms of the labor legislation.

The existence and mode of operation of these various federations in Quebec is another manifestation of the roots of Quebec life and the more lively political climate in the province. For reasons of nationalist identity, the Quebec Federation of Labor (F.T.Q.), since 1974, has taken over wholly the responsibility for labor education from the C.L.C., and one view is that in the assertion of that identity in the present political climate, it takes on the appearance of being even more militantly Quebecois than the purely provincial federations. The C.S.N. began as the Catholic Federation of Labor with roots in the Knights of Labor in the U.S., which were predominantly industrial unions, with a strong Roman Catholic church connection, and a belief in arbitration rather than strikes. In more recent years, the C.S.N. became more militant. Then some of the larger industrial unions, such as those in steel and textiles, split away and formed the C.S.D., leaving the C.S.N. with a major component of public service unions. Both of these federations have grown a great deal in recent years; between 1962 and 1976 the number of branches in the C.S.N. rose from 347 to 1,079, while the C.S.D. now has 146 branches. While Table 5 shows the number of members of C.S.D. as being 24,987 in 1976, a recent report by Labor Canada states that the C.S.D. membership was then 42,500 (Labor Canada, 1977–78).

This volatility is reflected in the level of activity in labor education in the province. The Labor Canada report shows that in 1977–78 more education projects were approved in Quebec under the "independent unions" category of the Financial Assistance Program than in any other province—twelve compared to nine in Ontario and five in Alberta. And this was apart from a series of projects submitted and carried out by the C.S.D., which received funding under a separate agreement with Labor Canada. The 1973 study of education in unaffiliated unions by Dickinson, showed that 50 percent of locals in the C.S.N. and 19 percent of locals in unaffiliated international unions in Québec had education budgets, compared with 10.3 percent in the prairie provinces (Dickinson, 1973:14).

The C.S.N. appears to be the most active, other than the teachers' federation. Until the early 1970s the F.T.Q. did not have an education department, and its activities were confined largely to assistance given to constituent members, whereas the C.S.N. has for many years run its own school for union officers in preparation for dealing with specific problems encountered by the union movement (Verner, 1975). A study in 1972–73 suggested that while the education budgets of the central F.T.Q. organizations and independent unions in Quebec were minimal, that of the C.S.N. amounted to about 5 percent of its total budget, while that of the teachers' federation was between 10 and 24 percent (Kerr and Deault, 1973).

In terms of policy, the Kerr, Deault study observes that the intensity of educational activity in a trade union depends more on a sense of priorities and the degree of commitment to syndicalist practice than it does on the working conditions of its members. The existence of a unit for labor education is more a consequence or a reflection of eductional concerns than it is a cause of such concerns (Ibid.: 217). This observation may explain the relatively active educational work in the C.S.N. and the teachers' federation, both of which are militantly unionist. They are, as well, both concerned with unionism as a part of a wider class struggle. Frenette, the education director of the C.S.N., states the objectives of labor education: "to encourage and organize a united front of workers, first of all in the factories, then in their neighborhoods, in their towns, in their industrial sector and even their country.... Labor education is never merely an individual education, but rather always a collective education; that is a collective action arising from the community" (Frenette, 1975). One of the objectives is to develop working-class consciousness. The teachers' federation's militancy is illustrated by the fact that in 1972, it adopted a resolution to set up a working group to analyze the role of the school and the teacher in a capitalist society (Centrale de l'Enseignement du Québec, 1977). In the same year—to illustrate support for the wider cause of adult education—it recommended that as an organization it should consider continuing education as an urgent social need, from the point of view of the development of individuals and of the collectivity of Quebec, and as a dimension of socio-cultural action (Ibid., 1972).

Statements of this sort are common in Quebec, in contrast with the more muted voice of labor in Alberta. The two environments, as they have been described in earlier parts of this study, make this fact not surprising. In Quebec the voice has become stronger since the early 1970s. In 1978 the four major central labor organizations, the F.T.Q., the C.E.Q., the C.S.N., and the U.P.A. presented a strong brief to the Minister of Education on public funding for labor education. That brief spelled out the following recommendations, among others: union education is a right for workers and farmers, as well as being an essential element in a just and democratic society; union education for workers and farmers is a matter for their own organizations; the Quebec Government should recognize this right by providing to these organizations adequate financial resources for education programs; this provision should be based on an allocation of one dollar per head (of membership), which should be increased annually until it reaches two dollars per head in 1982–83; this should be a program specifically for trade unions, and in addition to the budget for the O.V.E.P. program of the ministry; the ministry should institute a program of free access for the public to all equipment and facilities in public education institutions at all levels, for popular education, cultural promotion, and programs of collective development in collaboration with central labor organizations, all within a perspective of service to the community (*à la collectivité*) (C.E.Q., C.S.N., F.T.Q., U.P.A., 1978).

There is now a program of assistance to labor organizations under the Ministry of Education's Directorate General of Adult Education, the purpose of which is to facilitate instruction about the economic and social realities confronting unions and the labor movement, to stimulate thought concerning action to be taken by union members with regard to the development of the community, and to equip union officers and employees to be more effective in their work. For 1978–79 the total budget was estimated at $571,000, based on a per capita allocation of one dollar to the C.S.D. and the U.P.A., 93 cents to the C.E.Q., and 66 cents to the C.S.N. and F.T.Q. Disbursements would be made against project submissions from unions

and/or central organizations. This agreement signified both the influence of the unions and the attitude of the Quebec Government in
contrast to the situation in Alberta. It also indicated that financial
assistance from the Quebec Government was very much higher than
from the federal government under its financial assistance program.

As in Alberta, central labor organizations in Quebec have begun
to talk to and negotiate with universities and to promote labor education programs. They have gone so far as to negotiate detailed agreements, along the lines of the one negotiated by the U.P.A. with Sherbrooke University. In 1976 the C.S.N. and F.T.Q. jointly entered
into an agreement with the University of Quebec in Montreal
(U.Q.A.M.) and the F.T.Q. has a similar agreement with the University of Montreal. In each case a co-ordinator on the staff of the university works with the unions in formulating a program of research and
teaching to meet the unions' needs. In the first year of the C.S.N./
F.T.Q./U.Q.A.M. agreement, research was initiated in the subjects
of educational leave, transport in Quebec, and the financing of post-
secondary education institutions. Courses were arranged in job evaluation, anti-inflation laws, business organization, the Canadian Labor
Code, the economic situation, the Quebec copper industry, the training of animators, and wages and profits.

This list of courses shows a similarity in scope with that of the
A.F.L./Athabasca University program in Alberta. The difference is
in the process certification in Alberta, as distinct from the less formal,
ad hoc nature of the Quebec programs. Such a distinction parallels the
one between the Athabasca University and Télé Université approaches, referred to in Chapter 6. In general, there are similar
emphases in the labor education programs in Alberta and Quebec on
subjects relating to union organization and management, and roles of
union members and officials. There is some evidence, however, of a
greater emphasis in Quebec on wider economic, social, and political
issues. This was also the case in the earlier 1970s, when Verner found
some evidence that programs offered in Quebec related more to both
functional union operations at the local level and to social and philosophical issues, than those offered elsewhere. (Verner, 1975).

As to the matter of educational leave, the process of analyzing the
5,000 collective agreements had not been completed in Quebec at the
time of this study, so the proportion of those in which unions had

negotiated some such provisions was not known. Interest in this matter is signified by the fact that in a report to the Minister of Education in October 1978, the Superior Council on Education included a recommendation that legal provision be made in the province for the right to educational leave for Quebec workers. The Council placed this whole question firmly in the context of the need for a clearer and more comprehensive policy of éducation permanente, including manpower policies (Conseil Supérieure, 1978). So consideration of the application of the principle of the I.L.O. convention on paid educational leave appears to be more advanced in Quebec than in Alberta.

References

Alberta Statistics. 1979. *Statistical Review*. Edmonton: Bureau of Statistics.

Centrale de l'Enseignement du Québec (C.E.Q.). 1972. *Education Permanente*: *Project de Politique pour la C.E.Q.* Quebec: C.E.Q.

———. 1977. *Origine et Développement de la C.E.Q.* Quebec:C.E.Q.

Centre for the Study of Post-Secondary Education. 1979. *Labor Education in Alberta*: *An Assessment of Activities, Needs, and Preferences*. Edmonton: Athabasca University.

C.E.Q., C.S.N., F.T.Q., U.P.A. 1978. *Le Financement Public de l'Education Syndicale Autonome*. Montreal: C.E.Q., C.S.N., F.T.Q., U.P.A.

Conseil Supérieure de l'Education. 1978. *Eléments d'une Politique d'Education des Adultes dans le Contexte de l'Education Permanente*. Québec: Ministère de l'Education.

Dickinson, G. 1973. *Education in Unaffiliated Unions in Canada*. Ottawa: Labor Canada.

Dickinson, G. and Verner, C. 1973. *Education Within the Canadian Labor Congress*. Ottawa: Labor Canada.

Frenette, G. 1975. "Basic Issues in Labor Education Policy." In *Labour Education in Canada*, ed. B. Pearl. Ottawa: Labor Canada.

Kerr, K. and Deault, J. 1973. *Résumé et Conclusions de l'Etude – L'Education Syndicale au Québec*. Montreal: Université de Montréal, Service d'Education Permanente.

Labor Canada. 1977–78. Activity Report: Labor Education Program. Mimeographed. Ottawa: Labor Canada.

Pearl, B., ed. 1975. *Labor Education in Canada: Report of the National Conference on Labor Education*. Ottawa: Labor Canada.

Verner, C. 1975. "Educational Activities of Trade Unions: Some Research Findings." In *Labor Education in Canada*, ed. B. Pearl. Ottawa: Labor Canada.

10

Provincial Adult
Education Associations

In a sense, the provincial associations representing adult education interests in Alberta and Quebec are linked in terms of their provenance. The Quebec association began as an offshoot of the Canadian Association of Adult Education (C.A.A.E.) in 1936, and became an autonomous body, the Institut Canadien d'Education des Adultes (I.C.E.A.) in 1946. While based in Montreal and mainly concerned with Quebec affairs, it claims to represent francophone adult education interests across Canada, being not simply a provincial organization. Its contacts and involvement outside Quebec, however, are limited. It is the francophone counterpart of the C.A.A.E. The two associations have close links at the executive level.

The Alberta Association for Continuing Education (A.A.C.E.) originated in a conference in 1967 at which Dr. Roby Kidd, a former executive secretary of the C.A.A.E., was a resource person. One of the initial questions debated by its founders was whether it should be a provincial arm of the C.A.A.E., or an autonomous provincial body (Tewnion and Robins, 1978). The decision was that it should be an autonomous body but be affiliated with the C.A.A.E., on whose board it now has a member.

The Alberta group's decision not to be an arm of the C.A.A.E., at a time when a number of other provincial associations were, stemmed partly from the traditional Alberta feeling of counter-dependence in relation to institutions seen to emphasize or reflect central Canadian interests—even though the C.A.A.E. had cross-Canada representation (*see* Chapter 4). More recently the awareness has grown that since education is a matter of provincial jurisdiction, and that adult education is a part of the total, lifelong education system, a strong and representative provincial body is required to advance the state of adult education by attracting provincial government support (Roberts, 1978).

The Alberta Association for Continuing Education

The A.A.C.E. was established originally as an association of institutions, including some of the government departments engaged in adult education, and its objectives were related primarily to improving the operations of and the communication between those institutions. The objectives were to collect and distribute information on the programs of the member institutions, to help identify program needs in the province, to encourage the development and training of adult education workers, and to constitute a kind of pressure group with all levels of government to obtain assistance to meet "the extensive and growing adult education needs of the Province of Alberta" (Tewnion and Robins, 1978).

The association did not—and still does not—have a permanent staff or headquarters, relying as it does on the volunteer work of its members and the part-time assistance of a member of staff of one of its member institutions. It receives no outside funding. This follows from one of the views of its founding group, that the new association should start by being self-reliant, and dependent not on direct government funding but on the resources of its members. In many ways, including the preparation and distribution of all documents, board minutes, and monthly letters, and the payment of costs for some board members to attend monthly meetings, it depends on the support of its institutional members.

For the first few years, the association's activities conformed with the first three of its objectives. First one, and then two, meetings were held each year as means of making and retaining personal contacts and running workshops on specific topics of interest to the member agencies and their staffs. One of those early meetings was used as a vehicle for making presentations relating to adult education to the Worth Commission on Educational Planning (refer to Chapters 4 and 5).

But in the early 1970s a number of developments in the province suggested the need for a different emphasis in the association's scope. First, with the formation of new community colleges and Alberta vocational centres, and greater activity in adult education on the part of larger school-boards the number and variety of educational institutions grew. Second, the beginning of the Local Further Education Council movement in the province introduced a new kind of organization, with an expansion of the body of individuals working as volunteers in the field. So the constitution was changed to provide for the membership of individuals and local councils. The association then saw the need and accepted the responsibility for training council members and workers in their various roles and responsibilities.

For some years a certain tension continued between the interests of the older and formal adult education institutions, mainly urban, and those of the largely volunteer councils, which were mainly rural. As a reflection of its early constitution, the representatives of the larger institutions dominated the board. The middle and late 1970s saw efforts to reconcile those interests and to create common ground. More representatives from rural centres were elected to the board, and more conference workshops were directed at problems being encountered by rural councils, until at the end of the 1970s the association reflected and represented the interests of its whole constituency fairly well.

In the early years, and continuing to some extent into the present, the energies of the association were devoted to building up and maintaining strength. The focus was mainly inward, directed at the organizational needs of its members (though at the annual meeting in 1974 it did look beyond the province at developments in other parts of the country, including Quebec, and in subsequent years it co-sponsored annual conferences with the C.A.A.E. and the North West Adult Education Association respectively). In 1979 it gave its support, within the province, to the C.A.A.E. in its joint venture with the CBC – "People Talking Back" – a nationally broadcast television and discussion program on Canadian issues.

But the concerns of the association were mainly functional. It sought to help its constituent members to improve their internal and co-operative functions within the social and educational environment in which they and the association existed. It did not devote much energy to the fourth objective of "the development and presentation of collective views and interpretations, and guidance relating to the issues and needs in continuing education in Alberta" – in other words, activity as a political pressure group. The reasons for this were not only the preoccupation with internal consolidation as a new organization, but also the relative prominence of government departments and government-controlled education institutions in a small membership.

In the late 1970s the association's constituency expanded to include councils in over fifty communities across the province, as well as the major adult education agencies and government departments, and those councils began to include more citizens beyond the local members of government departments. By mid-1979 the total membership was 37 institutional members (including the major adult education agencies, Alberta Teachers' Association, Alberta School Trustees' Association, and major school-boards), 61 Local Further Education Councils, and 205 individual members. The leadership of the association began to turn to broader issues in adult education in Alberta and to the desirability of developing strategies to represent those issues to government and, where appropriate, to other centres of influence. An Issues Committee was formed in 1976, which initiated the formulation of a number of resolutions relating to the financing of adult education, the need for more training of a formal nature, for persons working or wishing to work in the field, the implementation of the philosophy of lifelong education in the education system, and the need for better co-ordination of government activities in the field. In 1977 the board began what was intended to be a series of annual meetings with senior officials of the Department of Advanced Education and Manpower. The first meeting was an occasion to discuss the resolutions adopted at a general meeting of the association in November 1977. The board later met the Minister of Advanced Education and Manpower for what was again intended to be the first of an annual series of discussions. The following year, despite efforts on the part of the board, no such meeting took place, nor has one taken place since then.

This raises the question of the government's strategy for dealing with the approaches of such associations. In Chapter 5, in the discussion of the role of the Minister's Advisory Committee on Further Education, it was pointed out that the original composition of the committee had included two representatives of the A.A.C.E., and representatives of other institutions concerned with adult education, which indicates one of the original purposes of the committee, which was to provide for professional as well as citizen advice, and which provided the association with formal recognition as an advisor and representative of people in adult education. The change in the composition to eliminate the representative nature of the committee, and subsequent appointments to the committee, have in effect weakened the committee's body of expertise and its commitment to the field. The changes were made with the intention that the committee should not be a lobby or pressure group.

This change would be offset by an arrangement for annual meetings with the Minister of Advanced Education and Manpower. However, in 1979 the premier established a series of caucus committees, i.e., committees of government back-benchers (all but five members of the whole Legislature), to act as the channels for public representation in various areas of activity, in other words, to divert public representation from Ministers and the Executive Council. The declared purpose was that associations and organizations, which in the past had had access to ministers, would henceforth make their representations to these committees. One of these committees is the Caucus Standing Committee on Education, which has a mandate covering all education interests from early childhood education to adult education. Judging from the level of debate in the Legislature on the part of the great majority of government back-benchers, and on the lack of independence of thought revealed by such debate, these committees are likely to be more appropriate to the designs and mode of operation of the government, in which there are more than insignificant signs of *hauteur*, than to the interests of the public.

The Issues Committee of the association continues in its responsibility for initiating the study and discussion of questions affecting the development of adult education practice in the province, and the association continues to become more representative of the field. In recent years such diverse organizations as the Alberta Federation of Labor and the Society of Management Accountants have become members. Within the association the role of actively representing the interests of all varieties of adult education attracts more effort. How strongly and effectively the association is able to pursue this role in the face of discouraging signs of government policy and practice with regard to public representations remains to be seen.

L'Institut Canadien d'Education des Adultes

The institute differs from the A.A.C.E. in a number of important respects, quite apart from an intention to represent francophone interests beyond Quebec's borders. These differences relate to the disparity in age of the two associations, in their respective environments, in their structures, and in their operations. The last two differences are a function of the first two.

With regard to the age of the institute, the fact that it has been operating since 1936 and has been an autonomous Quebecois institution since 1946 means that it has had time to explore a variety of operating philosophies in a sensitive area of the changing Quebec scene, and its leadership has a surer sense of the circumstances and the appropriate strategies. As we have seen, the Alberta association has only recently begun to emerge from its formative organizational phase to devote energy to such wider issues and strategies.

This is not to say that the Quebec institute is full of accord, and a smoothly running organization. As we have seen in Chapter 4, there are a number of currents of political philosophy in the province from Conservative to Marxist-Socialist, and this variety is reflected in the membership of the institute. In recent years there has been evidence of disappointment with institute policy and activity on the part of some members and among the executive, some of whom have withdrawn from the institute. In other words, the institute as a whole is a reflection of the volatility of the Quebec political and social scene.

The institute has had a longer period of passing through the various phases of member dominance, which are only just beginning to be observed in the A.A.C.E. In earlier years it reflected the interest of some of its leaders, such as Claude Ryan, in catholic action, and in trade union development. This declined in the mid-sixties when regional school-boards became a dominant influence. The movement toward support of popular citizen movements began in 1974.

Another circumstance that reflects the ages of the two associations is their size and complexity as working organizations. The relatively new A.A.C.E. is still a voluntary organization in all senses. It has no full-time staff, and no permanent executive director to provide administrative direction to the staff or policy initiatives to the board. The Quebec Institute has a full-time director-general and a unionized staff of about a dozen. The internal process of management/labor negotiations is again in the context of a relatively volatile Quebec management/labor environment. But it gives to the I.C.E.A. a continuing fund of experience and expertise in relation to a wide range of education matters, which is accessible to other groups and organizations. It also gives the institute a capacity for research, project formulation, document analysis and publication, either on its own or in conjunction with or in the service of other groups.

The membership of the institute is grouped in five categories: socio-economic organizations, which include the Quebec Teachers' Federation, the C.S.N., the Canadian Labor Congress, the U.P.A., and the Co-operative Council of Quebec; teaching institutions, which include the universities, a number of regional school-boards (about one-third of the total), and CEGEPS; popular social action groups, which include the Centre for Professional Training, the Centre for Rural Development, the Outaouais Centre for Family Action, the Association Feminine d'Education et d'Action Sociale, and the Quebec Latin America Secretariat; organizations of social animation and education, which include some Local Community Service Centres, Frontier College, the Quebec Assembly of Bishops, the Pastoral Institute, and SUCO, (the francophone counterpart of the Canadian University Service Overseas); and individuals. The number of individual voting members may not exceed the number of institutional members at any time.

This partial list indicates the scope of the institute's interest and operations. It has both rural and urban representation; it has strong trade union representation (it had the Quebec Employers' Federation as a member until the latter withdrew in protest against the institute's heavy opposition of a second francophone commercial T.V. channel in Quebec); it represents leading social education and social action groups, thus lending support to this approach to, and practice of, adult education; and the connection with SUCO and the Latin American Secretariat indicates an interest in adult education outside Canada. It is not surprising, therefore, that among its important objectives, the institute sees itself as being a *carrefour*, a crossroads, for groups interested in the democratization of public education at all levels, and of the mass media, and the promotion of informal, practically oriented, education (*éducation populaire autonome*) through citizen groups, as a means of collective development (*promotion collective*). By weighting its activities on this side of the balance, rather than being a more neutral meeting ground for all shades of adult education philosophy, the institute was questioned by members, some of whom withdrew, including the Department of Androgogy of the University of Montreal.

These general indications of the institute's interest and objectives can be illustrated by reference to some of its activities during 1977–78 (I.C.E.A., 1978): participating in approaches to the Minister of Education by the O.V.E.P.s for more support and funding; working with and drafting a brief on behalf of the four trade union federations, requesting more funding from the Minister of Education for trade union education; setting up committees to analyze the role of education institutions in professional and technical training for adults and the role of the federal govenment; taking on a researcher, under a government grant, to analyze the mechanisms for a technical education in industry, and the reactions of workers to such training; producing a document intended to sensitize educational institutions to their role in popular social education; producing an information paper on economically oriented adult education—who provides it, with what obectives, for whom and by what means; working with the Front Commun des Communications (F.C.C.), in terms of providing secretarial, co-ordinating, and documentation services; holding seminars on popular methods of education for those working with Latin

American groups, both in Canada and Latin America; and working with SUCO in literacy training for the General Union of Senegalese Workers.

These examples show the wide scope of the insitute, as well as its dominant image. Some of its publications reinforce that image: *Methods of Popular Education*, December 1977; *The Work of a Popular Education Centre in Mexico*, August 1978; *We Must Democratize Radio Quebec!*, 1977; *The Dossier of Collective Development*, June 1978; and *The Collective Cultural Development of the Underprivileged Classes*, May 1975. Both its work and its publications indicate the institute's need for, and use of, a document centre, to provide a resource for its own workers, for researchers, and for other interested people. The I.C.E.A. sees itself as the principal documentation centre for francophone Canada in adult education.

The institute's clientele in 1977–78 comprised 8.4 percent I.C.E.A. members, 22.4 percent I.C.E.A. staff, 5 percent other trade unions and citizen groups, 9.9 percent other teaching institutions, 23.4 percent students, 5.3 percent foreign, and 25.6 percent other.

Unlike the A.A.C.E., the I.C.E.A. receives the major part of its revenue from government; in 1977–78, out of a total of $344,074, $130,000 came from the Quebec Ministry of Education and $95,000 from the Secretary of State, in recognition of its claim to have a wider province than just Quebec. A total of $80,723 came in the form of project financing in research and development, from such bodies as the Canadian International Development Agency, the Canadian Council for Rural Development, and the Ministry of Education; membership subscriptions generated $20,925.

The financial support from the federal as well as the provincial governments places some restraints on the institute's ability to swing officially and ostensibly in one direction or another in the Quebec independence issue. It accepts the need for some caution in being seen to be critical of or favorable toward one government in relation to the other, and the diverse views of its own members on this issue are also good reason for such caution. The executive and program committees of the institute are not, however, reluctant to criticize the Quebec Directorate-General of Adult Education where they feel it is justified. In their report to the General Assembly in June 1978, they criticized the D.G.E.A.'s financing proposals and programs for the O.V.E.P.s for "being based principally on the need to facilitate the administrative work of the bureaucrats of the D.G.E.A rather than on the need to help the O.V.E.P.s in their educational activities" (I.C.E.A., 1978). It accused the ministry of relegating popular education for citizens to a second-grade ghetto, and even denying its legitimate place in adult education. The report indicates some similarity with the Alberta scene in pointing out that 1977 saw the first meeting between representatives of the O.V.E.P.s—including the I.C.E.A. representative—with the Minister of Education "despite repeated demands to successive ministers since 1972." It may or may not be relevant that this was the period of the Bourassa Liberal government and that a P.Q. government was elected in 1976.

The considerable difference in age and experience of the two provincial associations calls for some caution in making comparisons between their current structures and the scope of their activities. The A.A.C.E. is still in a fairly early stage of development compared with the I.C.E.A., and the two associations might grow to be similar in these respects as the A.A.C.E. becomes older. But it is not unreasonable to conclude that the environment of Quebec—political, cultural, economic, as well as educational—and the membership of the institute itself, appeared to be more conducive to the more political and action-oriented philosophy and practice of the I.C.E.A, whereas the Alberta environment and the membership of the A.A.C.E., including as it does so many government representatives, are not so conducive to such a role.

There is another difference in activity that may reflect more than simply a difference in stages of development. In Alberta, much of the effort of the A.A.C.E., particularly in its twice-yearly meetings, has been in professional development, in more recent years aimed increasingly at members of and workers for local further education councils. This has been a response to a strong need on the part of new people coming to the field, and a lack of such learning experiences elsewhere in the province during that period. The learning has tended to emphasize basic organizational and programming skills, publicity, marketing, and procedures under the government's Further Education Policy Guidelines and Procedures, in other words, a higher level of professionalism in the kind of adult education that is prevalent in Alberta. In Quebec the I.C.E.A., insofar as it has been involved in any form of training, has tended toward the skills of social animation and citizen action. Among some of its leaders there is, in fact, a mistrust of a trend toward professionalization in the field of adult education, and the removal of the initiative from popular groups to "professionals." There is more concern for questions of the philosophy of adult education. In its annual report of 1977–78, the institute emphasizes its role in popular education for citizens, in being a technical resource and a support for reflection on present practices. "It is more and more evident that we should put more energy into reflection, i.e. that the I.C.E.A. should place itself more at the heart of the reflection that is more and more evident at the level of popular groups and trade unions" (I.C.E.A., 1978). And this would be done both through meetings and through the publication of documents. This emphasis on reflection and basic questioning is in contrast with the emphasis on instrumentalities in Alberta, and it appears to illustrate general characteristics in the approach to adult education in the two provinces.

References

Institut Canadien d'Education des Adultes (I.C.E.A.). 1978. *Report to Annual General Assembly.* Montreal: I.C.E.A.

Roberts, H. 1978. "President's Message." *Journal of the Alberta Association for Continuing Education*, vol. 6, no. 1.

Tewnion, J. and Robins, K. 1978. "The Origins of the Alberta Association for Continuing Education." *Journal of the Alberta Association for Continuing Education*, vol. 6, no. 1.

Part IV
The Outcomes

Introduction

The analysis of roles and activities of government and other large institutions in Parts II and III has indicated how the weight of policymaking and programming in adult education in the two provinces is balanced. Those indications are that in Quebec, besides a strong concern for economic development and occupational training, there is a strong concern for "national" culture and the reinforcement of that culture at local levels through support for socio-cultural activities. This emphasis is reflected in the approach of labor and agricultural organizations. In Alberta, the indications are of a strong emphasis on economic development and the kinds of adult education that contribute to it. Support for cultural activities is in a narrower range of meaning of culture (music, art, literature) and bears in mind the multi-cultural nature of the population of the province. Union and agricultural education is, in the main, influenced by the dominant economic values, but there is evidence of an earlier concern in the province for socially relevant adult education in the agricultural sector which counteracts to some extent the dominant economic ideology.

In both provinces the picture of adult education among native people is one of mixed aspirations: a concern on the one hand to obtain the knowledge and skills—mainly occupational—needed to survive and progress in the dominant white culture; and on the other hand a desire to revive and strengthen their own culture as a stronger base of group and personal identity with which to confront the dominant culture. The latter effort provides a counteracting influence to that culture.

The analysis in Part IV begins with a description of the different approaches to needs assessment in the two provinces. We compare the allocation of financial resources by the governments, in other words, the results, in quantitative terms, of the policies and departmental responsibilities outlined in Part II. Using one table, it is possible to set out this quantitative comparison—in some respects, a contrast rather than a comparison—in a more direct way than is possible in describing philosophies and structures.

The analysis of government expenditures addresses the ascription of needs by the funding authorities. To complement that analysis, the study examines the relationship between ascribed and felt needs, and seeks evidence of the manifestation of the latter. This is shown to be a difficult quest. A perception of two sectors of education emerges: the public sector and the private sector. This perception is discussed further in Chapter 12, which draws some conclusions from the evidence of the study as a whole. In the course of this discussion, modifications are suggested to the two models proposed in Chapter 3, relating to a continuum of purposes of adult education, and to the relationship between forces influencing the patterns of adult education.

11

The Ascription of Needs
and Allocation of Resources

In Chapter 3 we discussed two sets of forces that are suggested as influencing the pattern of adult education in Alberta and Quebec: the dominant social philosophy, and the principal institutional structures. In discussing the non-government institutions, we have begun to discern outcomes, in the form of educational programs offered by those institutions, and we have seen that in some respects these latter institutions show that they are possibly counteracting, or at any rate modifying, the influence of the dominant public ideology. An example is the socially oriented programs offered by some agricultural organizations in Alberta, and in cultural programs offered by some native institutions in both provinces.

Now we look at the other two factors that influence the pattern: the perception of needs, and the availability and allocation of resources. It is here, and particularly in relation to the latter, that the pattern of outcomes emerges.

In one sense, there is not necessarily any relationship between needs and resources. If we consider needs from the point of view of those possessing them, it does not always follow that resources in terms of funds, facilities, and personnel are available to meet those needs. We have seen indications of this lack of consonance in adult education provided for native people in the two provinces. But in another sense, the relationship is close. Houle has distinguished between felt needs and ascribed needs (1972:233), that is, between needs as perceived by the persons possessing them, and needs as perceived by some other observer and hence ascribed by that observer. In this study an important, even central, observer is the government, and to varying degrees some of the other principal orders, as Mills and Gerth call them, are the economic and religious orders (1964). We have seen that whereas in Alberta there is a close affinity between the ideologies of the political and economic orders, in Quebec there have historically been, and there continues to be, some strain.

This is not to say that the relationship between felt needs and ascribed needs is such that they always stand opposed to each other; the relationship is a complex one. Felt needs may in some cases be deeply personal and autonomous to the individual or to a group, and perhaps counter-cultural, but with a human capacity and tendency to adapt one's perceptions and expectations to the dominant social pressures and avoid cognitive disssonance and conflict. Felt needs will tend to coincide with the needs ascribed by dominant orders. Furthermore, in Alberta, where a relatively large proportion of the population has immigrated from elsewhere in recent years, many have presumably chosen to do so because they saw the dominant economic and social climate as being congenial to them and their needs.

There is another point to be borne in mind. The extent to which people can satisfy their felt needs independently of the availability and allocation of government-controlled resources can be related to the amount of disposable income of those people. So in some societies with relatively high levels of income, and for some people with high personal incomes in all socieities, the ability to command education at whatever level, falls outside the limitations of government and other funding. In general, however, it will be an assumption of this study that the availability and allocation of resources for adult education, and therefore the amount and content of adult education, are closely related to the ascription of needs on the part of the providers of resources.

Needs Assessment in Alberta and Quebec

Nevertheless, there have been earnest efforts in both provinces to assess the needs for adult education and training as seen by potential learners, and the approaches to this enterprise appear to reflect characteristic features of the two provinces as outlined in Chapter 4.

In Alberta, assessments of needs in adult education have been dispersed among many agencies—practically all the agencies in the field. In more or less (usually less) formalized ways, individual agencies have conducted their own assessments, employing such devices as user advisory boards, the distribution of advertising material through monitored postal drops, contacts with community groups and services and professional organizations, and testing the market with program offerings. Many of the Local Further Education Councils in smaller centres and rural areas have employed teams of students under the Student Temporary Employment Program (STEP), to conduct local surveys in the summer using simple questionnaires and interview techniques.

A few general surveys, initiated principally by groups of councils or agencies, have been carried out on a broader scale, covering larger, but still fairly localized, areas of the province, while others have been directed at particular target populations in the province. These have used more sophisticated questionnaires and survey techniques amenable to electronic computation.

The first of the general surveys was commissioned jointly by the Alberta Department of Advanced Education and Manpower and the Saskatchewan Department of Continuing Education, to survey the need for a Community College in east-central Alberta and west-central Saskatchewan. This survey, which led to the establishment of Lakeland College in Lloydminster, was commissioned in 1973 and conducted by the Department of Educational Administration of the University of Alberta. It included a questionnaire directed at the learning needs of adults in the area (Ingram et al., 1974). A survey of adult needs covering four communities in west-central Alberta—Edson, Hinton, Jasper, and Grande Cache—initiated and conducted by the University of Alberta, in co-operation with Athabasca University (Small and Roberts, 1977), then followed. Using the same instruments as in this study, a group of four local councils in north-eastern Alberta conducted a similar survey in their area (Lagassé, 1976). All these surveys received support and funding from the Department of Advanced Education and Manpower, but the initiative for the two latter surveys came from the agencies and councils involved. In other words, the provincial government was supportive, but apart from the matter of the establishment of a formal college under its direct jurisdiction, it left the initiative to others.

Another survey of a general not pre-selected population, was one initiated in 1978 by two individuals interested in the possibility of having a literacy program produced by ACCESS, using videotapes, radio, and print material (Messaline and Newhouse, 1979). The first objective was to identify the extent of adult functional illiteracy in the province, so as to be able to justify, or not, a literacy program of the sort being investigated. Again, the initiative came from interested individuals, though the purpose was to persuade ACCESS to mount an education program to meet the needs.

The second kind of needs assessment that has been conducted in Alberta surveys the needs of pre-defined groups, with particular kinds of education and/or training in mind. One such survey has been referred to in Chapter 10 – the survey of labor education needs in the province conducted by the University of Alberta Centre for the Study of Post-Secondary Education, on behalf of Athabasca University and the Alberta Federation of Labor (Konrad, et al., 1979). The main findings of this survey have been discussed in Chapter 10. Of two other surveys of this kind, one was directed at the needs of persons working in the field of adult education (Campbell, 1977), and the second was directed at professional development needs of administrators in higher education (Konrad, et al., 1976).

In Alberta there has been a dispersed effort and a variety of surveys more or less localized in terms of territory or target population, and more or less sophisticated in terms of research techniques. There has been no concerted plan or comprehensive survey. The nearest the province has come to a comprehensive statement of guiding philosophy was the work of the Life-long Education Task Force of the Commission on Educational Planning (Worth Commission) in 1971, some of whose views were reflected in the Commission's report (Commission on Educational Planning, 1972).

In contrast to this almost *laissez-faire* and *ad hoc* approach in Alberta, the situation in Quebec reflects some of the more deliberate consciously directed and centralized aspects of public life in that province alluded to in Chapter 4. The enterprise of assessing the needs of adults was part of the larger enterprise of seeking new directions and new political and administrative patterns that flowed from the quiet revolution of the 1960s. The Parent Commission had recommended a study to create an inventory of adult education organizations and an assessment of needs, and in 1964–66 the Comité Barbin indicated the need for better information about adult education needs in the province. In 1964 a number of Comités Régionnaux de Planification Scolaire (C.O.R.E.P.S.) were set up, supported by a team of civil servants in the Ministry of Education, aimed at sensitizing and consulting the public in matters of education. This exercise, "Opération 55," resulted in the consolidation of school-boards into fifty-five Catholic Regional School-Boards and nine Protestant ones (D.G.E.A., 1970: vol. 1, p. 5).

Then, in 1967, the ministry mounted "Opération Départ," with a broad set of objectives directed at regional and provincial levels. At the regional level there were action objectives, comprising the diffusion of information, consciousness-raising, co-ordination of effort, providing a working framework for adult education, and starting a "dynamic process;" and research objectives, comprising needs assessment, an inventory of programs, a resource survey, and the union of needs and resources. At the provincial level the objectives were: creation of a documentation centre, standardization of terminology, determination of a provincial program, and collection of material to allow the formulation of a Quebec policy of éducation permanente (Ibid.: 38). The administrative apparatus for Opération Départ consisted of a team of ministry officials to prepare and direct the plan, sixteen consultants working out of regional offices of the ministry, and fifty-seven regional committees representing regional school-boards and various other education institutions, and institutions such as trade unions, employers' organizations and the media. These regional committees involved 1,742 people, representing 2,308 interest groups (Ibid.: 58–61).

The process followed by the committees was: the examination of census statistics, the examination of existing adult education offerings, an assessment of needs in both economic and cultural terms, the formulation of a regional plan, and the reporting of the plan to the ministry.

With regard to the assessment of needs, Opération Départ directed its attention to two main aspects of education: academic and professional education for economic development; and popular cultural education. In the former case, the committees focused on six population groups: women, young adults, farmers and farm workers, the unemployed, people on welfare, and "special groups." This part of the exercise amounted to a fairly conventional manpower needs survey, using projections of existing trends, and it identified the training of factory workers, farm workers, and workers in service industries as primary areas of need. In respect of popular cultural education, which was defined as non-formal education not leading to a qualification and with an individual, social, and/or cultural orientation, the process was a mixture of reflection and discussion among regional committee members, consultation with the associations and groups they represented and with local adult education agencies, and in some cases the distribution of questionnaires.

Parallel with Opération Départ, the Ministry of Education initiated another exercise: a systematic study of the concept of éducation permanente and its integration into the education system as a whole. This study was conducted by sociologists and educationalists from the Planning and Research Service of the Ministry. The authors of the report of this study, called *Opération Départ*, ranged through the writings of such people as Marcuse, Illich, Carl Rogers, McLuhan, Roszak, and Buckminster Fuller, and came up with a model of the relationship between individual growth and the educative society. The group suggested that there were interlinking relationships between the autonomous learner, the educational environment, and an educative society, all of which made up an educational system (D.G.E.A., 1971). The authors were frank in stating at the outset of their report that it would make no concrete recommendations, propose no plan of development, and suggest no organizational or administrative structures. It made no distinction between the education of the young and of adults, so as to accent the similarities in the process of growth (Ibid.: 1–3).

These, then were the two broad approaches to needs assessment in Alberta and Quebec: the one diffused, ad hoc, an activity mainly for the agencies concerned; the other planned as a province-wide enterprise, directly guided by the government, and part of a broader search for a systematic philosophy. The latter approach is suggested by Renaud (1978) as characteristic of Quebec public life in the 1960s and early 1970s.

The findings of the various needs surveys in Alberta provide a more detailed profile of expressed needs than does Opération Départ. In all the general surveys in Alberta, i.e. the east-central, north-eastern, and west-central regional surveys, the subjects of study that ranked highest in the responses to the questionnaires were business and other vocational courses, including locally important occupational choices such as farming. In the Lakeland College (east-central) survey, academic and university transfer courses were high in priority, probably because of the prospect of the establishment of a college in the region as a result of the survey, while in the west-central survey a reasonably high response was shown to the possibility of long-distance university-level courses, such as those offered by Athabasca University. In the east-central survey, "community service" programs were in the bottom rank, while in the other areas such topics as community studies, social sciences, and Canadian issues and problems were generally of low priority. There was a varying level of interest in subjects such as fine arts, crafts, and languages. A common feature of all these surveys was a relatively low response rate to questionnaires and, apart from the clear dominance of a demand for vocationally-oriented programs, a wide spread of low-number responses over a wide variety of other topics. The findings tend to underline some of the weaknesses of such surveys: the difficulty of inferring real levels of interest from a small number of responses and from general statements not requiring any real commitment, and the way responses tend to reflect expectations built up in the respondents by the purposes of the survey and the formulation of the questionnaires, for example, that courses at the college and/or university level would eventuate. They also illustrate a dilemma of agencies making such surveys: that the agency may not be able to meet the expressed expectations because of their thin spread over a variety of subjects. Insofar as such needs assessment are conducted by agencies themselves, with their fixed patterns of funding and program resources, the tendency is to tailor the assessments to the populations whose means correspond to the agencies' funding requirements and whose interests correspond to the agencies' program resources. There is a strong element of pre-selection of populations, and therefore a prejudgment of needs. Probably the greatest weakness of this whole approach to needs assessment is that it elicits responses from, and therefore reveals the needs of, only those elements of the population who are confident and motivated enough to respond. It does not get at the needs of groups who, in the French terminology, are *défavorisés*.

Opération Départ revealed its own limitations. Because the regional committees relied mainly on statistics of previous trends, and on the views of existing agencies and organizations, they tended to project the past and present into the future. For example, it was found that the number of courses in popular cultural education had declined as a percentage of all courses, from 75.6 percent in 1960–61 to 45 percent in 1967–68, so it was forecast that there would be a slower growth of need for such classes in the future. An independent assessment of the operation judged that it had done a good job of formulating an inventory of existing offerings, of consciousness-raising, and of co-ordinating activities, but that it had been weak at assessing future needs, partly because regional and local personnel were at that time new to the field.

The authors of the report acknowledged the limitations of their work. Their conclusion was that it had left gaps in the perception of needs, especially in respect of academic and cultural education. "Harmonizing resources and needs is a laudible objective, but the major unknown remains the state of the needs, not only because it is not easy to identify them quickly, but also because real needs are often unarticulated, and are hidden by all kinds of superficial needs—passing needs or stereotypical needs which come to the fore." (D.G.E.A., 1970:vol. 1, p. 307). When they go on to ask, "must [cultural education] constantly be the poor sister of other types of education?" (Ibid.), they reveal, perhaps, the disappointment of those whose biases are not corroborated, but also the strong commitment in Quebec government circles to socio-cultural development, which is identified in Chapters 4 and 6. They refer to the need for conceptual reflection that will lead away from the beaten path: "Adult education cannot be limited to the renewing of academic and professional education, filling in the gaps of the regular education system, past or present, or a short-term recycling process to cope with the difficulties of this or that group which finds itself in an endangered situation relative to its professional life. It much be thought of in terms of the future" (Ibid.).

This whole process of commissions and committees, from the Parent Commission to Opération Départ, and these expressions of philosophy that contain a strong element of idealism, illustrate what Renaud characterizes as the three-act scenario of Quebec state actions: Commissions of Inquiry whose recommendations cause high expectations; the initiation of ambitious plans, the restructuring and reshuffling of government structures and some cohesive mechanisms for implementation; and disappointment because of unsuccessful attainment of social democratic ideals (Renaud, 1978:3).

The Allocation of Government Resources (Ascribed Needs)

The assessments of needs discussed above are less than comprehensive, even within their own scope. They are even less so when it is borne in mind that their scope has been focused on, and to all intents and purposes restricted to, the concept of education enshrined in the formal education system. We have seen in Chapters 5 and 6 that in both provinces the scope of adult education responsibilites and activities extends far beyond the jurisdictions of ministries of education. In looking at the allocation of resources to adult education in its various forms in the two provinces, it is therefore necessary to go back to that broader framework. Table 6 gives an indication of the allocation of government financial resources within that framework. It is not possible to make precisely detailed comparisons between the two provinces on the basis of these figures, because of different allocations of responsibility between ministries, and the fact that expenditure on forms of adult education cannot be exactly equated with some of the listed appropriations—for example, for first-line social services in the Quebec Ministry of Social Affairs, and for advisory services in the Alberta Department of Agriculture, and for Radio-Television in Quebec and ACCESS in Alberta. But the parallels are near enough to justify some conclusions about the importance and direction given by the governments to adult education in the two provinces.

Table 6 brings expenditures together under a number of headings, identifying the ministries and departments that contribute under those headings. This attempts to overcome some of the difficulty of matching variations in ministerial responsibilities in the two provinces. One important point must be kept in mind: as far as it is possible to make a distinction from budget estimates, these figures show appropriations for direct program support, and do not include appropriations to institutions such as universities and colleges, from which provision for the administration of adult education programs is made internally, nor for the administration of programs by the respective ministries and departments.

Here are some broad comparisons that can be drawn from the figures as they relate to total expenditures in the two provinces. In Alberta the total expenditures listed in Table 6, $89,091,711, amounts to 1.9 percent of total estimated provincial government expenditure in

Table 6
_____

Allocations of Government Expenditure to Various Programs of Adult Education, 1979–80

Ministry and Service	Alberta	Quebec
1. *General adult education* i.e. non-vocational and non-specialized		
Advanced Education and Manpower	$2,445,000	
Consumer and Corporate Affairs	614,886	
Education		$32,664,100
	3,059,886	32,664,100
2. *Professional and Vocational Training*		
Advanced Education and Manpower	29,880,018	
Transportation	1,441,142	
Education		91,495,200
Labor and Manpower		14,480,000
Tourism, Hunting and Fishing		9,324,100
	31,321,160	115,299,300

3. *Social and Health Education*

Social Services and Community Health
—Metis development	691,010	
—vocational rehab. services	9,192,120	
—handicapped services	1,526,260	
—preventive social services	5,153,480	
—preventive health education	75,480	
—alcohol and drug abuse educ.	703,965	
Native Affairs	1,028,000	
Corporate and Consumer Affairs	472,641	
Ministry of Social Affairs		
—first-line social services		56,681,300
—support for volunteer organizations		4,962,800
—handicapped services		66,781,600
—social service information		309,700
	18,842,956	128,735,400

4. *Cultural Development*

Culture
—visual arts	604,144	
—performing arts	3,275,086	
—film and literacy arts	170,716	
—libraries	3,132,555	
—archives	478,900	
—museums	4,233,127	
ACCESS (Executive Council)	7,618,000[1]	
Cultural Affairs		
—arts and the visual environment		9,810,700
—interpretive arts		20,021,700
—book publication		2,164,100
—libraries		12,805,900
—archives		2,024,000
Communication		
—cinema and audio-visual		1,068,600
—Radio T. V. du Québec		26,409,300[1]
	19,512,528	74,304,700

5. *Leisure and Recreational*

Recreation and Parks	3,271,761	
Education (High Commission for Youth)		21,955,200
	3,271,761	21,955,200

6. *Agricultural Development*

Agriculture
—advisory services	5,112,174	
—4-H	964,675	
—home economics branch	2,458,362	
—agricultural training		7,820,500
	8,535,211	7,820,500

7. *Environmental and Conservation Education*

Energy and Natural Resources	1,397,978	
Environment	548,507	
Lands and Forests		1,610,000
	1,946,485	1,610,000

8. *Staff Training and Development (Government)*

Executive Council	467,085	
Solicitor General	359,904	
Public Service		5,467,500
	826,989	5,467,500

9. *Status of Women*

Executive Council	129,000	1,595,000

10. *Immigration Education and Orientation*

Immigration	—[2]	10,017,600

11. *Occupational Health and Safety Education*

Executive Council	1,653,735[3]	
Labor and Manpower		480,000
	1,653,735	480,000

12. *Grand Total*

	89,091,711	399,948,900

Source: Alberta and Quebec Estimates of Expenditures, 1979–80.

1. The figures for ACCESS and Radio T. V. du Québec are inclusive of programming at all levels, and therefore do not relate specifically to adult education. It is possible to break down the ACCESS figure, by virtue of the fact that 25% of the programming should be allocated to adult education, but such a breakdown is not possible for the Radio TV du Québec figure, so the two figures have been included in their entirety.

2. No amount is shown in the estimates, but in mid-1979 the Department of Advanced Education and Manpower announced a special appropriation of $2.3 million for the settlement of Vietnamese boat people. Quebec may have done likewise, over and above the budgeted amount.

3. Since April 1979, the responsibility for occupational health and safety education has come under the new Department of Workers' Health, Safety, and Compensation.

1979–80. In Quebec the total listed in Table 6, $399,948,900, amounts to 2.6 percent of total estimated provincial government expenditures in 1979–80. The ratio of expenditure on adult education to total government expenditures is considerably higher in Quebec than in Alberta. When the grand totals in the table are divided to show the respective expenditures per head of adult population (that is, persons over eighteen years of age as of June 1977) in each province, the result is that Quebec is seen to spend 30 percent more ($91 per head), than Alberta ($70 per head). This difference might be slightly greater if 1979 population figures were used, because of the relatively higher increase in Alberta through migration in the last few years.

On the basis that the adult population of Quebec is roughly three times that of Alberta, there appears to be relative parity of provision in only two of the program areas: professional and vocational training, and cultural development. In the first of these, this parity may be a reflection of the fact that so much of manpower training is financed by the federal government.

Those areas in which Alberta leads, both in absolute and relative terms, are agriculture, environmental and conservation education, and occupational health and safety education. The first probably reflects the long-standing prominence of agriculture in Alberta life and economy and the political activity of farmers over many years. The second may reflect the fact that resource development and its environmental repercussions have become a strong public issue in Alberta in recent years. The third may reflect the growing concern in recent years about the high accident and death rate among oil exploration workers. What is surprising is that in view of the strength of trade union activity in Quebec, compared with that in Alberta, provision for occupational health and safety education is so far behind in that province.

In the other program areas listed in Table 6, the interesting feature is not only the disproportionately high provision in Quebec compared to Alberta, but the disposition of funds within those totals, in terms of purpose and, in some cases, procedures.

In respect of general adult education, in Alberta the funds made available through Advanced Education and Manpower for further education programming are provided in grants for courses on a per-hour basis, the levels being $8 per hour for general interest courses;

$16 per hour for basic literacy, French or English as a second working language, and citizenship for immigrants; and $30 for the study of significant local problems and issues. The effect of the grants is to reduce the fees for an average ten-week course by between $6 and $10. Approval of all courses for grant purposes is delegated to Local Further Education Councils (Chapter 5), except that $30 per hour grants must be confirmed by the Department of Advanced Education and Manpower. In the event, agencies and councils have been advised, from the initiation of this policy in the mid-1970s, to exercise great restraint in submitting proposals for courses on significant local problems and issues, because of the small amount of money available. Consequently, the support goes almost entirely to general courses directed mainly at personal interest, and English as a second language.

The policy and procedures in Quebec are quite different. Courses offered by school-boards under the heading of popular education, which are designated by the Director-General of Adult Education as being of some social benefit, are subsidized to the extent that the fee for an average thirty-hour course is reduced from between $45 and $55 to $12. Subsidized courses include those such as basic home skills, pre-retirement, the citizen and power, and the citizen and the law. Non-subsidized courses include those such as jazz ballet, yoga, and oil painting. The extent of government funding for socially oriented programs goes beyond this, as outlined in Chapter 6. First, under the Services Educatifs d'Aide Personnelle et d'Animation Communautaire (S.E.A.P.A.C.), counselling and other services are provided to individual students, and in addition, a variety of community services is offered through regional school-boards, such as the services of *animateurs* to facilitate development of community groups and to support co-operative action studies of social and economic issues; help in the assessment of needs of people and organizations in the region; and the co-ordination and exchange of services between different resources in the region. Second, the servicing of Organismes Volontaires d'Education Populaire (O.V.E.P.) entails direct funding from the D.G.E.A. to various groups such as trade unions, co-operative associations, and women's groups for the purposes of helping members of such organizations to take more control in the development of their lives. The increase in activity under these latter two services is indicated by the fact that the number of community animation projects under S.E.A.P.A.C. rose from 22 in 1976–77 to 38 in 1978–79 and the number of O.V.E.P. projects rose from 270 to 600 in the same period (Ministère de l'Education, 1979).

Nevertheless, that the government is under continuing pressure to do more in this direction is shown by submissions from the Institut Canadien d'Education des Adultes and the provincial labor federations. See, for example, the submission in 1978 referred to in Chapter 9; additional funding was provided in the O.V.E.P. budget as a result.

For the purposes of this study identification of the purposes of the adult education programs is even more important than the total figures themselves, and to look behind the figures under the other headings confirms an emerging conclusion that government resources in Quebec are directed considerably more to social and community purposes than is the case in Alberta. In social and health education, an important element of the expenditure on first-line social services goes into Local Community Service Centres (C.L.S.C.), through which, as we have seen in Chapter 6, a good deal of social animation is promoted. A graphic account of this type of activity in one C.L.S.C., in Sherbrooke, is given by Lavigne (1978), as well as an account of the resistance such work encounters from some more conventional government officials. In leisure and recreation education funded by the High Commission for Youth, Leisure, and Sports, there appears to be more emphasis on socio-cultural activities than is the case for programs funded by the Department of Recreation and Parks in Alberta.

With regard to the promotion of culture, the interest in Quebec appears to be focused particularly on the promotion of Quebec "national" culture, a counter-force to the dominant international anglophone culture of the rest of Canada and North America. The heavy expenditure on the promotion of the interpretive arts and on Radio-T.V. du Québec, and the expenditure on book publishing and the cinema, are especially devoted to this purpose. Moreover, some of the Radio-T.V. funds are used to assist local community T.V. groups, again for "national" socio-cultural purposes. The pursuit of this purpose is clearly behind the expenditure on the adaptation of immigrants through the Immigration Department (the existence of this Department in itself exemplifies the Quebec stance on its own culture.) There is no counterpart to this thrust in Alberta. There, cultural development is seen in terms of the multi-cultural, but dominantly anglophone, nature of Alberta society in the context of a broader international, but mainly American, culture.

In his discussion of the new middle class in Quebec, Renaud (1978) raises a point that appears to bear on the relatively high expenditure on government staff training and development in that province. This expenditure seems to be a reflection of Renaud's proposition that because the higher, and even middle, ranks of business and industry in Quebec have been virtually closed to francophones, the latter have found or made their way into the government service, and any policy and activity to extend both the quantity and quality of the government sector is seen by this class of people to be good. The increased professionalization of the public service would be seen by such persons to be of benefit to the whole province—or, in the eyes of many of them— to *l'état*, for there is a strong Quebec nationalist element in the senior ranks of government. The establishment of the National School of Public Administration as a unit of the University of Quebec may reflect this feeling; the school is delegated the responsibility for the continuing professional education of public administrators in the province, and it conducts a comprehensive program in this field (Ecole Nationale, 1978:73).

In Chapter 6 it was noted that in Quebec there was a tension between various streams of political philosophy. Though there has, particularly since the early 1960s, been a growth of democratic socialism, there is nevertheless a significant middle class that supports small and/or large scale capitalism, and which is residual of traditional Quebec and anglophone societies. There is also the new francophone administrative class, which appears to be particularly established in the government service, and although, according to Renaud, this group espouses, in general, both Quebec nationalist and social democratic ideals, it has become a strong technocracy, with a tendency to conservatism that often characterizes such a development. This brings it up against the third stream of thought, referred to in Chapter 6: a more militant and in some respects Marxist socialism, allied in the trade union movement to syndicalism. It is from people in this group that much critical analysis has emerged of the actual outcomes of government policy and action, and of the lack of support for francophone working people. The critical analysis by Lafleur of Multi-Média mentioned in Chapter 6 is an example of this line of criticism.

This analysis of government expenditure indicates that in Alberta the highest priority among the various program areas is given to professional and vocational training, and that in Quebec this is also given a high priority. Seen from the governments' perspective, such expenditure can be interpreted as the implementation of a social policy with a social purpose of improving the living standards of the population. Most of the funding, however, comes from the federal government under manpower training agreements, and frequent allusions made in Quebec to the incursion of federal influence and the mechanisms in that province for the allocation of federal funds, as described in Chapter 6, appear to signify some concern about the consequent distortion of provincial priorities. Such a concern would appear to be consistent with the pattern shown by the figures in Table 6 taken as a whole, which indicates that in general, and notwithstanding the serious concerns of those who see the need for much more dedication to grass roots popular education, the ascription of needs for adult education in Quebec is far more in the direction of social and cultural development than is the case in Alberta.

The Manifestation of Personal Choices (Felt Needs)

It has been suggested earlier that the relationship between ascribed needs and felt needs is a complex one. On one side, felt needs will be a product of individual motives and circumstances. On another side, through the directions of its expenditures or ascription of needs, a government expresses a public philosophy and strongly influences the whole culture of its domain, including the perceptions and needs of its citizens. On yet another side, government and its public philosophy can be seen as a representation, more or less imperfect, of the major aggregations of needs felt by its citizens. To obtain a sense of whether the general pattern as seen from the government's perspective and indicated by Table 6 is similar when seen from the perspective of the students, we must seek information about the choices exercised by the consumers of adult education services when they pay for various kinds of programs.

It has been pointed out that the figures in Table 6 indicate the kinds of adult education for which the governments provide direct financial support, but they do not indicate the volume or direction of programs offered by the wide variety of agencies, including schools, colleges, and universities. And these are the programs through which the public demonstrates its felt needs. Unfortunately, in this area, comparable statistics are difficult to obtain for the comparisons being made in this study. Statistics for private agencies, such as Y.M.C.A.s, Y.W.C.A.s, and church organizations are very elusive. Statistics Canada has in the past published figures of continuing education registration in each province by field of study and by principal institutions (schools, colleges, and universities), but the fields of study so identified do not permit a satisfactory breakdown into the continuum of purposes used in this study. Therefore, Table 7 is an analysis of figures appearing in the Annual Report of Alberta Advanced Education and Manpower, 1977–78, and the Quebec Ministry of Education's Statistics of Advanced Education, 1975–76, published in 1978. They deal with non-credit part-time courses. In the case of Alberta, they cover such courses offered by the Alberta and community vocational centres, colleges, and universities – those institutions relating to the Department of Advanced Education and Manpower. In the case of Quebec they cover courses offered by colleges and school-boards, that is institutions relating to the D.G.E.A. for adult education purposes. The categories are those identified in the Alberta report, and the course titles listed in the Quebec report have been grouped into the same categories for the purposes of this table. With adult basic education on the left, the categories move through a continuum, which can, to a reasonable degree, be reconciled with the categories used for this study: remedial, coping, person-oriented, socially-oriented, and counter-cultural.

The important comparison is not so much between the provincial aggregates, either in total or under each heading, as between the percentages, which show the relative weight given by consumers to the different categories of programs. In Alberta, clearly the largest category comprises courses aimed at increased professional and vocational competence. In other words, besides the emphasis in this province on manpower training programs financed by government, there is a similar emphasis on other professional and vocational programs for which the students pay. The bulk of these are taken through the universities and they take the form of management, supervisory, and continuing professional education courses. The purpose can reasonably be suggested as relating to the need to cope with occupational pressures and to a desire for personal advancement (and the same can probably be said of the government-financed Manpower training courses, when looked at from the point of view of the student). If similar courses offered by Quebec universities, such as McGill, Montreal, and Quebec, were taken into account, the balance between the two provinces in this respect would probably be evened up somewhat, particularly with regard to more senior professional courses, since this element of the Quebec figures would show a proportionate increase.

On the other hand, judging from a breakdown of the course offerings made by all the principal agencies in Edmonton and Calgary, including the school-boards, the Y.M.C.A. and Y.W.C.A., in the fall session of 1979, if the registrations by the school-boards in Alberta were added to those in Table 7, the already comparatively heavy demand for courses related to personal development would be even heavier, both in comparison with Quebec and as a proportion

Table 7

Registration in Non-Credit Part-Time Courses

	A.B.E.	Professional and Vocational	Physical Ed. and Recreation	Arts and Crafts	Personal Development	Liberal Studies	Home Skills	Community and Family	Total
Alberta (1977–78)	4,027	32,632	5,747	7,187	5,337	6,508	11,653	1,405	74,496
%	5.4	43.8	7.7	9.6	7.2	8.7	15.6	1.9	100
Quebec (1975–76)	20,951	30,564	22,113	43,780	11,841	781	83,378	33,051	246,459
%	8.5	12.4	9.0	17.8	4.8	0.3	33.8	13.4	100

Source: *Annual Report*, Alberta Advanced Education and Manpower, 1977–78; *Statistics of Advanced Education, 1975–76*, Quebec Ministry of Education, 1978.

of the total Alberta registrations. This picture is strengthened by an analysis of the offerings on the part of the principal adult education agencies in the two cities of Edmonton and Calgary in the fall of 1979. Among 18 such agencies in Edmonton, including the universities, the Y.M.C.A. and Y.W.C.A., school-boards, and the Family Life Education Council, 93 percent of the courses offered fell within the "coping" and "personal development" part of the continuum, while 3 percent were remedial, 3.6 percent related to social development, and only 0.4 percent were of a counter-cultural nature. Among nine similar agencies in Calgary, 95 percent of the courses offered fell within the "coping" and "personal development" range of the continuum, while 3 percent were remedial and 2 percent related to social development (*Edmonton Journal*, 1979, and Calgary Board of Education, fall 1979–winter 1980).

The most striking imbalance between the two provinces is in registrations for programs aimed at community and family problems. In Alberta, they make up less than 2 percent of the total, whereas in Quebec they are over 13 percent.

Within the Quebec figures there is an interesting feature. Of the 30,564 registrations in professional and vocational courses, only 117 came within the subsidy arrangement of the D.G.E.A., and 30,447 were what in the Quebec terminology are called *cours auto-financés*, that is, the full course fee is paid by the student. In Alberta virtually all these courses are of that kind. Under "personal development" in the Quebec figures, 9,785 out of 11,841 registrations, and under "physical education and recreation," 21,559 out of the 22,113 registrations were in these cours auto-financés. So, regardless of the direction of government assistance in adult education, there is a public demand for the kind of course that leads to personal advancement, economically, physically, and/or emotionally. In other words, to some extent the pursuit of felt needs is independent of the ascription of needs by government or other funding agenices. It is not possible to say for certain in this case, but judging from the profiles of adult education students that have appeared in many studies, this independence is largely a function of disposable incomes (and levels of previous education). It might not be incorrect to suggest that there are two adult education economies or sectors: one in which the satisfaction of needs depends on the potential learners' receiving financial assistance from government and/or other sources, and therefore analagous to the public sector in the economy, and the other in which the satisfaction of needs is within the potential learners' own financial capacity, and analogous to the private economic sector.

The evidence of this study appears to suggest that in an environment dominated by an individualist, capitalist ideology, the pattern of adult education in both sectors will tend to be similar; the emphasis is on programs that are economically and personally beneficial, as in Alberta. This is particularly so where the level of personal income is relatively high, making it possible for many people to pay for courses leading to personal satisfaction. In such an environment, the private sector of adult education is large—even larger than the public sector. In an environment dominated by a strong socialist ideology, and in which the level of personal incomes is relatively low, such as in many less developed countries, there will be a tendency for the public adult education sector to emphasize programs directed at social and national development, and the private sector will range from relatively low to non-existent. Quebec seems to lie somewhere between these two positions. It has, in its government, a fairly strong leaning toward democratic socialism, and in its population a significant percentage of low income people; its unemployment rate is between 20 percent and 50 percent higher than in other parts of Canada, and its level of personal income per capita is 12 percent to 15 percent below the Canadian mean (Renaud, 1978). An important thrust in adult education in the public sector is toward improved standards of social and community functioning, and toward the acquisition of home skills, which either help people supplement their formal income or reduce their dependence on expensive home service industries. This latter category of program is a fairly significant element even in the private sector in Quebec; out of the total of 83,378 registrations in this category, 14,566 were in cours auto-financés.

But Quebec also has a significant private sector, made up of professionals and middle and senior managers in industry and commerce. As Renaud points out, in the industrial and commercial sectors this group has in the past comprised mainly anglophones, while the new francophone bourgeoisie has tended to be in the senior ranks of the government and government agencies. This element of the population is large enough to exercise a significant demand for adult education that aims at various forms of personal satisfaction – professional and recreational. Though in the long run, as Boshier points out, this kind of adult education may have a more or less profound social effect, its immediate focus is personal (Boshier, 1978).

References

Boshier, R. 1978. "Future Functions of Adult Education." *Canadian Journal of University Continuing Education*, vol. v, no. 1.

Calgary Board of Education. *Calgary Continuing Education Opportunities*. Fall 1979–Winter 1980.

Campbell, D.D. 1977. *Adult Education as a Field of Study and Practice: Strategies for Development*. Vancouver: Centre for Continuing Education and I.C.E.A.

Commission on Educational Planning. 1972. *A Choice of Futures*. Edmonton: Queen's Printer.

D.G.E.A. 1970. *L'Opération Départ*. Quebec: Ministère de l'Education.

———. 1971. *L'Opération Départ* (Montreal). Quebec: Ministère de l'Education.

Ecole Nationale d'Administration Public. 1978. *Annuaire 1978–79*. Quebec: Université du Québec.

Edmonton Journal. 1979. "Learning Is Living." 27 August 1979.

Houle, C. 1972. *The Design of Education*. San Francisco: Jossey-Bass.

Ingram, E.T., Kelsey, J.G.T., Konrad, A.G., and Small, J.M. 1974. *Towards an Interprovincial Community College*. Edmonton: University of Alberta, Department of Educational Administration.

Konrad, A., Baker, D.B., and McNairn, W.W. 1979. *Labour Education in Alberta*. Edmonton: Univerity of Alberta, Centre for the Study of Post Secondary Education.

Konrad, A.G., Long, J.C., and Small, J.M. 1976. "Professional Development Needs of Administrators in Higher Education." *Canadian Journal of Higher Education*, vol. 6, no. 1.

Lagassé, L. 1976. *North-Eastern Alberta Needs Assessment Survey*. Mimeographed. Edmonton: Department of Advanced Education and Manpower.

Lavigne, J. 1978. "L'Action Communautaire au Centre Local de Services Communautaires 'Sud-Ouest' de Sherbrooke." *International Review of Community Development*, no. 39–40, Summer 1978.

Messaline, P. and Newhouse, M. 1979. *ACCESS Alberta: Adult Literacy Project Research Digest.* Edmonton: ACCESS.

Mills, C. Wright, and Gerth, Hans. 1964. *Character and Social Structure.* New York: Harbinger Books.

Ministère de l'Education. 1979. *Rapport des Activités 1976–77 et 1978–79.* Quebec: Editeur Officiel.

Renaud, M. 1978. "Quebec Middle Class in Search of Social Hegemony: Courses and Political Consequences." *International Review of Community Development*, no. 39 –40, Summer 1978.

Small, J.M. and Roberts, H.W. 1977. *Continuing Education Needs in the Edson, Hinton, Jasper, and Grande Cache Areas.* Edmonton: University of Alberta, Department of Educational Administration.

12

Conclusion

The evidence of this study of two provinces in Canada appears to support the hypothesis set out in Chapter 3, that the extent to which the general pattern of adult education activities in a country or region shows an emphasis on social development, the collective good, as distinguished from personal development, the individual good, is determined by the dominant social philosophy or ideology of the region.

In Alberta the dominant ideology can, according to the analysis in Chapter 4, be said to emphasize individualism, the encouragement of private enterprise, and the measurement of advancement by economic criteria. Moreover, there is general agreement on this ideology in both the political and economic orders of Alberta society. The political term, conservative, can fairly be used to characterize the situation. There is, however, a vestige of an earlier rurally based co-operativism in the province. In Quebec the picture is not quite so clear. There remains a strain of the conservatism of the earlier, church-dominated, and rurally oriented Quebecois society, which has been joined more recently by a similar tendency among some of the newer francophone bourgeoisie, and for a long time there has been the more individualistic business-conservatism of the anglophone population. But since the early 1960s a current of democratic socialism has been joined to that of Quebec nationalism, and this has flowed particularly strongly through the political and civil service channels of Quebec society. As a result, there is a tension between the still predominantly anglophone and conservative economic order and the more recently dominant social democratic francophone political order, with the latter enjoying the support of an aroused Quebecois cultural nationalism.

These differences are not immediately and markedly apparent in the structure and interrelationships of government institutions. In general, the same kinds of ministries and departments exist in the two provinces, and as far as adult education is concerned, there is a similar spread of responsibilities among various portfolios for one aspect or another of this field of activity. In both provinces the support for vocationally oriented training, general or "liberal" adult education, and cultural development, is provided through government departments that appear to have roughly parallel jurisdictions. The difference, however, becomes clearly apparent in the way and the extent to which these ministries and departments allocate resources to adult education. It is in this respect that one sees the relationship between the provision of adult education through government agencies and the dominant ideologies of the governments. Chapter 11 shows that it is fair to say that in respect of government-supported adult education, there is far more emphasis in Quebec on that part of the continuum which relates to social development than there is in Alberta.

In other words, the ascription of needs, as far as adult education is concerned, is related directly to the dominant social philosophy of the government. This is exemplified in Alberta by the quite rapid and marked change in attitudes, policies, and direction of expenditure under the new Progressive Conservative government in the early 1970s. Though in a general sense the previous Social Credit government had been of an individualistic and conservative mold, it had continued to reflect some of the populism and social idealism of earlier Alberta society, and had, particularly in its dying years, directed substantial resources into social development programs. The Progressive Conservatives represented a clear break from such vestigal prairie populism, and the espousal of a harder-headed conservatism – with expedient deviations now and then into such ventures as the purchase of Pacific Western Airlines.

This kind of ascription is evident not only by government. Fordham (1976) has suggested that adult education agencies reveal a broad political inclination in their styles of programming, the direction of their need assessments, and their staff recruiting, the third of which determines the other two in the final analysis. And certainly in Alberta, the author's personal experience and observation of the staffing and programming policy of the principal agencies, particularly the university extension units, supports that suggestion. Needs are assessed within the predetermined boundaries of staff interests and competencies, and of institutional policy, and this is generally congruent with the dominant socio-political climate of the province. In Quebec there is, likewise, some evidence that the staffing and policies of some of the social service agencies, such as community T.V. groups and local community service centres, reflect the strain of democratic socialism in the province.

The analysis of this study suggests that the relationship between the elements cited in Chapter 3, Figure 4, as affecting patterns of adult education, requires restating. Alongside the field of government-supported adult education, there is another field, the extent and nature of which is determined by the level of disposable private funds. In both provinces there is a considerable demand for programs aimed at vocational advancement, personal growth, and recreation, provided by all the principal adult education institutions, and by a wide range of other agencies this study has only alluded to. The demand comes from that section of the general public that can afford such programs.

As far as programs of a professional and business nature are concerned, and particularly those offered by universities and colleges, the demand comes from the management of business institutions and from professional associations. These two kinds of institutions exercise a demand for adult education that is independent of the influence of government institutional structures and of government funding. It would not, however, be entirely correct to suggest that these programs constitute a response to the felt needs of the learners as distinct from the fulfillment of ascribed needs. A second order of ascription is evident here. Though much of the demand for continuing professional education appears to arise from the personal intrinsic needs of the people concerned, many students participate not because of such personally, intrinsically felt needs, but from extrinsic motives; advancement in their occupations is contingent on their attendance at such courses. The phenomenon has in recent years attracted the label of Mandatory Continuing Education, and has aroused growing opposition to what is seen as an insidious movement toward compulsory lifelong schooling (Lisman and Ohliger, 1978). In these circumstances, such education can fairly be placed in the "coping" section of the continuum of purposes that forms the basis of this study, when it is viewed from the students' standpoint, though from the standpoint of the employer it might be avowed to have a broader social purpose.

Another observation that can be made about this same phenomenon is that it calls into question a proposition frequently made among adult educationists: adults come as volunteers to learning. This is sometimes suggested as a characteristic that distinguishes adult education from the education of children, when in fact it applies to only certain kinds of recreational and personal-oriented programs.

Figure 8 sets out the revised schema in diagramatic form. While in the public sector the relationship between social philosophy, social structures, needs, and resources remains the same as suggested in Figure 4, consideration of the private sector, i.e. programs offered in response to, and paid for by, private corporations and associations, and by persons who have disposable incomes for that purpose, adds an additional element to the model.

Needs perceived by persons in the official government structures can be seen as ascribed needs, which then lead to the provision of resources to meet those needs. Alongside this, in the private sector the corporations and associations ascribe certain needs in respect of their employees or members, and they make available resources for programs to meet those needs. These programs may be provided by the corporations and associations themselves, by private educational and/or training agencies, or by formal institutions such as universities and colleges. They may be especially contracted by the corporation or association, or the latter may pay the tuition and other costs for their employees or members to attend programs already available. The other component of the private sector consists of the provision by individuals, from their own disposable incomes, of funds to meet their own felt needs.

The relative strengths of the public and private sectors of adult education in a country will depend on the level and distribution of

Figure 8
_____

Relationships Between Forces Influencing Adult Education

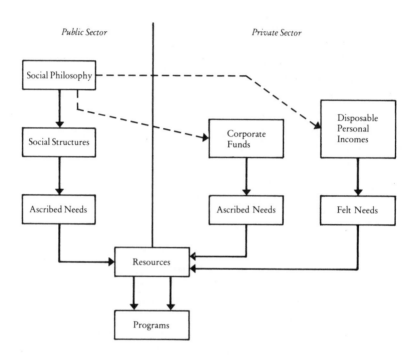

personal disposable incomes and/or of corporate and association funds made available for education and training. In highly government-directed and in less developed countries, the bulk, if not all, of adult education will fall in the public sector. In less developed countries there have, however, been instances of prominent private sectors of adult education, stimulated by large resource industries finding a need for employee training of various kinds, and allocating funds for the provision or purchase of appropriate programs. An example of this can be seen in Zambia, where since the early 1960s the copper mining companies, the largest employers in the country, have been active in providing or purchasing various types and levels of skill training for their workers.

Figure 8 shows how the public and private sectors contribute to the pool of resources—human, material (including financial) and organizational—available for various kinds of programming in a country. The dotted lines between *social philosophy* and *corporate funds* and *disposable private incomes* are meant to suggest that the dispositions of the latter are not immune from the influence of the dominant social philosophy of the region or country.

We have identified three specific types of non-government institutions that, in Alberta, Quebec, and all the other provinces, exercise an influence on the adult education scene: labor unions, agricultural organizations, and associations of native people. In Alberta and Quebec the demands expressed through these institutions, and the resources available to them, reflect to some extent the dominant pattern, but they also reveal some trends counter to that pattern.

With regard to the labor unions, a clear difference between the provinces is the much greater strength and militancy of the union movement in Quebec than in Alberta. This arises partly from economic and partly from political and cultural conditions. In Alberta economic conditions since mid-century have improved both absolutely and in relation to other provinces, bringing a climate not conducive to the development of strong or militant unions. At the same time, and not independently, the political trend has been toward government that barely tolerates union activity. In Quebec, on the other hand, levels of unemployment and incomes give better cause for labor organization, while the common relationship of francophone labor to anglophone management has given a broader cultural base to union activity. The result is that in Quebec the unions have more internal funds for trade union and workers' education, i.e. the training of union members and officials in union matters and the broader education of workers in political and economic affairs, and they have more interest in such education as a political and economic necessity. Moreover, there is a closer affinity between the purposes of the unions and those of recent provincial governments, which results in the possibility of better funding for union education, though not enough in practice to satisfy the unions.

In general, therefore, the state and extent of labor education in the two provinces tends to conform to rather than distort the dominant patterns of adult education. In Alberta, this is not just by choice of the unions, but by a paucity of choice resulting from a paucity of funds for independent activity.

What has been said about labor unions applies to some extent to agricultural organizations. In Quebec, partly on account of the same historical and cultural factors referred to in regard to union organizations, an important thrust in agriculture has been toward the syndicalization of small farmers and laborers in farming and forestry. The Union des Producteurs Agricoles is, in fact, a registered trade union, with interests similar to those of other unions as far as the education and training of its members and officials is concerned. Its main educational function is in activities directed toward improved organization, syndicalist activity, and political understanding. In Alberta, agriculture has historically been a more prominent element in the life of the province, and it provided the roots of government in the years up to the 1960s, so there is a tradition of socio-political education among farm organizations. This tradition continues in the 1970s and 1980s through the Rural Education and Development Association, almost as an aberration from the mainstream of adult education in the province. There are interesting similarities, for different historical reasons, between the educational interests of the U.P.A. and the R.E.D.A. Parallel to their activities, there is in both provinces a strong stream of practical, production- and marketing-oriented education through producer organizations, often in conjunction with government and educational agencies.

An examination of the educational interests and activities of native organizations puts a particular focus on certain elements in the continuum of purposes. At one end of that continuum we have adult education with a remedial purpose, adult basic education, literacy, and some second-language courses.

Table 7 indicates that in both provinces the number of registrations in adult basic education courses of various sorts, as a percentage of totals in all courses, is relatively low, though it is more than proportionately higher in Quebec than in Alberta. In both provinces there are groups of the Movement for Canadian Literacy, who are concerned to alert the public and governments to the need for better programs, in quantity and quality, and to combat the high rates of functional illiteracy revealed by statistics of educational levels among Canadian adults. In Alberta, 20 percent of the population over fifteen years of age had less than grade nine education in 1976, and in Quebec the equivalent figure was 36 percent (Statistics Canada, 1976 Census). In both provinces, the governments have been accused, by members of the Movement for Canadian Literacy, of doing little to remedy this problem (Snider, 1979; Hautecoeur, 1979).

These statistics refer not to native people, but to other Canadians who have simply failed to learn to read and write but have managed to get through at least some schooling. For native people, the problem is particularly acute. In Chapter 7 we have seen that the emphasis in most programs designed for or available to native people is on preparing them for occupational and social responsibilites in the dominant white culture, in other words, on remedying their lack of skills (including language skills), knowledge, and attitudes appropriate to this culture. This is the common interpretation of the term, "remedial education."

But in the case of the native people and their relationship with the dominant white culture, and the Quebecois in their relationship with the dominant North American anglophone culture, there is another aspect to the process of remediation. For many such people, that process is seen to start, not with an adaptation to the demands and ways of the dominant culture, but with a strengthening of their own identity in terms of their own culture. Searching into their own roots and strengthening their self-awareness through a renewal of the values and ways of their culture becomes the means of confronting and being able to cope with the other culture. Thus, counter-cultural and remedial education are joined. In the metaphor of the continuum of purposes of adult education, the linear representation becomes a circular one, with remedial and counter-cultural merging into each other, and all of the categories touching in the centre. The lines between the categories are blurred. This relationship is represented diagramatically in Figure 9.

There is an analogy between this social phenomenon and the experience of individuals in a learning process. Counsellors working with alcohol and drug addicts, trying to help them break out of a darkness of self-loathing and self-punishment, confirm that a necessary part of the process of change is a prior recreation of a favorable self-concept, a respectable self-image.

One interpretation of the learning process, in Gestalt/cognitive/field theory tradition, is that learning, for any person, is a continuous transaction between the self-concept (the "very essence of me"), the phenomenal self (the self as perceived and felt in particular external

Figure 9

Purposes of Adult Education (Revised)

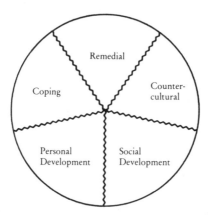

situations), and the phenomenal environment (the continually existing and changing outside world as seen by the individual) (Combs and
Snygg, 1959): "The need (for learning) is need from the behaver's point
of view, not that of an outsider" (Ibid.: 194). The process involves an
interactive and interdependent relationship between the self and the
environment.

There is an interesting analogy to this theoretical approach in the
propositions made by the committee that produced the report of
Opération Départ (Montréal), referred to in Chapter 9. This group
sought a theoretical framework for the relationship between personal
and social aspects of learning, as it related to the concept of éducation
permanente. The report defines education as being centred on the autonomous learner (s'éducant); learning by the autonomous individual
takes place in an educative environment, which, in turn, is seen as
existing within an educative society. All these elements make up what
the group calls an educative system (D.G.E.A., 1971: 1–7). This proposition does not have the phenomenological perspective of that of
Combs and Snygg, but it reflects the same relationship between the
inner being of the learner and the social environment in which people
learn and act.

The elegance of the model in Figure 9 is, however, marred by the
absorption of the subordinate culture into the dominant one. It fails

to take account of the continuance of separate cultures, even though they are modified by one another. In the original representation of the continuum of purpose, Figure 2, the solid line from *remedial* to *social development* was extended to *counter-cultural* as a dotted line, because it was suggested that counter-cultural education was of a different dimension, taking us outside the paradigm into which the other categories fitted. It is now suggested that within the dominant culture the range of purposes extends from remedial to social development, and that the dominant social philosophy in that culture will influence the balance of purposes of adult education programming.

It is likewise suggested that the same set of relationships between the dominant social philosophy and the purposes of adult education exists in each culture, for example, in the native and the Quebecois cultures in Canada. The counter-cultural element of a situation arises when there is interaction between people of different cultures. We can use the analogy of two gear wheels being brought into contact. The gears may synchronize and begin sharing energy, or they may crash and damage each other. The meeting of the two cultures is an educational process—a process of negotiation, adaptation, the mutal respect of identities and values, and what T.S. Eliot calls, "a consideration of useful diversities" (1948:52). It is a two-way process of learning. Figure 10 gives a diagramatic presentation of these relationships.

That is one aspect of the term, counter-cultural. Crowfoot and

Figure 10

The Relationship of Cultures

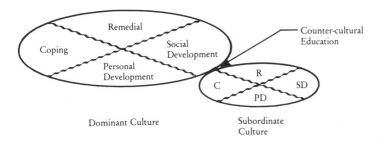

Coping
Remedial
Social Development
Personal Development

Counter-cultural Education

R
C
SD
PD

Dominant Culture

Subordinate Culture

Chesler's use of the term in Chapter 2 gives it a broader meaning, one that sees the process not as being against the dominant culture, but as going *beyond* existing mundane cultures, embracing them in a more universal search for understanding, seeing our planet in a larger cosmos. Some of the ways in which this aspect of counter-cultural education shows itself are in the formation of "new age" communities, the groping for a new scientific paradigm on the basis of current research in sub-atomic physics, and for a new social paradigm on the basis of co-operation and synthesis rather than competition and analysis. While, as we have seen, there is some evidence in the two provinces that are the subjects of this study, of counter-cultural education of the first kind, that is, among the native people and in Quebec, evidence of the latter kind would call for more careful and detailed research than is possible in this study. Such research could, however, be important for expanding the boundaries within which adult education in these and other provinces constrains itself.

References

Combs, A.W. and Snygg, D. 1959. *Individual Behaviour.* New York: Harper and Row.

D.G.E.A. 1971. *L'Opération Départ (Montréal).* Quebec: Ministère de L'Education.

Dion, L. 1976. *The Unfinished Revolution.* Montreal: McGill-Queens University Press.

Edmonton Journal. "Illiteracy plagues 1 million Canadians, seminar is told." 5 April 1979, p. E8.

Eliot, T.S. 1948. *Notes Toward a Definition of Culture.* London: Faber and Faber.

Fordham, P. 1976. "The Political Context of Adult Education." *Studies in Adult Education,* vol. 8, no. 1.

Hautecoeur, J.P. 1979. "Pour Le Développement de l'Alphabétisation Au Québec." *Le Grain de Sel,* numero spécial, mai 1979. Quebec: Ministère de l'Education.

Lisman, D. and Ohliger, J. 1978. "Must We all Go Back to School?" *The Progressive,* vol. 42, no. 10, October 1978.

13

Postscript

Recent developments in Quebec serve to underline one of the differences that has been shown by this study, between approaches to the organization of adult education in Alberta and Quebec. In the latter province there is a tendency toward large, comprehensive designs, involving more systematization and centralized government involvement than is the case in Alberta.

From the early 1960s and the Parent Commission and Ryan Committee, there has been, in Quebec, a succession of comprehensive studies, at the provincial level, of various aspects of educational and cultural development. With regard to adult education, there has been, on the one hand, a searching among government administrators for a comprehensive adult education policy, and on the other hand, increasing pressure from a number of organizations for better educational services to adults in the province. These organizations include the Adult Education Commission of the Superior Council of Education (*see* Chapter 6), the Institut Canadien d'Education des Adultes (*see* Chapter 10), and the Federation of CEGEPs, the Federation of School-Boards, and the University Council. These pressures distinguish the situation in Quebec from that in Alberta, where there has been virtually no active representation by such educational lobby groups on behalf of adult education, and where in the case of the Alberta Association for Continuing Education there has actually been some resistance among the membership against such a representational role. Moreover, on the Alberta government side, there is no evidence of a comprehensive overview of the field of adult education in its many forms. Indeed, there is recent evidence of a lack of such an overview, which will be alluded to below.

It is as a result of these internal searchings and outside pressures that the Quebec government set up, in January 1980, a Comission d'étude sur la formation des adultes. We will, for our purposes, use the term Jean Commission, the president being Michèle Jean. The commission comprised persons representative of adult education in the CEGEPs, school-boards, universities, unions, and industry and business. It was responsible to an interdepartmental committee of Ministers of Social Development, Labor and Manpower, Education and Cultural Development.

The scope of the commission's work was very wide; it adopted for its purposes the UNESCO definition of adult education, set out and discussed in Chapter 2. Its mandate was expressed in its full title; in other words, it was to examine the two spheres of vocational and socio-cultural education, and formulate a comprehensive adult education policy for Quebec. To pursue its objectives, the commission set up a program to obtain public input, and to meet with "movements, associations, and organizations concerned" (Jean Commission, 1981:3). Not only did it publicize itself widely, asking for people's views on the subject of its mandate, but it established eighteen regional offices for the receipt of comments. It organized, in the autumn of 1980, a series of regional study sessions, other meetings, and work committees. It heard from 245 groups and 5,000 individual adults, and received 651 briefs.

As a second step in its process, after obtaining these initial submissions, the Commission prepared a working document entitled *Adult Education in Quebec: Possible Solutions*, which it distributed widely in order to obtain reactions. As part of the feedback process, a conference in Quebec City was organized in May 1981, to which over

400 persons were invited from the field of adult education in the province. The initial findings of the commission, as expressed in the *Possible Solutions* document, including the following: "No one is happy with the present system. Adult education strikes us as being a fragile sector, imperfectly understood, and a constant source of dissatisfaction" (p. 5); with regard to the administrative structure of adult education, "we can well speak of an administrative jumble" (p. 205); "In Quebec the public and various organizations, community groups, union, business firms and co-operatives regard education as an essential component to be used when called for. It remains now to give this conception a practical form" (p. 6); despite the combined efforts of experiments such as Opération Départ, SÉSAME, TEVEC, and Multi-Média, adult education within the academic institutions remained a low priority (p. 33); and "The democratization, accessibility and sharing of knowledge will be achieved only if there is co-operation, assumption of responsibility regionally, and rapid access to information and guidance of adults" (p. 9).

These selected observations from the interim document provide a flavor of the commission's perceptions at that point. The commission saw a widespread dissatisfaction with existing conditions, a lack of administrative cohesion, a growing demand for adult education services for the many social and economic institutions, failure on the part of academic institutions to give priority to adult education, and the need for a mechanism of co-operation and regional responsibilities. Such perceptions appear to have provided the basis for the commission's main proposals, which were as follows: the government should enact a general law recognizing and delineating the field of adult education, and providing better access to the field for adults in the province; there should be created, by legislation, "an agency for collective action in adult education"—the office of adult education, with a centre for distance education—which should be a para-governmental structure; this office should have a Board of Directors representing the different milieus involved in adult education, including users, and the president should have the rank of Deputy Minister and should report either to the Prime Minister or a designated minister; the office of adult education should be given jurisdiction over all the adult education resources so far controlled by the Ministry of Education, and should administer the funds resulting from the Canada-Quebec agreements on adult vocational training; it should create a comprehensive model of education by integrating the existing sectors—general, vocational, and socio-cultural; under the central office should be established about 25 regional centres of adult education, which in turn should have local service points and local "sectorial" committees; these regional centres should make educational agencies aware of local concerns and demands, so that offerings could be tailored accordingly, and they should offer services such as counselling to adults; the educational agencies should withdraw from the activities of publicity directed at adults, community animation and support for social action, guidance services, and the identification of adult education needs, and they should do little more than respond to requests from regional centres; and there must be a serious questioning of cost/capacity ratio of services in all educational institutions, including the universities.

It is clear that such an array of proposals would be seen as a direct threat to the roles and functions of existing educational institutions, some elements of which have from time to time been active in supporting local social-action groups, and all of which, to some degree, see themselves responding directly to public needs. It is not surprising, therefore, that at the conference called by the commission in Quebec in May 1981, there were heated objections to these proposals. There was, among some Quebec adult educationists, a revival of an earlier antipathy against what had been seen as an inappropriate French influence that had introduced the concept of éducation permanente to the Parent Commission in the early 1960s. In this later case, there was a feeling that the characteristic French penchant for centralist control of education was a factor in these proposals. In the final report, entitled *Apprendre: une action volontaire et responsable,* the proposal for a central office of adult education, with regional centres of adult education, remained, subject to a three-year phasing-in period (Commission d'étude, 1982:567–78). It will be interesting to see to what extent this model will be accepted by the Quebec government.

While the commission was gathering data and comments, the government brought out its estimates of expenditure for 1981–82, which showed a total for adult education programming of $138,600,000, a decrease of $8,231,000 or 5.6 percent from the 1980–81 estimates, which showed $146,831,100.* This prompted a note in the *Possible Solutions* document to the effect that such cuts "make us aware of the vulnerability of the rights of adults to education, and the effects of the absence of an overall policy based on precise principles and aims."

There are interesting parallels to be drawn between one or two of the Jean Commission proposals and some that emerged during the process of the Worth Commission in Alberta almost ten years previously. The Jean Commission (1981:303) revived an idea that has been abroad in the last decade or so, namely, that there should be a system whereby everyone would have the right to fifteen years of full-time education and that those who have not used up these fifteen years should be eligible for subsidized education up to that limit. This parallels a Worth Commission proposal (1972:202) that there should be a national education bank or fund that credits each person with fifteen years of freely chosen schooling at public expense. The recommendation of the Jean Commission that ten or eleven of the fifteen years must be taken between the ages of six and sixteen (compulsory attendance) indicates its agreement with the Worth Commission's conclusion that, though ideally, in a true and equitable regime of lifelong education, there may be no need for compulsory basic education, in present circumstances it is justified. In the ten years since the Worth Commission, the educational bank concept has not been brought anywhere near reality, either provincially or nationally, so it

---

* This figure of $146,831,100 was allocated between vocational training, training management, and general and socio-cultural training, and the latter was allocated $39,588,000. This figure therefore corresponds to the $32,664,100 for 1979–80, in the Quebec column of the first section of Table 6 in Chapter 11; in other words, there was an increase between 1979–80 and 1980–81 of $6,923,900. The two comparable figures relating to Alberta in that table – $2,445,000 and $614,886 – became in 1980–81 $2,699,175 and $490,974 respectively, a total increase of only $130,263. However, in the Alberta estimates for 1981–82 these figures jumped to $3,740,500 and $569,060 respectively, a total increase of $1,119,411, which reflects the rise in further education course grants and administration grants to local councils. Unfortunately, since in its 1981–2 estimates the Quebec government breaks down its total adult education allocation in a different way, between school-boards, public colleges, and other organizations, we cannot carry the comparison in Section 1 of Table 6 forward to that year.

will be interesting to see if it eventually has any effect on educational policy and practice in Quebec.

A more important parallel lies between the proposal for an office of adult education in the interim Jean Report, and a somewhat similar proposal that appeared in the report of the Lifelong Education Task Force, which was one of three task forces feeding into the Worth Commission process in Alberta. The other two task forces were in N-12 education and post-secondary education. Each task force produced an interim report with recommendations, and these interim reports were the subject of a series of public meetings and comments from a selected group of leaders in the respective fields of education in North America and Europe. The Lifelong Education Task Force proposed a High Commission for Lifelong Education, whose duties and responsibilities would be to oversee the total picture of lifelong education. It would work toward opening all education agencies to all learners at the appropriate levels of learning; obtaining co-operation between all educational agencies at regional and provincial levels; a system under which work experience, vocational training, and wider education could be more consciously integrated; and, where appropriate, contracting for the provision of educational services to community groups. It would be authorized to bring to the attention of the cabinet, matters in which the concept of lifelong education was affected by decisions and developments in other fields—economic, social, and political.

This commission would exist alongside a Universities Commission, Colleges Commission, a Commission on Educational Planning, Research and Development, and the Department of Education (Lifelong Education Task Force, 1971:11).

In other words, there was a sense, among some people in Alberta in the early 1970s, of the need for co-ordination and systematization of adult education, that the Jean Commission perceived in Quebec ten years later, though the Alberta proposal was not as comprehensive and controlling as the Jean Commission's. The interim report of the Lifelong Education Task Force met with a good response in public meetings in Alberta, and from seven eminent adult educationists in North America and Europe to whom it was sent for comments. Its proposal for a Commission for Lifelong Education did not, however, survive into the final Worth Report, which made no reference to such a mechanism of co-ordination, though it did acknowledge the need for co-ordination of adult and continuing education and leadership training, through a Further Education Divison of the new Department of Advanced Education (1972:136).

This question of co-ordination draws attention to a recent development in adult education in Alberta which is still, at the time of writing, not clear as to its outcome. In Chapter 5 we discussed the roles of the Local Further Education Councils in Alberta, the policy of community education, and the very recent phenomenon of educational consortia. Local councils, funded in terms of the Further Education Policy of the Department of Advanced Education and Manpower, have been in existence since the mid 1970s; they have directed their attention to promoting and meeting the need for non-credit adult education throughout the province. Each local council's main energy, in the smaller centres, has been focused through a local part-time coordinator, who can be paid up to $7,000 per annum ($10,000 in the 1981–82 budget). The community education policy was only beginning to get under way in mid-1981. It, too, provides for co-ordinators, working out of designated schools and promoting forms of adult education in the surrounding community, based on the community school. And in 1981, consortia of educational institutions were in place or were being set up, in five regions of the province, each region covering a number of Local Further Education Council jurisdictions. The primary role of these consortia was to deliver credit courses to their respective regions, through their constituent institutional members. Each consortium was served by a local advisory board and a full-time director, earning, generally speaking, more than three times the income of the Local Further Education Council co-ordinators. There were, by mid-1981, signs that some consortium directors were beginning to extend their role to cover non-credit programs.

This brief account reveals the possibility of overlapping, confusion, and locally perceived inequities, which does not seem to have been taken into account in the formulation, in different parts of different ministries, of these various policies, particularly in the case of the consortia, which came into being with so short a gestation period as to have what has been termed an immaculate conception in a study commissioned by the Alberta Association for Continuing Education (Byrne, 1981:15). This study, by Dr. T. Byrne, a former Deputy Minister of Education in the province, and first President of Athabasca University, was aimed at clarifying the picture in which these three policies were featured, and providing a basis for raising questions about their implementation. The author of the study makes the following recommendation relating to co-ordination and administration of continuing education: "That to improve the central coordination of the Further Education and Consortium Policies the Association should request the Minister of Education and Manpower [sic] to include the administration of both policies within the same departmental branch under the direction of a senior civil servant with a status comparable to that of Assistant Deputy Minister."

There is a broader issue involved in this discussion of co-ordination, commission reports, and the roles of various agencies and of government in the field of adult education. It is the issue of the future disposition and organization of adult education, both within large institutions such as colleges and universities, and in society as a whole. On the one hand, there is a growth of adult education enterprises serving the private sector, particularly in the corporation-controlled part of that sector, as interpreted in Chapter 12, which shows signs of increasingly outgrowing and outmoding respectively the volume and methods of adult education offered in the public sector. As is indicated in Chapter 2, that is matter for another study. On the other hand, and here is matter relevant to this study, there are indications that as adult education, represented by its practitioners and some of its clients, seeks a more central place in the formal systems of education, and more institutional and public funding, it exposes itself to the possibility of direction, if not control, from host institutions and/or government or quasi-goverment bodies. Within institutions such as colleges and universities, in Alberta and elsewhere, the extension/continuing education operation is recently more under the eye of senior administration and more subject to pressure to be consistent with broader institutional goals. Outside those environments, adult education activities are increasingly influenced by government funding policies. whether those policies are internally consistent, coherent, and centralized, or inconsistent, incoherent, and dispersed. In Alberta, the introduction of a further education policy, and a system of funding under that policy, have absorbed the energies of agencies, local councils, and the provincial association, and have shaped much of their thinking, planning, and programming. In Quebec, the funding and support policies of the government have influenced the growth and activities of the O.V.E.P.s, other community groups, and the formal institutions. In both provinces, and all others, a wide sector of adult education, that is, manpower training in its various forms, is shaped by provincial and federal government policies together.

That this is an issue not only in these two provinces, but also in others, is indicated in a discussion paper issued by the Ontario government at about the time of the publication of the Quebec paper. Entitled *Continuing Education: The Third System,* it explores the role of government in this field, and concludes that, "the co-ordination of efforts in continuing education presents many difficulties, but it also provides opportunity to consolidate the third system. It remains central to any development of an integrated policy for continuing education" (Ministry of Education, 1981:50).

References

Byrne, T.C. 1981. *Towards a System in Continuing Education.* Edmonton: Athabasca University.

Commission d'étude sur la formation des adultes (Jean Commission). 1981. *Adult Education in Quebec: Possible Solutions.* Quebec: Ministère des Communications.

———. 1982. *Apprendre: une action volontaire et responsable.* Quebec: Ministère des Communications.

Commission on Educational Planning (Worth Commission). 1972. *A Choice of Futures.* Edmonton: Queen's Printer.

Lifelong Education Task Force. 1971. *Interim Proposals.* Mimeographed. Edmonton: Commission on Educational Planning.

Ministry of Education. 1981. *Continuing Education: The Third System.* Toronto: Ministry of Education and Ministry of Colleges and Universities.

Index

adult education, defined: Alberta, 17–21; Quebec, 18–22; UNESCO, 15–16

adulthood, 16

agrarian populism and cooperativism, 64

agriculture–producer organizations, 182

Alberta: distrust of eastern interests, 64; ethnic composition, 62–63; religious non-conformity, 62–63; social philosophy, 64–75 passim

Alberta Association for Continuing Education (A.A.C.E.), 111, 112, 211, 212–16, 217, 219, 262, 267

Alberta Education Communications Authority (A.E.C.A.), 96

Alberta Education Communications Corporation (ACCESS), 96–97, 230

Alberta Federation of Labor (A.F.L.): 195, 199–202; education committee, 199–200

Alberta government: Advanced Education, 71, 81; Advanced Education and Manpower, 83–85, 86, 87, 99, 126, 148, 215, 229; Advisory Committee on Further Education, 86, 111–12; Agriculture, 87, 88, 180–82; Caucus Standing Committee on Education, 215; Community Education Co-ordinating Committee, 99; Consumer and Corporate Affairs, 87, 89; Co-ordinator of Continuing Education, 78; Culture, 87, 91–92; Education, 78, 86, 87; Executive Council, 87, 95; Labor, 82, 83; Municipal Affairs, 87, 96; Native Affairs, 87, 95; Recreation and Parks, 87, 91–92; Social Services and Community Health, 87, 92–94; Transport, 87, 95; Workers Health, Safety, and Compensation, 87, 89

Alberta Native Communications Society, (A.N.C.S.), 160–62

Alberta Teachers Association (A.T.A.), 205

Alberta Vocational Centres, 81–87 passim, 95

animation communautaire, 33
animation sociale, 33
Antigonish Movement, 10
Athabasca University: 97–98, 136; labor education survey, 200–201; and trade unions, 208

Banff Centre, 180, 182
British North America (B.N.A.) Act, 49, 147, 148, 164

cable television, 98–99
caisses populaires, 191–92
Canada Manpower and Immigration, 148, 153, 154
Canada Manpower Industrial Training Program, 85
Canada Manpower Training Program, 85
Canadian Association for Adult Education (C.A.A.E.), 9–10, 32, 139, 211
Canadian Broadcasting Corporation (CBC), 139, 173, 187
Canadian Employment and Immigration Commission, 148, 165
Canadian Farm Problems Radio Series, 187
Canadian Labor Congress (C.L.C.): 195–98, 199; education department, 196
Centrale de l'Enseignement du Québec (C.E.Q.)/Quebec Teachers Federation, 204, 206, 207
Centrale des Syndicaux Démocratiques (C.S.D.), 204, 205, 207
Collèges d'Enseignement Général et Professionel (CEGEP), 118, 119, 137, 186
Commission d'Etudes Sur La Formation Professionelle et Socio-Culturelle des Adultes (Jean Commission), 262–66
Commission on Educational Planning (Worth Commission): 17–20, 69, 71, 96, 265; functions of adult education, 17
community development, 33

community education, 33, 102–3, 267
Community Vocational Centres, 81, 85, 87, 89, 160
comparative adult education, 3, 12, 34–35
Confédération des Syndicaux Nationaux (C.S.N.)/Confederation of National Trade Unions, 197, 204–8 passim
consortia, 103–4, 267–68
Co-operative Commonwealth Federation (C.C.F.), 65
co-operatives: Alberta, 183–84, 192; Quebec, 191–92; Inuit, 170–71; T.V. and radio, 134–35
co-ordination: 269; Alberta, 99–102; Quebec, 137–38
cultural pluralism, 24
culture: defined, 23–25; Quebec, 57

democratic socialism; 59, 250
Duplessis regime, 53

éducation permanente, 19, 20, 114, 116, 231, 232
educational communications: Alberta, 97–99; Quebec, 132–36
educational leave, 202, 208–9

Farmers' Union and Co-operative Development Association (F.U.C.D.A.), 184
Farmers' Union of Alberta, 65
Faure, E., 20
Federation of Metis Settlements, 159–60
further education, 17–18, 83
Further Education Policies, Guidelines and Procedures, Alberta, 100–101

government expenditures on adult education, 235–40
guiding hypothesis, 4, 12, 27, 43

Human Resources Development Authority, (H.R.D.A.), 79
Human Resource Development White Paper, Alberta, 66–68

ideology(ies), 53–55
Inagtigut Tunnagavinga Nunaminni (I.T.N.), 171, 173, 174
Indian Act, 147, 153, 158
Indian Affairs and Northern Development, 148, 151, 153, 157, 163
Indian Association of Alberta, 151, 153, 154, 156, 160
Indian associations of Quebec, 165–66
Indian control of Indian education, 149, 155
Indian cultural and education centres: Alberta, 156–58; Quebec, 168–70
Indian news media, 162–63
informal adult education, 22
Institut Canadien d'Education des Adultes (I.C.E.A.), 139, 211, 216–21
Inuit: 147, 150, 163–64; cultural education centre, 175; in Quebec, 170–75

James Bay Agreement, 165, 166, 171, 174

Labor Canada, 196, 197
Laval University, Faculty of Agriculture and Food Sciences, 186
Lesage government, 53–55
lifelong education, 15, 16–18, 57, 61
Lifelong Education Task Force, Alberta, 80, 99, 266
literacy: 30–32, 256–57; in Alberta, 32; in Quebec, 32
Local Community Service Centres, 130–32
Local Further Education Councils, 83, 99–102, 111, 213, 267
Lougheed, P., 68, 71

mandatory continuing education, 42, 253
Manning, E.C., 66, 74
McGill University, Macdonald College, 186, 187
Metis: 148, 149; in Alberta, 150, 158; in Quebec, 170
Metis Association of Alberta, 151, 154, 159, 160

multi-culturalism, 73–74
Multi-Média, 60, 120, 135

National Farm Radio Forum, 187
National Indian Brotherhood, 149
nationalism: 58; in Alberta, 68; in Quebec, 68
Native Outreach, 154, 155, 160
needs in adult education: ascribed, 43, 228, 251, 253–54; assessment of, in Alberta, 229–30, 233, in Quebec, 231–32; economic, educational, political, psychological, social, 39–40; felt, 43, 228, 254; individual *vs* societal, 6; of minorities, 43
non-credit part-time course registrations, 244–47
non-status Indians, 147–49, 170
Northern Quebec Inuit Association (N.Q.I.A.), 168–74 passim

Office of Radio-Television of Quebec, 133
Opération Départ: 231–32, 234; (Montreal), 258
Organismes Volontaires d'Education Populaire (O.V.E.P.), 119, 120, 240

Parent Commission, 18–19, 22, 53, 61, 107, 109, 113–15
Parti Québécois, 55–57, 61, 124
"People Talking Back," 10, 214
people's culture, 59
philosophies of adult education, 5, 8–9
prairie socialism, 65
private sector of adult education, 253–54
Progressive Conservatives, 70, 79, 81
public sector of adult education, 253–54
purposes of adult education: 5–12, 16, 21–22, 259; in Alberta, 70, coping, 31–32; counter-cultural, 31, 33–34, 259–60; personal development, 5, 16, 21, 28–29, 33; provincial comparisons, 241–43, 244–47; remedial, 30–32, 257, social development, 5, 16, 21, 28–29, 33

Quebec: categories of adult education, 21; conservatism, 53, 59, 250; early educational system, 106–9; ethnic composition, 63; nationalism, 53, 54, 58–60 passim, 73; separatism, 59; socialism, 59; social philosophy, 52–61 passim, 72–73

Quebec Federation of Labor/Fédération des Travailleurs du Québec (F.T.Q.), 196, 204–8 passim

Quebec government: Direction Générale d'Education des Adultes (D.G.E.A.), 117, 119, 121, 168, 207; Agriculture, 119, 128, 186; Cultural Affairs, 119, 132, 163, 164; Communications, 119, 133–34; Education, 19, 21, 53, 61, 113–15, 116–23; Green Paper (1977), 56–57; Immigration, 119, 127; Labor and Manpower, 119, 124–27; Lands and Forests, 119, 129; Municipal Affairs, 119, 129; Social Affairs, 119, 130–32; Tourism, Hunting, and Fisheries, 119, 128; White Paper (1978) 57–59, 61

quiet revolution, 53–57 passim, 190

Radio Quebec, 134

resources in adult education: 36–42 passim; government allocation, 235–43; private and public sectors, 253–54

Roman Catholic church, influence of, 52, 72, 188

Rural Education and Development Association (R.E.D.A.), 183, 184–85, 190, 193, 256

Russell Report (U.K.), 6

Ryan Committee, 21, 113, 114

Schwartz, B., 20, 116

Services Educatifs d'Aide Personelle et d' Animation Communautaire (S.E.A.P.A.C.), 120–23 passim, 240

Social Credit: Alberta, 64–70; Quebec, 72

social democracy, 55, 58

social philosophy: 36–37, 43; Alberta, 64–75 passim; national, 49–51; Que-

bec, 52–61 passim, 72–73; and socio-economic conditions, 58

social structure, 38–39, 43

sociology of education, 35

status Indians: 147; in Alberta, 151–58; in Quebec, 165–70

Superior Council of Education, Quebec, 110–13 passim, 123, 127

Tagramiut Nipingat Inc., (T.N.I.), 173

Télé-Université, 135–36

Television and radio co-operatives, Quebec, 134–35

TEVEC, 120, 135

trade unions: Alberta, 74, 198–203; Quebec, 73, 203–8; and universities, 208

UNESCO: 3; adult education, defined, 15–18; General Assembly, 4, 15, 17; International Commission on the Development of Education, 20

Unifarm, 183

Union des Cultivateurs Catholiques (U.C.C.), 189

Union des Producteurs Agricoles (U.P.A.), 186, 188–91, 193, 207, 256; and universities, 190–91

union education, defined, 195

United Farm Women of Alberta (U.F.W.A.), 179, 183

United Farmers of Alberta (U.F.A.): government, 64, 65, 179; H.W. Wood, president, 64

United Kingdom Ministry of Reconstruction, 1919 Report, 5

universities: Alberta, 85, 87; and trade unions, 201, 208; and U.P.A., 190–91

University of Alberta: Faculty of Agriculture (and Forestry), 180, 181; Department (Faculty) of Extension, 180–82

voluntary organizations, 42

Women's Institute, 183

Workers' education, defined, 195